HORSES
ARE MADE TO BE
HORSES

HORSES
ARE MADE TO BE
HORSES

FRANZ MAIRINGER

Summaries by Kay Irving

HOWELL BOOK HOUSE INC.
230 Park Avenue, New York, N.Y. 10169

Library of Congress Cataloguing-in-Publication Data

Mairinger, Franz.
  Horses are made to be horses.

  Reprint. Originally published: Adelaide ; New York :
Rigby, 1983.
  Includes index.
  1. Dressage. 2. Horsemanship. 3. Dressage–
Australia. 4. Horsemanship–Australia. I. Irving, Kay.
II. Title.
SF309.5.M327 1986   798.2'3   85-27027
ISBN 0-87605-855-1

Distributed in the United States of America
and Canada by Howell Book House Inc.
230 Park Avenue, New York, N.Y. 10169

First published in the United States 1986

God grant me the serenity to accept
The things I cannot change,
Courage to change the things I can,
And wisdom to know the difference

ACKNOWLEDGMENTS

Before his death my husband had been working on the material for this book. However, he rarely had much time to devote to it, and his lectures, addresses, notes, and annotations were therefore left in a random and unco-ordinated form. For their generous assistance in preparing these pages for publication I sincerely thank the following people:

Mr Clive Cochrane, E.F.A., Ascot Vale, Victoria
Sir Alex Creswick, Avenel, Victoria
Miss Kay Irving, Coldstream, Victoria
Mr Albert Jacobs, Narre Warren, Victoria
Miss Janice Johnson, Sydney
Miss Cecile V. Kamenade, Wonthaggi, Victoria
Mr John Kelly, Caramut, Victoria

Mrs Ina Maria Knospe, Bungendore, New South Wales
Mr Neale Lavis, Braidwood, New South Wales
Mr Laurie Morgan, Tarcutta, New South Wales
Mr Ron Paterson, Albany Creek, Queensland Rider Magazine
Mr Colin Thiele, Wattle Park, South Australia
Mr W. W. Thompson, Eglinton, New South Wales
Mrs Tina Wommelsdorf, Terry Hills, New South Wales

Last but not least I thank my son Franz, my daughter Martha, and their families, for their help and support.

Erna Mairinger
Bowral, N.S.W.

FOREWORD

It is with much pleasure that I write this Foreword to the work of a person to whom I owe so much. I have read the manuscript with great interest, some parts repeatedly. Although it was difficult for Franz to translate his knowledge and his thoughts from his own native language into English, he gets through to the reader with remarkable zest and spirit.

I have spent many pleasant and informative hours with Franz, discussing various ways of overcoming physical and mental problems with horses, and Franz had an answer for them all.

There has not been, and there is never likely to be, any person in Australia who could psychoanalyse a horse better than Franz. This is apparent in his search for perfection in the various movements. To the inexperienced it would no doubt appear unnecessary to carry out all the little basic exercises that are so time-consuming— especially if one believes that the same result can be acquired in a fraction of the time. It is not until later, when attempting more advanced movements, that one realises how the short cuts have created problems that are going to be much more difficult and time-consuming to overcome. I shall always remember Franz saying, 'A building is only as good as its foundations'.

I sincerely hope that readers will gain as much pleasure and value as I did from the knowledge passed on to us by Franz Mairinger.

I raise my hat to the gentleman to whom I, in particular, and Australian equitation in general, owe so much.

LAURIE MORGAN

A TRIBUTE

Those who read this book shall do so, hopefully, with a wish to acquire the wisdom that is unfolded within. It delves not only into the mind of the reader, but into the mind of man's fastest and greatest companion in the animal kingdom—the horse. Human and horse psychology are considered with equal sensitivity; essentially both are complementary, being dependent upon action and reaction. On the one hand, an animal of quite limited intelligence but possessed of tremendous physical strength and endurance; on the other, man, the most intelligent species on earth, but of relatively insignificant physical prowess.

Franz Mairinger, whom I am proud to call my friend, the respected mentor of a multitude of horsemen and horsewomen, explains where and how the twain shall meet on a foundation of mutual respect. The result is a contented, trained and willing horse, whose owner has experienced the ultimate satisfaction in showing his ability to work with his horse and, through the bonds of physical contact and considerate accord, extracting from it the end product.

Indeed fortunate are those who live on to inherit Franz's concepts, which have been faithfully correlated and published through the tireless efforts of his wife, Erna.

It is a singular honour to have this opportunity to write a tribute to this man's life work, which will influence the equestrian sphere for generations yet to come.

NORMAN JUDGE, B.V.Sc,
M.R.C.V.S., M.C.A.V.Sc.

CONTENTS

INTRODUCTION

This book is a memorial to a man who has done more than any other single instructor for riding in Australia. He trained no less than six Olympic equestrian teams and was preparing the seventh when his untimely death came as an unexpected blow to the horse world.

He was a philosopher with a great love and understanding of his equine friends. The book, if read carefully, brings a very necessary message to all people who love horses and who strive to educate the horse so that he is able to give his best and last longer, whatever the purpose of his training. All serious riders who desire to compete in dressage, showjumping, or three-day eventing should make this book their bible. Anyone who is prepared to put Franz Mairinger's advice into practice will be rewarded with success.

This book has been put together from the accumulated notes of lectures and demonstrations given by Franz Mairinger throughout Australia. Unhappily, he died before he was able to prepare the manuscript. Accordingly his wife, Erna, gathered all the available material and, with the help of various friends, pupils, and followers of his teachings, arranged it in the form in which it appears here.

Great care has been taken not to interfere in any way with the character and spirit of the original. The people concerned knew Franz Mairinger as a great riding master for more than twenty-five years; they studied under him and admired his extraordinary wisdom and skill in educating the horse. The utmost thought has therefore been given to the manuscript to ensure the accuracy of the text.

Franz Mairinger was born in Vienna on 11 December 1915, the son of an engineer, who encouraged him to pursue a similar career. However, Franz's real interest lay in horses—an interest which developed even more strongly from the day he enlisted in the Austrian Cavalry in 1935. At that time it was customary for some of the top riders to be sent to foreign cavalry schools, and Franz was soon rewarded for his ability and dedication by being selected to attend the highly regarded Cavalry School of Hanover in Germany which was famous for its achievements in jumping and 'military' (three-day eventing).

Franz spent two years there, receiving a thorough training in those disciplines. Although dressage was part of the training he was at that time more interested in jumping, cross country, and steeplechasing.

Dressage really captured Franz's attention

when he attended the International Horse Show in Hanover where the Spanish Riding School of Vienna gave a number of guest performances. Their horses were stabled at the Cavalry School—an arrangement which later proved to be very fortunate for Franz because, unknown to him, Colonel Podjhasky (the Director of the Spanish Riding School) had been observing the Cavalry riders working out. Franz was asked to ride one of the Spanish Riding School stallions, and he so impressed the Director that on the following day he was offered a position at the School. A few months later he was back in his beloved city of Vienna.

Reflecting on the beginnings of his career with the most famous classical riding academy in the world, he once said:

> I thought I could ride well, having been invited to join the Spanish Riding School. My head was very swollen, but it took them only two days to shrink it. I really came down with a thump. I suddenly realised that by the standards of the school I could not ride at all. I also realised that had I given my horses at the Cavalry School only 10 per cent of the schooling given to horses in Vienna how much better they would have performed.

After six years at the School, and after many examinations, Franz was appointed a *Bereiter* (Senior Rider) and continued for twelve-and-a-half years with great success.

One of Franz's significant contributions to Austria occurred in April 1945, when he performed the difficult courbette in front of America's General Patton at the historic demonstration at Wels in Upper Austria where the Lippizaner stallions were stabled during the latter part of the war. The impromptu performance by selected riders convinced General Patton of the need for the immediate transfer of the Lippizaner mares from Czechoslovakia which was in the process of being occupied by the Russian army. The success of this daring venture has since been depicted in a well-known film.

After a period as a private instructor in Switzerland following his resignation from the School in 1951, he made the decision to leave Europe, which was slowly recovering from the war, and begin a new life in Australia with his family. This move was made on the suggestion of a former pupil, Major Sandford, who gave him introductions to friends in Australia who were hoping to assemble a group of their best equestrians to start preparation for the Olympic Games in Stockholm.

Miss Kay Irving, M.B.E., was instrumental in Franz's becoming the first trainer of an Australian Olympic Equestrian team when she suggested that Franz be asked to conduct a suitable training course for potential competitors in 1955. Franz accompanied the team to Stockholm where Australia stunned the international equestrian world by gaining fourth place. This success brought the sport of eventing into the public eye in Australia and clearly demonstrated to team members and aspiring Olympians what proper training could achieve. Even greater success followed, with a gold medal in Rome in 1960, and with world respect for Australian achievements in subsequent Olympics. Franz's international successes with riders from a country which had suddenly achieved world standing did not go unnoticed by the Spanish Riding School or the Austrian Press. On several occasions he was approached by the late Director of the Spanish Riding School, Colonel Handler, to return to Vienna and bring his skills back to the world mecca of dressage. However, because of his family ties and his great ambition to set up a National Riding Academy where he could pass on his knowledge to aspiring Australian equestrians, he declined the offer.

When Franz died on 10 May 1978, dressage was really emerging and becoming an accepted sport in Australia, almost solely because of his untiring efforts. His death was not only a tragic loss to Australian riders, who need his guidance more than ever, but to the international equestrian world where he was one of a small, élite group who possessed skills passed on by the great masters for centuries.

Had he lived he could have seen the fruits of

decades of dedication, and could have started the most advanced riders on the way to the classic *haute école*. Franz had great hopes for Australian riders. He once said, 'Australia has many talented riders and some of the best horses in the world. If they applied the classic training methods with patience and understanding they would be consistent top performers in international competitions'.

We have lost Franz Mairinger but we can still follow his teachings. They are summed up in his own words:

The foundation of all equitation is the correct position of the rider, the application of the correct aids, combined with patience and feeling for your horse's movements. It will enable you to ride your horse forward, straight, supple, balanced and calm. On this foundation you can build with confidence; you will succeed in any riding discipline, be it classical dressage, jumping or eventing.

INA MARIA KNOSPE AND GEORGE KINNIBURGH

CHAPTER ONE

A PERSONAL PHILOSOPHY

What is the difference between you and your horse? According to Charles Darwin, nothing except appearance. Both receive the gift of life from the same source, from the almighty God, from Buddha, Allah, or whatever deity you believe in. It does not really matter whether you believe in God or Buddha, or whether you think the universe just developed itself through millions of years. It is here and you are part of it. It is not my intention to try to answer questions that I cannot answer.

All I want to do is to make you think, to make you realise that there are things far beyond our wildest imagination. To make you see the greatness of creation. I want you to see that everything in life follows a pattern, and that everything we do, and the way we do it, is forced upon us and dictated by the laws of nature. Try to imagine the universe expanding for about 200 billion light years. Try to comprehend that you are rushing with the Earth at about 112651 kilometres an hour along its orbit around the sun, and that you have a speed of about 1608 kilometres an hour around the polar axis of the Earth. If you are still filled with your own importance, I give you up as a lost cause!

One season follows another. Water runs downhill. Anything you drop falls down. Ever thought why? Perhaps there was no reason to, because you were told at school about the laws of gravity and many other things; but you may not have been told that you should draw logical conclusions from this, and act and react according to the given facts.

If you jump into a lake and you can't swim you will drown; that's why you don't jump in. If a fish were to jump out of the lake, he would suffocate, which is really the same thing. Ever thought why? Well, it is just the pattern of life. We can't live in the water and the fish can't live out of the water, and if the Earth did not circle around the sun and make summer and winter, we would not live at all. A bird can fly and some animals can change their colour (some people can do it too but they are not very well liked). There are millions of different insects, reptiles, birds, and animals all neatly ordered in groups and classes, and one of the classes is the mammals which include, among others, the whales, monkeys, you and me, and our horses.

From Mother Nature's point of view, what is the difference between you, your horse, and everything else that crawls, runs, swims, or flies? We accept the fact that we can't fly or live under the water, but why do we accept it? Because we know that we would have to pay with our lives if we didn't. We accept it subconsciously, but I want you to bring it into full realisation. I want you to see the guiding hand of God. I want you to see that anything walking, crawling, flying, anything alive on this Earth, was created or developed to suit its purpose, to meet the requirements of its environment, to be equipped with the best possible means for its survival.

How could a tiger stalk if he had hooves instead of paws? How could a gazelle run with the legs of an elephant? How could a fish swim with legs and no fins? The tail of a cow would be useless for a monkey, and the ears of a mouse would be too small for a donkey.

There is no doubt: Nature knows best. If you care to take a closer look you will find out for yourself how ingeniously the different bodies are designed. You don't have to look far. Look at yourself. Isn't your body a wonderful instrument, a miracle? We should bow very low in respect to the genius who designed it. We are equipped to perfection to carry out the task of living. The way we do things—work, run, jump, carry—is the way we *have* to do it, because that is the way the mechanics of our body function best. Everything is based on the laws of nature. Nature has developed our body to enable us to carry out the task of being alive, and the task of maintaining our life, in the easiest possible way—in order to make us last longer, in order to give us, or let us achieve, the maximum result with the minimum effort.

Naturally, we do a lot of things we should not do. We undermine the delicate organs of our body and destroy our health by smoking, drinking, and using all sorts of drugs. But we have to pay for it in the end because we cannot cheat nature. However, as long as we waste or ruin our own health, our own vitality or strength, we have to pay for our mistakes, our ignorance, our lack of thought, our failure to realise the greatness of life itself.

All this talk is leading up to our horses, but before you can understand what I want to tell you about horses, you must understand me first. That's why we are having another closer look at our own bodies. Not that I mean to give you all the details concerning the structure of your body; that alone would fill more than one book. But I want you to realise that you have a frame of bones, your skeleton. The bones are held together in joints by strong fibrous ligaments; otherwise the 206 bones of your framework would collapse in a heap. I don't think you would have much hope of piecing yourself together again. All the bones of the joints fit snugly into each other. Every joint has a certain amount of flexibility, in certain directions, and to a certain degree, and the ligaments have to be just the right size to allow that movement, *that planned movement*. The bones and ligaments alone would not take us far: it is our muscles that put everything into motion. We can order our muscles to contract or relax. We can lift our legs. We can close our fists, we can stretch the fingers, we can do anything. But we would not be able to do anything if we did not feed our muscles. We must give them energy. We cannot produce energy, we can only transform it: we have to eat food and we have to digest it.

If you have given all this some deeper thought, you will have realised that although you can do a lot with your body you have your limits. You will understand that nature forces you to do things in a certain way, but in that certain way you can move about with the greatest of ease, comfort, and security. Everything is perfectly balanced, ideal.

As I have said before, we belong to the same class—the mammals—as our horses do. Can you give me a single reason why nature shouldn't have developed the horse to be a horse as perfectly as nature has developed us to be human, or as it has made a fly, a tiger, a whale, a crocodile, or any other creature you can think of? The way we move, if undisturbed, is the way we are supposed to move. The way the horse moves, walks, trots, canters, is the way nature has made him move, because in that manner he achieves maximum result with minimum effort.

Do you see what I mean? If you want to

know how a horse should be ridden, see how he moves by himself when free. How he walks, trots, and canters. How he jumps. Have a close look and see the beauty, the rhythm, and harmony of his movements. Then, sit down, close your eyes, and try to burn this picture of effortless grace, beauty, and harmony deep into your mind, your heart. Never forget it. Because that is the way you should ride your horse. There in a few words is all the knowledge of the world, and your training goal!

Preserve his natural gaits. Preserve his personality. Preserve his instinct to go forward. Do this and you must be successful because you are respecting nature's wisdom.

Give him back his natural balance, with your additional weight on his back. That is the essence of schooling, training, or *dressage*, as the rest of the world prefers to call it. Do you still think that dressage is a mystery? Or, as Harry Carpenter said in the *Daily Mail*, 'Something foreigners do damned well'. No, I am sure you will agree with me that it is the most natural thing one could think of.

So, we know why we should reproduce the horse's natural balance. But, to make sure, I will condense everything said so far into a few words: if you think that you know more than nature, why not prove it and jump in the lake and stay there? Now, let's move on.

So far we have looked at the horse from a general point of view, but the next step will bring us close to him, although we will not yet touch him. We are still trying to prepare ourselves psychologically for our task of schooling him later on. I am telling you all this because I am convinced of the vital importance your deeper understanding, your attitude towards your horse, will have when we start to talk about the actual schooling.

A man's nature and his way of life are his fate, and what he calls his fate is but his disposition. We can't just blame fate for the things we do, for, as Menander said, 'He who conquers himself will conquer the World'. Look a bit more closely and we can say that when something does not turn out as we planned, it is

usually because it was not planned properly. Whatever we do in life, we must approach it in the right way to be successful, and this is very true with handling horses.

Generally speaking, the more money a project costs the more planning goes into its preparation. When you build a house you get the advice and help of experts before you start because you may have your life's savings at stake and you can't afford a mistake. For most people, riding a horse is not as expensive as building a house, but if you want to train a horse successfully you will have to be as thorough as an architect in your preparations.

When you ride a horse do you really prepare yourself? Do you know exactly what you should know? Do you think about it? I will do my best to explain what you should do, how you should do it, and why you should do it. But I will not be able to tell you how the different movements will feel when you carry them out, and that is of the greatest importance—feeling when you are right and when you are wrong, feeling when the horse is moving properly, when his rhythm is right and his impulsion is right. No book can explain this satisfactorily.

If you follow my words and work hard enough you will develop the feeling. Mind you, it will take longer than it would if you were on a horse and under my observation. I would then be able to tell you when you were right, and when the horse was right, so that you could remember the feeling. You would try to re-create the same feeling. You would get it, lose it, get it again, lose it again, and finally reach a point where, at every step, you were sure whether you were right or wrong.

Before we go on to details, let's get our approach right. As I said in the beginning, approach is everything. We are approaching the subject of riding a horse, of schooling a horse to the highest possible standard.

I recall an incident in Sydney when we had a lame horse with a very bad tendon, and the rider wanted to start the horse the next day. We asked Roy Stewart, the veterinary surgeon, and he said, 'Yes, that's the trouble. People

always think that horses are made for man, but that's not true. Horses are made to be horses'.
I thought about that a lot, and decided that if ever I should write a book I would call it *Horses Are Made to Be Horses*.

The horse has evolved to its present form by meeting the needs of its environment with the best possible means of survival. To survive it has relied on its speed. It has relied on its ability to run from meat-eaters, but without having to bear and balance a load on its back.

You can do a lot with your body, but there are limits which force you to do things in a certain way. But in that certain way you will find that you can move about with the greatest ease of movement and security. When naturally balanced, everything is more or less ideal, but I am quite sure that none of you thinks about balance in your everyday movements. We are balanced and subconsciously we maintain our balance. We are naturally balanced. I say 'naturally balanced', not 'perfectly balanced'; there is a lot of difference between natural balance and perfect balance.

Is there any reason why a horse should not be as naturally balanced as we are? Is there any reason why the horse should not be as beautifully designed as we are? There is no reason why the horse's body should not function as well as ours. There is no reason why the Designer should not have wanted a horse to be a horse to the same perfection as with all other animals.

Give the horse back his natural balance with your additional weight on his back. That is the essence of schooling and training—the most natural thing one could think of, and it makes sense. If you think that it does not make sense, draw a line on the ground and walk along it. Find out whether you can walk the line and keep straight and at the same time be comfortable. I take it you are successful? Now, take a bag of oats, or a bag of chaff, or a small child, up on your shoulder and try to walk the same line. The heavier the weight on your shoulder, the better you will understand that without it you are comfortable but with it you are uncomfortable.

Don't laugh. Try it: if you really feel it you will know the difference. If you are uncomfortable with the weight on your back, there is no reason why a horse with an additional weight on his back should not feel as uncomfortable as you feel.

How should we look upon our horse? What attitude should we take? What should we see in our horse? It is important that we get our psychological approach right. Do you see him as a slave and treat him accordingly, or do you see your best friend in him? So far as I am concerned, slaves always want to run away and the horse is no exception. Freedom is surely no human invention. The urge to be free is something that nature has instilled in every form of life.

'Freedom' is the most misused word in any language. Millions of people have died for freedom and the fight is still going on. Anything that is not free will fight to be free as long as there is spirit left in its body. As I have said, slaves will try to run away; they will fight and resist and one will have to use force to get the work done. Xenophon, 2400 years ago, said, 'Force will never produce anything beautiful'. That means that because we want to produce something beautiful, we cannot use force with our horse. We want to show him in the beauty of his natural movements. Therefore, we have to treat, handle, and respect him as our friend. And what a friend he can be. Horses don't let you down. They have no treachery, and you can be sure that they will return love with love—something you can't be sure of with your human friends.

To use the capabilities of the horse to the best advantage we have to avoid making him fight. We have to put him at ease. We have to have his confidence. He must trust us. He must have faith in us, and then we can trust him and he will always try to do his best.

You expect your horse to carry you to victory—to jump clean and safe because you want to win, and not land in hospital. Common sense will tell you that the better you are united with your horse, the better the understanding between you, the better will be your chance of success, of achieving the round of honour. Your sweetheart may be in the grandstand, or somebody else whom you want to impress, but even if there is nobody watching it is always a good feeling to be first.

You may think that my exhortation to look upon your horse as your best friend is a bit far fetched. Then find someone else to compare him with, somebody who works with you, somebody you have to team up with, perhaps for climbing a high mountain where you are tied together with a rope to protect each other. You will find dozens of examples you can use. If you don't want to see your best friend in a horse, because he is only a horse, let's say that he is your servant. Everybody likes to have a servant.

How would you treat him? Would you treat him with kindness because it is your firm belief that every man has the same right to a fair deal in life, or would you treat him with kindness because you are scared that he might poison your dinner the next day? The servant I am talking about is doing his job to the best of his ability. Now, search your conscience and confess which group you belong to. The first? Well, you cannot go wrong. If you belong to the second group you will still treat him well; your fear of retribution will keep you on the right track. But what if you belong to a third group—all the little and big supermen—the men who do not believe, and because they do not believe have no fear? The men who rely on physical strength or the strength of their social position? Such men will always mistreat their servants. They have caused wars and revolutions and have made empires collapse. All the misery they have produced boils down to negligence—negligence of the rights of others. Negligence of freedom. The fight for freedom runs like a thread through the history of mankind, and the hope of every revolution is democracy.

Why democracy? Simply because democracy means freedom and guarantees freedom for every member of the community within the boundary of its duties towards the people. The meaning of freedom and democracy is often misinterpreted. Many people think that in a democracy everyone can do as he pleases, but that is not so. A democracy does not give freedom, it gives responsibility.

Freedom of the State is different from freedom of the individual. Freedom of the individual must be in proportion to his acceptance of duties and his recognition of other men's rights. We have to accept the fact that we can only be free if we are alone, for only then can we do as we please. We would need a lot of islands and a lot of oceans to give everyone freedom. When people live together, somebody must be the leader. Somebody must make decisions, and somebody must carry them out. Everyone has a place in a community and every place is of importance to the community. We have intelligence, and so we should be able to judge the extent of our capabilities; according to our own judgment we should submit ourselves to our place and do our job. Our duty is to do everything to the best of our ability. In theory there should be no need for a policeman, no need for an army, no need for a taxation officer. Everybody should control himself by realising and fulfilling his duties.

If water restrictions are necessary the local council is forced to send a man around to check up on whether you have your sprinkler going or not. I consider that to be a bad sign: that the individual in the community is not as free as he should be. Not because the fellow is spying on you, but because it is necessary to send a man around to make sure that you carry out your duties. If we don't do our job properly, restrictions and enforcements must be placed on us. The greater the support for the restrictions or laws in the community, the fewer the restrictions will need to be, and the less need there will be for enforcement. The smaller the support, the more restrictions are necessary and the more need there is for enforcement, the closer we are to dictatorship. The need for enforcement is reciprocal, proportional to the support given.

18

Somebody said that the Continental riders are all dictators; they dictate every step the horse should take. Well, you have read so far, do you think that I am a dictator? No, I am not. I want to build up a mutual understanding with my horse on a democratic basis. I want to educate him to submit himself freely to his duties without fight. I school and exercise him in order to enable him to carry out or perform different tasks joyfully and with the greatest of ease. By doing it in this way I gain his confidence, his co-operation, and I get the full benefit of his mental and physical potential.

The freedom of a State may not have anything to do with riding a horse, but the essence of the idea goes a long way towards giving us a base to work from. If you think that I am wrong, try to prove the basis of the idea wrong. You may have to rewrite the history of the world!

My introduction is getting longer and longer. I hope that I am not trying your patience too far. But I must make myself quite clear: there is more to it than just sitting on the horse's back. So far I have only been trying to explain my mental approach to the subject, and trying to get you on the same track. You must get your psychological approach right, because your approach to the subject will control the way you carry it out. It will guide your actions. It will keep you thinking. I want you to think along these lines for the horse's sake and for your own benefit.

Of course there is another angle to it too. Certainly it is our duty to look after the horse in the right way—after all he does not want anything from us and we are supposed to have more brains than he, although I have never seen a horse smoke or get drunk, or have late nights and cocktail parties. But the other angle is that I want to have an easy ride. I really want to enjoy myself. But how can a king enjoy his life if he is the king of slaves?

Yes, I want an easy ride, but we never get anything for nothing in this world. We have to do something first. We have to build a house first, and then we can move in. In the same way, we have to school our horse first, so that he will give us the easy and safe ride we want.

SUMMARY

Franz Mairinger was unique as a horseman and teacher. He believed that the relationship between rider and horse required something far deeper than mere ownership or performance. It demanded a sensitive understanding of the inter-relationship between all the earth's creatures and of 'the laws of nature'.

Above all, it required very special insight into the nature of the horse—its grace and speed, its beauty, strength, and remarkable 'personality'. Only when the rider approached the task of riding, dressage, and showjumping with such empathy and vision could the happiest results ensue.

CHAPTER TWO

UNDERSTANDING THE HORSE

So far, I have tried to make you realise, to see and understand, that a horse is made to be a horse. But what has enabled the horse to survive? Scientists say that its evolution took fifty-five million years. If something can survive for fifty-five million years, nature or creation must have taken good care of it.

A horse lives on grass, and grass does not run away. So why is a horse capable of running so fast? Because the horse's natural destiny is to go forward. The horse had to be fast because other animals were hunting it. Because life consists of the strong and the weak. There are a lot of animals stronger and better equipped for killing their prey than the horse. As a vegetarian the horse is not equipped for killing. His whole structure is designed for speed, and for covering long distances.

However, his speed would be useless if it were not combined with a highly developed sense of hearing, eyesight, smell, and shyness. His shyness is a suspicion of any sound or of any strange movement. That shyness is a trigger for his natural means of survival, his speed. If your horse shies at a little piece of paper flying about or at something he sees that hasn't been there before, do not try to punish him and get him past or close to the object by forcing him.

That would be against his natural instincts and would show that you do not understand the animal. If the horse shies, it is something he cannot account for, something he does subconsciously, something nature has made him do in order to survive, in order for him to make use of his equipment to survive.

The horse must go forward; if he does not go forward he is no good. His natural destiny is his speed; that is why he must go forward when we school him. If we school him and he does not go forward, we are sinners against nature and we pay that penalty even if we do not realise it. Perhaps because we are not bright enough to realise that we did not ride him properly we find some excuse to account for our failure.

The all-important part that governs the whole body, governs all movements, sound, method, and reason, is the brain. The brain helps a species survive. The brain is responsible for every single thing we do. In realising this we have to control our thinking. Anybody who is mentally tied in knots, tense, will never be able to react quickly, to be supple and cool headed. The horse's brain is really the same; it governs his body just as ours does. Only most of it he does by instinct, not by reason.

If we think that we can neglect the importance of the horse's brain we are far off the track. On the contrary, we have to take very special care of the horse's brain, just as we would with any other pupil. We must not forget that the horse hasn't as much intelligence as the human being, and because of that we must adjust our thinking to the horse's thinking. The biggest mistake most riders make is that they expect the horse to think in the way they do, which is impossible. It is the rider's duty to realise that he has to adjust his thinking and try to think and feel as the horse does.

Horses are intelligent even if they do not think or act as we do. In their way they are intelligent and I am quite sure that everyone has had experience of their amazing memory. They don't forget what they have been taught, so try and teach them the right thing—because just as they do not forget the good things, so will they not forget the bad things.

I remember something that happened to me shortly after my arrival in Australia. It was in Adelaide, and I was riding a horse that belonged to Mr A. J. Higgins. I was preparing and schooling the horse for the dressage test at the forthcoming Royal Show. We were working on the grounds of the Dressage Club in the parklands—circling, shouldering, halts, and rein back, cantering around in circles with changes.

While I was riding, another fellow was riding on the same ground, further away, on a very beautiful horse, a beautiful horse indeed. The only thing wrong with the horse was that the fellow could hardly ride him. The horse wouldn't walk, but was pulling at the rein, shaking his head, pulling the rider out of the saddle, not standing still. He didn't have a comfortable ride. As a matter of fact I wouldn't have ridden the horse because I thought he was mad.

At last the other rider had had enough, realising that he could not do any good, so he dismounted and just stood there and let the horse feed on the grass. As soon as the rider was off and the horse was feeding he became calm and as happy as could be. The rider stood and watched what I was doing for about 10 minutes until I had finished.

He said, 'Hey mate, what are you doing here?'
I replied, 'I'm preparing the horse for the dressage test at the Show'.
'What's dressage?'
'Dressage means to school a horse, and so on. If you keep on schooling him you can improve him all the time. Go from one test to a higher test until you reach the highest level, the Grand Prix at the Olympic Games.'
He answered, 'Not bad. Tell me, how long does it take to get the horse into the Grand Prix?'.
'Well, it depends a lot on the horse, and a lot on how much time the rider has. But in three years you could attempt the Games.'
The poor man was shocked. He said, 'What? Three years? Three years' schooling? Ah! You must be nuts'.
I said, 'Oh well, everybody likes to do something different. By the way, how long have you ridden that horse of yours?'.
Turning around, he pulled his horse's head up, looked him up and down in disgust, and then said, 'I've had him for five years, but he's no good'.
No comment from me.
Three years' schooling is madness, but five years of riding an untrained horse is perfectly in order!
The tragedy of the thing is that he is not the only one. You run across examples like that nearly every day, where you can see good horses (or what should be good horses) that are being spoilt through mistreatment, negligence, or just ignorance of the horse's need to be schooled.
Yes, a horse has to be schooled. How much schooling we give him depends a lot on the horse and, more so, on the rider—how much time you want to spend, how hard you want to work, and, most of all, how high you really want to go. If you want to go for the stars, if you want to compete in the Olympic Games, then you will have to do a lot of hard work.
How much can we teach the horse? This is very, very important to our thinking. What can we teach the horse? I say that we can't teach

him a single thing. So many times I hear people say, 'I am going to teach my horse flying changes', 'I am going to teach my horse to walk', 'I am going to teach my horse to trot . . . to canter . . . to jump . . . to gallop'.

Foals, three days old, make the most beautiful flying changes you have ever seen. Near my house, on Mr Horden's property, I saw a four-day-old foal frollicking. Suddenly it turned around and jumped a fallen log 1 metre high—its mother was on the other side. We see foals playing, turning, stopping, changing, rearing, and jumping around, and then a man who knows everything comes and says, 'I am going to teach him flying changes'.

A horse can walk by himself, he can trot by himself, he can canter and jump, turn left or right, wheel around as he pleases. He can do anything that is natural to a horse by himself. In a sense, then, there is nothing we can teach him. All we can do is educate him to do his natural movements when we want him to and not when and how he pleases.

I know how to wash dishes. My wife doesn't have to teach me. All she has to do is make me wash them when she wants them washed. It is the same with a horse. We must educate him to carry out our wishes without fighting.

The word 'education' brings us right to the meaning of dressage. It is a French term meaning to train, educate, exercise, and discipline. Can you imagine a human being without education and discipline? Nobody can educate without being educated, and that is why on the Continent horse-riding is a popular aid to education. I am quite sure that the realisation of the character-building properties of riding has had a lot to do with the tremendous growth of pony clubs throughout the world. Riding and caring for a horse drives home the children's responsibilities to look after the animal. In educating a horse the child begins to appreciate the planning and preparation needed for the job, and so he begins to realise the similarity with his own education. He learns that education must be made a step at a time with a definite goal in view.

For instance, I once spoke with a trainer about his horse. Just looking at her you would say, 'That mare would win a 3-kilometre race', she had everything necessary to do so. He had given her up as a race-horse and was trying to sell her as a hack. I said, 'She is a beautiful horse, she should be able to gallop'.

He replied, 'Yes, that's what I thought too. But I taught her dressage. You should never do it. I taught her to go sideways. I taught her to go backwards. When I put her on the track she would not jump from the barrier'.

Now, what does dressage have to do with the horse playing up at the barrier? Well, if I wear my left shoe on my right foot, and then say to you, 'For goodness sake don't wear shoes because they give you sore feet', that would be similar to saying that a horse taught dressage would only go backwards and not forwards.

By saying that, the trainer proved that he did not know what he was seeking. He did not know that the foundation of dressage, the foundation of everything we do, is to advance. The horse must go forward.

If you are in a high building and the lift breaks down you don't take a short cut to the ground floor by jumping from the window. Similarly, you can't take short cuts in a horse's education. The fellow with the race-horse did not realise that he was fighting the horse's natural inclination to go forward. He was taking short cuts in teaching a horse to do movements out of context with his aim to make it race properly. He was penalised because the horse would probably have made a good race-horse. But he did not blame himself and say, 'I did not know the basis of dressage'. No. He said, 'Bloody dressage'.

Unfortunately, in cases such as this, where horses are expected to do something that they have not been prepared for properly, the horses are the sufferers. They suffer in body and mind. The owner is penalised, but he is often not aware that it is his own fault. And there is no way of proving it to him. All you can do is say, 'If you had schooled that horse in a different way he would have jumped. He would have lasted five or ten years longer'.

There is no such thing as a fast job of horse training. It will always turn out to be a slow job. Horses, as a rule, are regarded as 'dumb animals'. But if they are dumb, why do people rush them through, not giving them time to learn or gain experience? The horse must always go from step to step to reach a higher standard.

When you went to school you started at the bottom and then went from grade to grade. You wouldn't take a bright youngster and ask him to sit for the Leaving Examinations. We don't expect our children or ourselves to do things without the proper preparation. You must increase your capabilities until you are able to achieve your goal. The child when faced with a task beyond his capabilities will try to get away from it. He is nervous: 'It can't be done'. Yet someone sees a horse by himself, jumping a fence, and says, 'Oh! He can jump. A natural jumper!'. So on with the saddle, and on to the showground they go. The rider expects his horse to jump a clear round. He sees the horse, green from the paddock, going into the open competitions, jumping against the clock, carrying all before him. He asks this of a 'dumb animal' without the power of reason. The horse can't say, 'No, I am not going to do it', or, 'I am not prepared', or, 'I have not enough confidence', or, 'I don't know how to handle the combinations; you have to give me time'.

He can't talk, but he can't do the job expected of him either. So the rider does something he should never attempt. He substitutes force for finesse.

The horse may in his own language tell us that he is not ready. In his own language he could say, 'I'm not going to jump any more; I'm going to stop'. Or he could say, 'I'm terribly excited; let me get over as quickly as possible'. As soon as he sees the fence he tries to rush. If he stops later on the rider will say, 'Last time he jumped as good as gold; he jumped it a few times and now he won't go near it'. He may take a whip and lash the horse. More fear; more excitement; less result. We can't do that. We must not do it.

We should act according to the standards of intelligence we are credited with. We must try to understand the horse. True, it will take a long time, but in the long run the time will be well spent. Nothing can be done at once. So don't expect the horse to do something without the proper preparation.

The psychological condition of the horse is something that is rarely taken into consideration. It is just a horse. 'He has no brains', people say. But does he really have no brains? Well, all you need say is that horses have an incredible memory. It would be impossible to school a horse to do anything if he did not have intelligence and memory. Mind you, even if the horse does not think and act as we do he certainly has enough intelligence to look after his own comfort. When he looks after his interests, however, he often does it in a way that makes him suffer. That's where he proves his lack of reason. Personally, I think the only time he does prove his lack of intelligence is when he attempts to do things that he is not prepared for. Because they are capable of jumping by themselves, horses with a rider on their back will often attempt jumps that they are not prepared for.

There are a lot of reasons why people ride horses. One rides on Sunday to help keep his weight down, another because it is part of his job, another because he enjoys it. I am not interested in Sunday riders. They provide a means of keeping riding schools going, but they are not really interested in improving their riding because that is not their object. I am interested in people who ride as part of their work. They usually like riding and they usually have consideration for the horse. The people who ride because they enjoy riding really interest me, because they are the people who are prepared to sacrifice in order to improve. The rider who wants to school himself and the horse properly will have to sacrifice a lot of comfort and time.

The men on the land who have to ride might not always have the opportunity to do what they would like to do. I have found that their

23

reaction is that they have to break in a horse in a few days or the breaker will be out of a job. Therefore, they can't take the time to school him and bring him along slowly. I understand their position. Still, if they love the horse I am sure that they will make their workmate's life a bit easier.

There are as many styles of riding as there are reasons to ride. The stockman has developed a style suitable for his work; the jumping rider has his style; cross-country rider, his style again; polo player, his style; dressage rider his; and the jockey has a different style again. But they all have one thing in common—they sit on a horse. I am sure that any rider will benefit if he tries to follow my explanations about how and why the horse should be schooled, and will, if nothing else, appreciate the horse's personality.

The fundamental requirement to play a violin is to hold the violin and bow, and rub them together to make a noise. The sound may not be harmonious but you will be playing the violin. Similarly, you paint by smearing paint on canvas. But you will not play like Paganini or Oistrakh, and you will not paint like Rubens, without immense study, practice, and determination. Your determination to succeed is very, very important. Abraham Lincoln once said, 'If you are *determined* to become a lawyer the job is more than half done already'.

One of the main requirements if you are to be able to ride a horse, is for you to sit on top of it and not fall off—but this is a long way short of being a riding master such as Lindenbauer or Pollak.

People on the Continent call the art of riding 'classical high school' (*haute école*). Why? Because riding has been improved from the ability not to fall off to an ability approaching perfection. Perfection in understanding the horse. Perfection in controlling the horse. Perfection in unity with the horse. Just as it takes much work to paint like an old master, it also takes hard work to reach that goal of classical high school, that perfect understanding between horse and rider.

Whenever you aspire to perfection you have

to work hard. There is no easy way out. You start from scratch by smearing paint, or you put your leg across the horse for the first time. Conventional art is simply reproducing nature, because you have the subject right in front of you, but the execution is difficult. The difference with modern art is that the conception is difficult and the execution easier.

The art of riding is as easy in its conception as other conventional arts. Very easy, because what we want to do is reproduce nature. Just as Michelangelo attempted to reproduce nature, so riding students in the art of riding attempt to reproduce the horse's natural movements, his natural grace and beauty under the rider.

When thinking about schooling a horse, we have to consider facts first. We have to find out the why before we talk about the how. We have to get our priorities into the right perspective— what comes first, and what comes after, the order in which we try to achieve the various goals we have set ourselves to obtain a successful result.

And the difficulty here is that we tend to apply principles by instinct. Because we often do things without having to think about them, we do not really know them. We are not aware of the facts. And when we are forced to be aware of certain laws and conditions we act in the most extraordinary way, as if we had never heard anything about them. And yet, as I have said, we use them all our lives without knowing it.

I started by saying, 'When thinking about schooling a horse', and that's exactly what I meant, *thinking*. Too many people approach various subjects and projects without giving them enough thought, enough planning, in the first place. And they finish up poorer financially, but richer in experience. If it was lack of planning, reading, or thinking that made the house collapse, you might be poorer but all you have to do is clear the rubble away, and as you are richer in experience you will plan better at your next attempt. You are dealing with brick and timber, so no harm is done.

But when you are dealing with a horse, which

is your equal in more ways than one, you are dealing with something alive,

- something with a heart,
- with a nervous system,
- with, above all else, a brain,
- with his own personality, will, and desires.

You are dealing with something which can learn and experience, and, most importantly, which can remember. And what a memory horses have! Any mistake in your planning, handling, and schooling will leave a lasting imprint in your horse's memory. Make sure, therefore, that what the horse learns and experiences is good and helpful for your further schooling.

You cannot throw away a wrongly taught lesson, a fearful experience for the horse, as you would some old rubble. The greater the mistake, the more experience and knowledge it takes to eradicate it and replace it with the right sort of lesson. If you do not have the experience to rectify the mistake, then for heaven's sake think first in order to avoid making it at all.

Of course most people think that if they don't fall off at every few steps, they can ride. One of my favourite questions before I start a new class is to ask the assembled riders, 'What in your opinion is the most important thing when riding a horse?'. Naturally there is a lot of guessing going on, and you wouldn't believe how technical people can get—they have been reading books. But rarely do they come up with the right answer, which is, 'Do not fall off'. The most important thing is to stay on. How makes no difference, but stay on.

Obviously, however, staying on is only the beginning. A student learning to play the violin, a cricketer, a golfer, or a tennis player—all have to practise how to hold the respective tools of their game. The violinist must learn how to hold the violin and the bow, how to adopt the best body position for doing so. When a person starts to drag the bow across the strings and produces some hair-raising noise, nobody—with the exception of his mother perhaps—would claim that he can play the violin, but he is nevertheless learning the fundamentals of playing the violin. To play the violin takes a lot of practice. Not to fall off is the first requirement of riding a horse. It takes a lot of practice, thinking, and understanding to ride the horse in all the beauty and grace of its natural movement, and to develop its given potential to the full.

More often than not the horseman rides not because of his skill but by the grace of his horse. The horse, unlike us, will perform even if the conditions are not the best. Even under very bad circumstances he will suffer the rider and still try his best—which can only be his best under these conditions and never the best he is really capable of.

To make it a bit plainer: the best, under rider-created bad conditions, may be to clear an obstacle 1·5 metres high, when the horse's true best is to clear at least a 2-metre obstacle. The riders, full of self-importance, think that they are marvellous because they have made the horse jump 1·5 metres, never realising how much they have in reality lost, and never really wanting to find out, because their ego could not stand the truth.

The main problem, of course, is inherited ignorance. Wrong thinking from the past produces the wrong mental approach in the present, with disastrous results.

In life generally, people tend to blame fate for their misfortunes. I have my own thoughts on the subject but this is not the place to philosophise on life. However, I do know that with horses there is no such thing as fate. If you school and work your horse properly you will have a good and reliable performer, mostly at the peak of his potential. Furthermore, and this is one of the most important points, the horse will be consistent in his performance until old age catches up with him. If you don't school him properly you will have a ratbag. Make no mistake: no matter how young you are, old age is catching up with *you* too, and it does not take long either. Many times I quote my Old Instructor during my lessons and say, 'My Old Instructor said . . .', and then I realise that when my Old Instructor actually said it he was younger than I am now.

Horses are extraordinary animals. They are unique, quite unlike any other animal. No other animal could be so misjudged, mishandled, mistreated, and abused, and still try to serve faithfully, willingly, to the best of his ability. Surely a masterpiece of creation.

Where, then, are the riders' mistakes? Where and how and why are the horses misunderstood and, as a result, mishandled, mistreated, and abused, even with the best intentions? So many riders believe that the right thing is being done. They act in complete innocence. But just as ignorance of the Law does not prevent punishment, nor can doing the wrong things innocently prevent failure and heartbreak.

If I did not believe that mistakes are being made innocently because of lack of knowledge, or misleading knowledge acquired through books whose authors based their theories on false assumptions, I would not be writing this. My reasons for writing are: firstly to help the horse, because I believe that such honest creatures deserve a fair deal in life; secondly, of course, I would like to help the riders who really are seeking the truth, who genuinely want to learn how to get the greatest enjoyment and success out of their glorious sport – a sport which, through association with a living being, offers a much greater challenge than any other sport. And it has a further advantage over any other sport: it can be successfully carried out even after old age has caught up with the rider. Age does not limit the capacity of the horseman as it does in other sports. On the contrary, with age comes experience, more understanding of the principles, greater tolerance, and, above all else, the deep and thorough realisation that one must hurry slowly. One of life's tragedies is that young people who have all their lives in front of them have no time; they are always in a terrible hurry, they want everything done yesterday. Older people, because of their accumulated experience, have a lot of time, in spite of the fact that their time is running out fast. A perfect contradiction.

Through practice and experience one learns to do things with as little effort as possible. The rider can enjoy his sport up to his last day, and can be capable of taking on all comers of all ages – witness, for example, General Poncracz of Austria competing at the Berlin Olympics at the age of seventy-six, Mrs Johnson of England in Munich at seventy-two, and Bill Roycroft in Munich at the age of fifty-eight, the oldest rider on the cross-country course yet he had one of the fastest rounds. Could you imagine some of the old heroes of past Olympics, swimmers and athletes, still starting at the Olympic Games? Impossible for any other sport, but possible for the horse rider because the horse rider has someone else who does the work for him.

Well, I said we must *think*. Where do we have to start? Where are most of the mistakes made? What produces more resistance, opposition, and even fight in the horse? What dooms the rider to failure or turns his riding into doubtful pleasure? What on the other hand is the key to success and happy enjoyment of the sport into old age? Simple. Applied common sense.

SUMMARY

1. The horse is designed as he is. We cannot change that.

2. What is the horse's means of survival? Scientists tell us that the horse's evolution took fifty-five million years. Therefore his means of survival must be pretty good.

3. He survives through his speed which enables him to flee from his enemies.

4. His speed is combined with a highly developed sense of hearing, sight, and smell.

5. The horse is thus built to go forward. If, when we school him, he fails to go forward we know that this can only be the result of incorrect schooling.

6. The brain governs all movements of all animals. The brain helps the species to survive.

7. To function and react smoothly and quickly the rider and the horse must be mentally calm and relaxed.

8. The horse has a very good brain but he does not reason as we do. He has a wonderful memory and so in schooling we must be very careful to teach him only the right things. He will not forget the right things nor will he forget the wrong things, especially if they cause him less effort.

9. We must understand the horse before we can school him. We cannot really teach him to do anything. He can do it all as soon as he is strong enough to trot. We can merely teach him to do his natural movements when *we* want him to. This is to educate him.

10. The meaning of the French word *dressage* is to train, educate, exercise, and discipline.

11. The rider, as well as the horse, must be involved in all these things. The character-building properties of riding account for the immense growth of pony clubs as a youth movement.

12. There is no fast way of educating a horse. He must have the proper preparation and advance slowly, step by step, allowing time for him to learn and understand. Because this is neglected and horses are not sufficiently prepared many horses suffer and many trainers are disappointed, not realising that the failure is their own fault because they lacked the patience to progress slowly.

13. When the horse fails to do the job expected of him the rider so often substitutes force for finesse. Then the horse usually jacks up altogether. Sometimes he attempts the jump, or whatever the task, but he will be mentally upset and so can never perform at a level approaching his best.

14. The rider who wants to school himself and his horse properly will have to sacrifice a lot of comfort and a lot of time.

15. There are as many styles of riding as there are reasons to ride—stockman, polo player, jockey, jumper—and they all involve sitting on a horse. I am sure that any rider will benefit if he tries to follow my explanations of how and why the horse should be schooled, and will, if nothing else, appreciate the horse's personality.

16. First you must sit on top and not fall off. But that is a long way short of the perfect understanding between horse and rider. Perfection means long, hard work. The conventional arts strive to reproduce nature. The art of riding is to produce the horse's natural movements, with his natural grace and beauty—under the rider.

17. In thinking about schooling the horse we must get our priorities in the right perspective—what comes first and what comes after?

18. There must be careful planning. If we plan our house wrongly and it falls down, we have gained experience and there is no harm done except the expense. Next time we will plan better and build better.

19. But if we plan our schooling poorly the mistakes will make a lasting impression on the horse's memory. We cannot just wipe it out and start again. We must remember that we are dealing with something alive, with a heart, a nervous system, and a good brain. The horse has his own personality, will, and desires. His wonderful memory will remember the bad things just as well as it will remember the good things.

20. Not to fall off is a beginning. But it takes much practice, thought, and understanding to produce the schooled horse under saddle in the gracefulness of its natural movements, and to develop its given potential to the full.

21. When conditions are bad for the horse he will still try but he cannot do his best. For example, with a rider who interferes with his mouth he manages to jump 1·5 metres. With no interference he could jump 2 metres. The rider, in his ignorance, does not realise what he has lost. He is proud of his 1·5 metres.

22. The main problem comes from inherited misunderstanding—wrong thinking in the past just copied blindly in the present with disastrous results.

23. Fate is often blamed for misfortune. With horses there is no such thing as fate. School him properly and you will have a reliable performer for years.

24. Horses are extraordinary and unique. No other animal could be so misjudged, mishandled, mistreated, and abused and still try to serve willingly to the best of his ability.

The trainer makes mistakes in all innocence, but doing the wrong thing innocently does not prevent failure and heartbreak.

25. If I did not believe that the mistakes are made innocently because of lack of knowledge, acquired through false theories in books, I would not be writing these words. I emphasise that:

(1) I want to help the horse to get a fair deal;
(2) I want to help the rider who is truly seeking the truth.

26. Riding is a sport which, because of its connection with a living being, offers a greater challenge than any other sport.

27. The rider can still ride in his old age. He has learnt understanding and tolerance and the value of the maxim *go slowly*, and so he is a better rider than the ever-hasty young.

Through practice and experience we learn to do things with as little effort as possible. This applies most particularly to riding. The horse does the work; the rider appears just to sit there. He can compete at eighty years of age if he has trained his horse correctly.

28. Where are most mistakes made? What produces resistance and fight from the horse? What, on the other hand, is the key to success and enjoyment in old age? The answer is simple —applied common sense.

CHAPTER THREE

POSITION AND BALANCE

We will start with the position of the rider. The way the rider sits on the horse, and the degree of body control, determines the rider's success. You might say, 'But a little while ago you said, "Stay on; *how* makes no difference"?'. And that's right too, but it applies firstly to the very beginner on an experienced and calm horse, and secondly to any rider in any emergency—on a bucking horse for example. If the beginner falls off, his confidence might be jolted, making him nervous for a long time, particularly if he falls awkwardly. Falling off has to be learnt too. If the bucking horse gets rid of his rider, the horse might have learnt a very important lesson, namely that he can get rid of the rider if he wants to, and that is the very last thing we want a horse to find out. In either case hang on, wherever, however, with whatever you can, but don't fall off. Even if you don't present a graceful picture remember that you will look a lot worse if you fall off.

There are two very fundamental reasons why the rider should position his body and sit in a certain way and develop complete control over his body.

Firstly, to carry the rider is a matter of balance for the horse. And here we run into the first difficulty, caused by the sheer simplicity of the fact. I know that it sounds contradictory but I still have to say it. Because it is so simple I will have to explain it in detail, and after you finish reading you will say, 'But I knew that all along and everybody else knows it as well', and I won't argue with you. I know that everybody knows, but I also know that when they get on a horse they forget that knowledge (don't ask me why that is so, but you can take it from me that it is a fact).

Now, what are the laws which we know and abide by, and yet are not aware of? The best way to understand what I am trying to explain is to go outside and find something you can carry on your shoulder. The best object would be one of the rails you use for showjumping. Pick it up, put it on your shoulder, carry it 20 metres, and drop it again. Then sit down and contemplate what you have just done. Try to find out how you did it, and why you did it the way you did. Even then you might not have the right answer. I will tell you. You placed the rail on your shoulder in a balanced way, but you did not think about how you would have to place it while you were adjusting its position on your shoulder. You just kept on shifting the rail's position on your shoulder until you felt as comfortable as possible in the circumstances.

But again you were not thinking of why you wanted to be comfortable, or why you were comfortable after you had the rail in the right position. You made every single move by feeling, *instinct* I am inclined to call it. This one example shows that you were acting according to the laws of gravity without being aware of what you were doing or why you were doing it. The rail might have weighed 10 kilograms, and yet you found it easy enough to handle after you had placed it in the right position on your shoulder.

Now, get up again, pick up the same rail, and again carry it 20 metres but—and this is important—place it in such a way on your shoulder that you have one-third of the rail in front of you and two-thirds behind. You will find that you can still carry it, but you will have the sensation that the rail is now a lot heavier than it was when it was in a balanced position, and you must make a greater effort to carry it the same distance. You find that the result does not accord with the effort. The increased pressure on your shoulder caused by the misplaced rail, the increased discomfort and effort you experience, is directly proportional to the degree of shift in balance of the weight you are carrying. You would never do it this way because you do it correctly by what I call 'instinct'.

Here is where man differs from the horse. Here is where the horse shows, and proves, his lack of intelligence. This is just as well because if he had the power of reason, which man does not use when dealing with the horse, we would not be able to get anywhere near him. We would have no horse sports. Let's thank creation that the horse is willing to do what man would not do, and that is to do it the hard way. You may think, 'What does a rail on my shoulder have to do with my position on the horse?'. The answer is simple—everything. Weight has to be carried whether you or I carry it, or whether it is carried by a ship, a truck, an aeroplane, or a horse. The weight, the load, must be balanced; otherwise there will be disaster. You or I might fall on our nose, a ship sink, a truck turn over, an aeroplane crash, and your horse break down

as so many do, when in reality no horse should break down, or would break down, if man used his intelligence.

Balance is a matter of life and death. Anything not balanced is doomed to destruction—or extinction, as with so many animals of prehistory. They could not adjust to the changed condition of the environment and balance themselves with nature, and therefore vanished from the face of the earth.

We know it, every designer is aware of it, yet when dealing with the horse we completely forget it and use a different yardstick altogether. The big question is why? The reason is the wrong thinking of the past, an inherited misconception accepted and applied without thought. Conclusions man reached a few hundred years ago have no right to exist in this age of the atom when astronauts are walking on the moon. For centuries the riding world has been under the illusion that the rider does, and can, balance the horse—a fact which at close examination turns out to be what I just called it, an illusion. The reasoning which started people thinking in this direction is another misconception. It was in the past believed, and it is still believed, that the horse because of his conformation carries more weight on the forehand than on the hindquarters, and because of this the rider has to raise the forehand and by doing so shift the point of gravity further backwards and establish an equilibrium. What utter rubbish! I can understand and forgive such thinking in past centuries. Men just did not know any better, though I think they should have known better, because the man who more than any other was responsible for conceiving and publishing these ideas—L. Seeger of Germany—did so in 1844, 150 years after Isaac Newton published his findings on gravity and the laws of motion. Whatever the reason for his ignorance, Seeger spawned one of the most disastrous theories, which I am sorry to say is followed to this very day. Why has this not been rectified a long time ago? Simply because all the authors who followed L. Seeger faithfully and thoughtlessly copied his findings. For example, 'to improve the balance of the horse it is necessary to raise the head and neck'. You can find that same basic theory in all books between Seeger and the present day, probably because Seeger's was thought to be a classic.

Naturally if the fundamental idea is wrong everything that follows must be wrong too, so let us find out why it is wrong. Is the horse by nature unbalanced and therefore carrying more weight on the forehand than on the hindquarters? When we look at the horse, at the head and neck—the forepart of his body—the horse does indeed look heavier on the forehand than on the hindquarters, and it is too. But, and here comes the crucial point overlooked by Seeger, only when the horse is at rest—standing still. Then the forehand, as crude tests have shown, is 27 to 36 kilograms heavier than the hindquarters. To overcome this natural shortcoming in balance nature has supplied the horse with an automatic system of suspension, which locks the forelegs into position without any muscular effort. That is why a horse never rests his forelegs as he does his hindlegs; if he should rest his foreleg then you know there is trouble because only injury of some degree will make him do so.

When the horse starts to move he will collect himself and balance his weight evenly on all four legs. If this were not so, not even primitive man would have had any idea of making use of the horse. Far less would the horse have inspired poets through the centuries to the most flowery descriptions of the glory of his movement and the nobility of his character. We would not have the horse at all, because horses would not have survived. The only thing we would know about the horse would be what we know about other extinct animals—from fossilised remains. Whatever you choose to look at in nature you will find to be balanced—chemically, ecologically, astronomically. The whole universe is in a state of balance and when that state of balance is upset there is disaster. Only man in his big-headed ignorance could have conceived the idea that he must improve on the Lord's creation and bring the horse into a state of

equilibrium to save it from extinction after only fifty-five million years of evolution!

However, all this philosophy does not answer a most important question—can or could the rider balance the horse? Is it mechanically possible? What does the law of gravity have to say? Whichever way you might wish to look at the problem the answer is always 'No', and must always be 'No', for the simple reason that the load cannot balance the support. It always is, and must be, the other way round. The support must balance the load, no matter what the load might be.

To make it even clearer, let us transfer the concept into other spheres of our life. If the load could balance the support, then railway lines would not have to be firmly and solidly laid because the train would keep them in place. No matter how one built a truck, an aeroplane, or a boat the load would keep it in a balanced position. One could think of a million examples and all of them would be equally absurd. Nothing would need any sound foundation—chairs and tables would need only one leg, houses no foundation. Earthquakes would lose their terror, avalanches do no harm—after all, it is the snow that keeps the mountain in its place! All this would be the case if we could balance the horse while sitting on it. As it is not so, it proves that man is not using his intelligence by abusing the laws of nature when dealing with the horse—laws which are accepted, and respected, in all other aspects of life. It all goes back to L. Seeger. I don't blame Seeger. Perhaps he had a right to be wrong because, after all, the great technological advances came after he had written the book. The catastrophe is not that Seeger was wrong, but that after 150 years we are still wrong although we are in possession of all the knowledge of modern science.

All these digressions started from a discussion of the rider's position. I wanted to prove to you that there is a lot behind my statement that position comes first, and everything else comes after. If the rider cannot balance the horse while sitting on top of it, and I hope I have proved my point, then what can the rider do?

Can he do anything at all to help and facilitate the horse's task? Yes, he can—sit still. That's the great secret. Sit still—no more, no less. The horse is by nature as well balanced as we are—or anything else you want to look at in nature. Take the whole range from a mosquito to an elephant and you will find that all of these creatures are perfectly equipped for their special task of staying alive, and within that for the survival of their kind. Their body structure, their way of life—is balance. Why should horses be an exception? Like the rest of nature they are naturally balanced.

Just as the carrying of a load upsets your own balance and you have to adjust to it, so does the added weight of the rider disturb the natural balance of the horse. Therefore, the corner-stone of our success in schooling lies within the horse's ability to re-establish his natural balance under the rider's weight. It is the horse that must find his balance. Therefore, once again, *sit still*. The role of the rider in this respect is a passive one. It is definitely not an active one, not attempting through body movements to help the horse find his balance and—horror of all horrors—definitely not raising the forehand with the hands.

To highlight what I just said about position I will tell you what happened during a lecture I held with the first team that went to England to train for the Olympic Games held in Stockholm in 1956. We had the lecture in Bunty Thompson's room at the hotel in Aldershot, and to emphasise the very thing I have just been talking about I asked Ernie Barker to put John Winchester on his shoulders and walk up and down a line in the carpet. Well, Ernie walked up and down without any difficulties at all. He was even going straight along the line until I gave John a little push as Ernie went past, and Ernie started to wobble about. I said to Ernie, 'Why don't you go straight?'. Ernie replied, 'I can't walk straight; he is not sitting still'. I said, 'Ernie, you have just said the most beautiful thing you could have said. Don't you ever forget what you've just said when you are sitting on your horse'.

If natural laws control our daily lives why should it be different with the horse?

Now all this discussion about position and balance was my first point. The second is equally important, and equally ignored and overlooked, because as long as we can get from A to B in some fashion we think everything is just fine. But is it? Most certainly not. We can only do what we can because the horse will do what man won't do—do it the hard way. That brings us back to how marvellous our horses really are. They not only carry us around even when far removed from the state of natural balance, they even guess what we want them to do, and that is a lot more than most people can do.

The second point about position is concerned with communication—generally called 'the aids'. Again I am compelled to develop the subject in an attempt to make it quite clear. As much as balance is misunderstood, so may communication with the horse well be even more misunderstood and muddled, and in a lot of cases not understood at all.

As a start to this all-important discussion we must go back to the question, 'How much and what can we teach the horse?'. As I said previously, when I ask the same question in my classes the replies run approximately along these lines, 'We teach the horse to walk, trot, canter properly; we teach him to jump, change legs in the air, anything we want to do'. Is that so? No, it is not. So far as movement is concerned we can't teach him anything at all, for the simple reason that he can already do everything that we might ever want him to do. He can walk, trot, canter, stop and turn, jump and change legs, go backwards—and he could do it all as soon as he was strong enough to stand on his legs, and that was very soon after he was born. Granted, wobbly and uncertain to begin with, but after a few days of practice he could do even the most beautiful capriole. All of course in his own good time, when he feels like it, when he wants to do it. Unconstrained by weight, unhindered by a foreign will except for an occasional disciplinary nip from mother—an otherwise happy, glorious, carefree childhood.

32

Then comes man with saddle and bridle, a swollen head, and a powerful sense of self-importance, believing that he is right but never having thought about it—a sort of 'my grandfather was a horseman, how could I be wrong' attitude. Worst of all, man comes into the life of the young horse after approximately two years. This alone is just short of criminal as the full calcification of the horse's bone structure is not completed before three-and-a-half to four years. But more about that later on.

I said that we can't teach the horse anything because he can already do it. He learnt it in the same way that we learnt to walk and finished by climbing trees. Nobody taught us, it just came naturally. The horse learnt it in the same way, all programmed into his genetic inheritance.

If we can't teach him anything, what can we do? What must we do to be able to make use of his power and movement, of his ability to go fast, to cover long distances, and jump over all sorts of obstacles? The magic word is 'education', which will give us the understanding of the horse and will produce the necessary discipline. Without discipline, riding is a nightmare, and nothing more or less than a case of getting from A to B somehow, and even that is often doubtful. Very few people have the ability to force the horse into submission to carry the rider. The very rare rider has the ability to force the horse and still get some sort of performance out of him—but that is the born horseman.

A lot of riders think that they are born horsemen but very few really are. I could count the born horsemen I have met in forty-five years of riding on the fingers of one hand and even then I would have some fingers left over. Most of us have to cook with water, in other words approach the subject with a bit more care and thought.

I said earlier that horses have a wonderful memory. Without that memory we could not do a thing with them; they would be dog's meat from the start. Unfortunately more horses than I care to think about are finishing up as dog's meat because the riders are ignorant of the most basic principles. They make the horse break down.

We have to try to understand one very important fact before we go any further because everything hinges on it. The rider must understand that he must make the horse understand. Believe it or not, if the horse understands what the rider wants him to do he will do it. Most of the confusion, disobedience, and fights are caused by the horse's not understanding. And because he does not understand he does not know what the rider wants, and he gets frustrated, and that frustration can take all forms.

Our brain controls the movements of our body. We are not aware of it, and so we don't realise that the horse's brain controls his body too. If the horse's brain controls his body movements we must make him understand what we want him to do. If he understands, he can and will do it—but only if he understands. As we have no means of communication with the horse other than our aids, the importance of body control, which in turn produces consistency of aids, is becoming apparent. This is not the place to discuss the aids in detail, but generally speaking there are:
- the aids with weight (nearly always misunderstood);
- the leg aids (mostly not used enough) and;
- the aids with the hands (more often than not used too much).

These are known as the 'natural aids', which are supplemented by the artificial aids like spurs and whips and all the various gadgets invented by riders to prove what savage brutes horses are, but which prove only the lack of ability and expertise of the rider.

To teach the horse our aids, and that is the only thing we can teach him, is like teaching somebody a foreign language. If, for instance, you want to teach Spanish, you will have to use Spanish words all the time, and not Spanish and then German, followed by Chinese and maybe a few other languages, otherwise your pupil will never learn Spanish but only become thoroughly confused. Of course you would not teach Spanish that way because it is stupid. You would not do it because you would be dealing with an intelligent being who more than likely would tell you that you were not right in the mind. With horses of course, it is different. They are 'stupid', they can't talk back. Heaven be thanked that they can't, or we would hear some awful language. Probably because they can't give us a piece of their mind, and for some inexplicable ignorance on our part when dealing with the horse, we apply the aids— which are our only language with the horse— in any old fashion. Anywhere, anyhow. We use all the languages in the world and then get cross if the horse doesn't understand, and misinterprets our mixture of world language. I keep on asking myself the same questions over and over again, 'Why is it so? Why are people so ignorant of such simple facts? Worse still, why are they ignorant of it only when dealing with the horse?'.

Horses are born with the ability to move and to learn, and we have been born with the same abilities. A baby born to English-speaking parents has not inherited the ability to speak English, only the ability to learn to speak. If you take the baby to Italian-speaking foster parents the child will grow up speaking Italian. The way a child speaks a language is in itself a fair pointer to the way the parents speak. The language indicates the background.

Horses are not born with a knowledge of the aids, only with the ability to learn them. You have to teach them, and rest assured that, once learnt and understood, they will never be forgotten. The memory of the horse is a tremendous asset to the rider, but it can also turn into a liability because horses don't forget the bad lessons either. The moral of the story is to teach them the proper things in the first place.

The better the body control of the rider is, the more consistent the aids are going to be. The more consistent the aids are, the faster the horse will learn, the greater the joy of achievement and the greater the success will be. And the partnership will last until old age catches up with our dear old friend. That's exactly

Franz Mairinger on Gay Pam, clearly depicting his ideal position

what your horse is going to be, your dear old friend, a member of your family. The body control of the rider must be such that the rider knows under any conditions what the different parts of his body are doing, and he must be able to use any part of his body independently from the rest of his body. The rider must be aware of his body. This is something that has to be learnt because in normal life we are not aware of what we do and how we do it; we just move and that is that. This may be good enough for getting up in the morning and going through your daily chores and going to bed again, but it is not good enough for schooling a horse. How this all-important control of the body can be achieved we will discuss later. For the moment all I want you to do is think, and prepare yourself mentally, because if your thinking is not right, what comes after can't be right either. Remember that with horses there is no such thing as fate. They are only a perfect mirror of you, as complete as a person—character,

34

temperament, intelligence, tolerance. They describe you better than any fortune teller could do.

So many words, and only two points covered! And even then, only the *why* of it, not even the *how*, which falls into another chapter. I have gone to the trouble of a detailed explanation because my experience in teaching has shown and proved that riders overlook the most simple facts, and because of this lack of awareness and its consequences they run into endless trouble. The tragedy is that with a little more thought all this could have been avoided.

Remember, riders don't have trouble with horses. It is the other way round. Horses have trouble with riders.

SUMMARY

1. Of first importance is the position of the rider. We hang on in any old way in an emergency, but there are two fundamental reasons why the rider should sit in a certain way.

Firstly: For the horse, the carrying of the rider is a matter of balance. If the rider sits straight and still in the middle the horse can carry him with the least effort. To carry a pole with the least effort you place its middle on your shoulder so that it is in balance and, therefore, easier to carry. Likewise, the aeroplane or the truck must be loaded in balance or there could be disaster. Balance is one of the laws of nature that we know and abide by but are not really aware of. Isaac Newton published his laws of gravity and motion in approximately A.D. 1700. About 150 years later a German, L. Seeger, wrote that the rider must balance his horse by raising his head and neck. But the horse is balanced by nature: he needs no help. Seeger is really saying that the load must balance the support . . . *rubbish*! The support must always balance the load. This misconception has led to many erroneous theories about schooling horses. Because of the horse having to balance the rider, *position comes first and all else after*. All the rider can do to help the horse is to sit still and straight.

2. *Secondly:* The second fundamental reason for a good position is communication—generally called 'the aids'. As we have said, the horse can do all the movements when he is free and unhindered by the weight or the will of his rider. He does them all naturally, when *he* feels like it. He learns them as we learn to walk and climb. Nobody teaches us; it is all programmed into our—and his—genetic inheritance. What is it that will give us command of all his ability? In one word—*education*. We educate the horse and the rider so that they both understand what is wanted. Once the horse understands he will do as he is asked. That is, he submits to discipline.

3. It is a very important point that the rider must understand the horse, his temperament and ability, and he must quietly make the horse understand what it is he wishes him to do. This can never be done by force. Confusion and

fights come from the fact that the horse does not understand what he is supposed to do, or the rider does not understand how to teach the horse. This must be done thoughtfully through his brain. His brain, like ours, controls all movements.

4. How do we make him understand? We teach him the meaning of the aids. He learns through 'feel', and this shows how important our own body control really is. We must be able to govern exactly the small movements of individual parts of our body so that they act in a clear and definite way. These small movements constitute the aids by which we communicate with the horse. The aids are weight, the leg aids, and the hand aids. These are supplemented by artificial aids—spurs, whip, and any gadget invented by man to cover his own lack of body control, knowledge, and understanding.

5. How do we teach the horse the meaning of the aids? The aids (to ask for a certain thing) must always be given in exactly the same way and place. When the horse responds correctly he is rewarded. Consistency is all-important. Many riders are careless. They give the aids in any old way and still expect the horse to interpret them correctly. The horse is born with the ability to move and to learn. He is not born with a knowledge of the aids, only with the ability to learn them if properly taught. We have to teach him, and once the horse has learnt he will never forget. His wonderful memory is a great asset to the rider, provided that he teaches his horse the right thing in the first place.

6. The better the body control is, the more consistent the aids will be. Then the horse will learn quickly and rider and horse will understand each other. The control must be such that the rider knows what every part of his body is doing and every movement must be independent of every part of the body. We do not normally think about what we do with our body, but to be a good rider we *must do so*. The rider does not have trouble with the horse; the horse has trouble with the rider.

CHAPTER FOUR

THE ART OF CONTROL

First of all you have to have a back that submits when you sit, a back that swings and is supple. Only then can you do something with it. If I say to an architect, 'Explain how to decorate a building without telling me how to build the house', I couldn't do a thing with the house. I would have to build it first. It is the same with the horse. The seat has to be developed first, then come the finer points. I remember a school in Perth where I said, 'Canter left'. You should have seen one fellow! His aids were exaggerated, to say the least. 'Where did you get that from?' I asked, 'I didn't tell you to do that'. He replied, 'I read a book and it said that to canter left you put your left hip forward and your right shoulder back'. This is true, but it is a finer point which comes into operation after you have learnt to sit still and square and know how to let your weight down, and when your horse is responsive to the legs. Then you don't have to move your legs so far. All you have to do is apply a tiny pressure with your hip. But that is far from being an exaggerated movement.

If you are inexperienced you are inclined to overdo things. The finer points come later by themselves. Every rider will develop according to his personality and temperament— a tiny bit here and a tiny bit there. The stallions from the School in Vienna, and the riders, are both schooled along the same lines, schooled for years and kept an eye on. When you rode the various stallions you found a thread of schooling common to all of them, but each one kept a little stamp of his master. With one you had to have a little bit more leg, with another a little less leg; one cantered on a bit better, another did a better piaffe, another a better passage, and so on. The reason for this is that no person is the same as another. Even though the stallions had been schooled along the same lines they all reacted in a different way.

The history of horses and horsemanship is a fascinating subject. Xenophon, 2400 years ago, said, 'No hoof, no horse'. He was really keen on breeding horses with very hard hooves. It's true enough— no hoof and you have no horse to ride.

Years ago the men who couldn't walk, or march, and carry heavy armour at the same time, were put on horses and were handicapped in one way or another. Man had to design some means of making the horse pliable and at the same time make the hooves hard. When knights were fighting in heavy armour, they had to have the horse as there was no other means of transport. And when you were fighting on horseback your life depended on the ability of the horse—how responsive, how fast he was— because if the other horse was better schooled than yours, your head would be cut off before you knew anything about it. The end result was to have the horse at your disposal when you needed him, and to keep him sound. It took a fair amount of time and work to get him responsive, to make him understand. If he was not schooled properly he broke down.

Dressage probably failed to take on in England because of the influence of the Duke of Newcastle, who studied on the Continent. Somewhere in a book he read the statement, 'What a pity; you school a horse for three years and then he breaks down'. The practical Englishman tended to say, 'Why should I fiddle around here? I would rather ride to hounds. Forget about dressage; it's no good'. Well, the initial schooling of those horses must have been wrong, otherwise they would not have broken down.

The whole point of dressage is to keep the horse serviceable for as long as possible. We have to achieve this goal through work. The true translation of *dressage* is 'to train'. 'To train' means exercise, education, and discipline. What do we want to exercise? We want to exercise the physical part of the horse. What do we want to educate? The mind. Dressage doesn't mean anything but the systematic development of the mental and physical abilities of the horse. Nothing else. Some people think that horses are stupid. Maybe they are, because otherwise they wouldn't put up with us. Fortunately, they don't know how strong they are.

Horses have a fair amount of intelligence. Their minds may not work like ours—they definitely appear to go only in a straight line— yet it is amazing how many times they get the better of the rider. The horse gets away with things; he does the things he likes to do, not the ones the rider wants him to do. He likes to do the things which come easily, that do not involve any strain, any exercise, any work. Isn't it true of us? Don't we try to do the things that don't involve any strain or physical exercise? This is because of the natural laziness of the body. If you work it is because your mind drives you; and if your mind doesn't drive you, all you do is lie in the sun. That is probably the reason why so many people buy lottery tickets.

The horse is buying lottery tickets all the time too, by putting it over the rider. Of course he does not know, and there is no way of verbally explaining to the horse, 'Now listen, horse, if you hang on, if you don't balance yourself, if you don't collect yourself, one day your leg will break down and you will go to the knacker'. You try to tell him, and there is only one way you can make him understand. You can talk to him through his feeling; there is no other way.

So many times at the jumping ground you will hear riders calling out 'Jump, jump, hup, hup'. A Dutchman in Adelaide cried, 'Joomp, joomp', each time he approached the jump. The horse didn't, but he did—and landed right in the middle of the oxer. You can talk to a horse as often as you like but you will only make him do something for you through the influence of your position. That is how you talk to him.

I have never heard of a broken-down wild horse, and I have never read any stories about one. You may have heard something in the bush, although I make it a point of asking when I come across people from the outback. Even in the American West no one has ever heard of it. This proves my point—horses don't break down by themselves. But as soon as we break them in and squeeze ourselves on to their backs horses are bound to break down right, left, and centre. I would like to know how many yearlings are sold, how many yearlings go to the racetrack, how many yearlings are racing after three or four years, and how many have broken down.

Nature supplies the horse with everything he needs for his survival, and one of the things he can do is to stand on his four legs and remain balanced on his four legs at whatever pace he goes. There is no joint connection in the front, but there is one in the hip, the engine, the driving force. All the power is developed in the hindlegs and transmitted through the spine, which pushes. The picture should, therefore, be one of the hindquarters pushing the front forward and not, as you often see, a case of the front going here and the quarters dragging behind—like pulling a wheelbarrow from the front instead of pushing from behind. All the muscles are there because he needs them. It is the same with human beings: all the muscles you have, you have because you need them.

If you pick up a bag of chaff, or if you say, 'I will make it my occupation to carry chaff around all my life', you don't have to grow a new set of muscles. You already have them. What you would have to do would be to strengthen the particular muscle groups that you intend to use. You would develop the means you have.

I had better explain what I mean by 'natural balance'. If I walk around I am naturally balanced and I have no fear of being top-heavy. Who taught me, or who taught you, to be naturally balanced?

I watch my little granddaughter crawling around on the carpet. She tries to crawl, but the poor little girl doesn't know that she has to bring her knees under her tummy in order to go forward. Instead she tries to drag herself forward with her hands, and as I watch her I wonder how I can help her. But I can't. She understands about as much of my language as the horse does. If I were to try to tell a horse what he should do he would just look at me with his big brown eyes full of trust and think that I had gone round the bend.

The process is a natural one. You just do it. As the proverb says, 'You must crawl before you walk, walk before you run'. But as you crawl, and then walk, and then run, you never know how it all happens. And then you start to climb boxes and do other things, and you never know how it all comes about. It's just natural.

The tragedy of the horseman is that he doesn't recognise that the horse develops in the same natural way. As soon as he can stand on his legs he can run and do everything else. Nature takes care of that. If this had not been the case we wouldn't have any horses at all. They would all have been eaten by wild animals.

So he develops his balance, his natural balance, which is effortless. And so do we. If I were to walk and forget to put my foot under my point of gravity I would fall on my nose. If I were to take that rail mentioned in the previous chapter and carry it with one end longer than the other I would really experience the effort needed to maintain a state of balance. The more someone leant on that rail the more effort I would have to put into maintaining my balance. It's directly proportional. If you put your load on properly and get used to it you can run around, but if it is not balanced it needs a lot more effort to carry the rail.

At every school that I attend, particularly where there is jumping, I let someone pick up a rail and carry it around. In fifteen years of doing this, only once did I strike a person who picked it up and carried it the hard way from the beginning. I had to send him back because he was no good to me. Either there was something missing or he did it on purpose. Every sensible person will pick up a load and balance it. It makes the job so much easier. As mentioned before, we try to have everything easy for ourselves. When the horse picks up a load that he doesn't like he unloads it every now and then. If something squeezes itself on his back, what is that load doing to the horse's natural and effortless balance? It unbalances him, it upsets the natural balance. If you pick up a very awkward load, you may have to sit down and work out how to place it so that it will stay in position. You will balance the load if you can, if you have the intelligence. The horse does not have the intelligence, because if he did I would be out of a job. He would tell you, 'Now look, old fellow, you do this and you do that'.

You may have heard of the American journalist who went out hunting in Ireland. He was to ride a grey stallion, and he mounted it and sat down with a thud. The stallion turned around and said, 'Have you done a lot of hunting, sir?', and the rider replied, 'Well, I'm afraid not'. The stallion said, 'Yes, I can feel that you haven't'. So off they went and they came to the first jump, and the stallion turned and said, 'Would you like to jump that one?'. 'Oh, yes, I would', the rider replied. 'Well, just leave it to me', the stallion replied. They jumped and landed on the other side, and the stallion turned around and really abused the rider. 'I told you to leave it to me. Why did you hang on to my head? It felt terrible?' Then they came to a big ditch and the horse said, 'Would you like to jump this one?'. The rider answered, 'Oh, yes please, yes'. 'Oh, would you?' the horse said, 'Well, I wouldn't', and *plop* he landed the rider in the ditch. It was full of mud. The stallion took one look at him, made a rude noise, and galloped off after the rest of the field. Two hours later he came back and overtook the rider trudging home, wet and muddy. The stallion filled him in on what had happened on the hunt, how they had got the fox out from cover, and in what paddock they had caught him. Then the stallion said, 'I suppose you would like me to take you home?', to which the rider replied, 'I would very much appreciate it'. 'I'm afraid you stink too much!' the stallion said, and went off home by himself.

Yes, if horses could talk it would solve all the problems. If they could speak English! Very often they do talk but we can't understand what they are saying. The stallion in the story would probably say, 'You so and so, you pulled on my mouth'. Some horses throw up their heads after they jump, and if they could talk they would probably say the same thing as the talking stallion, 'Oh, that hurt!'.

In a lot of other ways they try to tell us things, but we don't understand. Yet we have to try to understand everything. We must find out or figure out why this horse tosses his head; why he tries to run away; why he is lugging in with his shoulder; why he tries to buck me off; why he fights me. There is a reason for everything. He doesn't do anything without a reason, nor do you.

So we always come back to the horse, that machine, that creature with its natural balance which needs no extra effort to maintain graceful, elegant motion. Yet, put a rider on top and it's gone—gone is the elegance, gone that beautiful picture of power and symphony of movement. It can still be there, but the rider must know how to achieve it.

The rider must sit in a position such that if the horse were taken out from under him he would still be standing in a squatting position. The load must be balanced in itself. If you tilt the body back and have the feet forward, and then take the horse away, the rider would fall on his back. It is exactly the same principle as when you are carrying that rail on your back. If it is balanced you can let your hand fall loose, but if it is not balanced one end will fall down and the other will probably hit you on the head.

What must the rider be able to do to maintain the balance of that load? As I have said before, he must sit still. That's all there is to it. *Sit still*—just two little words. Do you find it easy to sit still? No, it's very difficult. In order to be able to sit still you must first understand the basic principle involved. This is a principle that we can't change because it is a law of nature. Believe me, there is one thing we can't cheat— we can't cheat nature. We may steal a ride for years, not knowing how much we have been penalised. But penalised we are—by going through a lot of horses, by having a sore backside, aching head and toes, broken ribs, and so on, as well as a most uncomfortable ride. That is how we are punished. And most of the time we don't even know that it could be any other way.

We once had a flat in Vienna. We were very pleased to get it and we were very happy there. Five years later when I returned to Vienna and walked down the street where we had lived and looked up at our old balcony, I said to myself, 'How on earth could we ever have been happy living in that dump?'. But we didn't know any better at that time and we were very happy. The rider who flops around all his life is quite happy because he doesn't know any other way.

To develop the controlled position which enables you to sit still you must avoid interference. You must not interfere with the way the horse moves. The art of riding is the art of not interfering. That's all.

The art of riding is called 'classical high school'. The foundation of the whole thing springs from the classical age of the Greeks. Xenophon wrote the first book on training horses, and I don't really agree with everything he says. But he says one thing that has not changed since that time, and will never change, and should not change. He appreciates the horse as a personality and he gives him the same right to a fair deal that we expect for ourselves. He treats him as something alive— with a head, a nervous system—something that can be frightened, something that can be brave, and something that can be sick and tired.

In essence Xenophon says, 'Be kind to your horse. Don't be rough and tough and hard. Don't punish him and don't hit him. Try to kid him along, try to show him'. Xenophon even goes so far as to say (and this is why I don't agree with everything he says), 'If you want your horse to jump over that ditch, take him by the lead and jump with him'.

It is important that you acknowledge the horse's right to a fair deal, to be treated properly and not knocked around. You have no justification for ill-treating him.

You have to try to develop gradually the ability to avoid interference, and that is the art of controlling your horse. When you stop interfering you give the horse every opportunity to use himself exactly as he would when he runs out in the paddock on his own. You treat him with intelligence, not with a constant stream of checks and upsets. Not with a *bump, bump* of the load on his back, a *jab, jab, jab* of the hands in the mouth, a *kick, kick, kick* with the legs, a *wobble, wobble* here and a *wobble, wobble* there.

Naturally, the more you move the more you interfere and the more efficiency you take out of his movement. If the normal length of his stride is from here to there, and suddenly *bump*,

bump, the rider comes down on top of him, he will take only a short step. He has, therefore, to take many more steps to cover the same distance than when he is striding without interference.

The road to this goal is a long and stony one, and because it is a long way people try to take a short cut. Now let me tell you—*there is no short cut*. There may be short cuts in making money. You may think that you don't have to be a Rembrandt to paint a picture, but that all you have to do is to get some paint, put the canvas on the windscreen and start the wipers going, or drag the dog across it, and then sell if for $500. That would be a short cut. But you can't take short cuts with the horse. There is no short cut. There is no short cut to the development of the control position, and there can't be. You have to sit there, and you have to stretch out, and you have to take a fair bit of *bounce, bounce, bounce* until you relax and let yourself go, let yourself into the horse.

Most people give up as they become worn and tired. The best cure for this is the treatment the Old Instructor gave me when I first came to the School in Vienna. For two years previously I had ridden with short stirrups for jumping. I could not do dressage at all. On first coming to the School every pupil starts off on the lunging rein, so I had 1 hour on the lunge rein and then the Old Instructor said to his crew, 'Bring me another stallion, he is still too stiff'. And then we went on for another hour. I didn't walk home very well that day! But this is really the only way, the hard way. You have to ride without stirrups or you will not overcome the greatest difficulty in your own body. For we are all one-sided. When I pick up a piece of chalk I pick it up with my right hand as I am right-handed. Everything I do, I do with my right hand. Some other people do it with their left hand, but there are more right-handed than left-handed people.

Horses unfortunately are one-sided too. They are inclined to go with the hindquarters to the right, and the tragedy is that there are more right-handed horses than left-handed horses. So, take a rider who is inclined to collapse his right hip—and by collapsing on the right the left leg is longer than the right leg, even if you are dead straight in yourself. He gets on the horse, which throws out his quarters to the right and so puts the rider in a position to the left.

So now there are two crooked ones, and out of the two crooked ones you are trying to make one straight horse. If you want to achieve straightness one of the two has to straighten out first. And who is that one to be? The rider—for the simple reason that it's a matter of mechanics, a matter of balance, a law of nature. As long as the weight of the rider is hanging on that side to the left, the horse cannot balance himself with ease and you have no hope of ever making him straight. He will curve himself to the right by himself. The foundation of all schooling is to get the horse straight, or flexed to the left, or flexed to the right, when we want to flex him. He has to develop the necessary suppleness so that he can do it.

Most horses hang on that left rein a lot more and don't want to take the right one. They curl up, and if you really try to drive them with the right leg, they are inclined to kick up or go against the leg. This is where education comes in. To make him straight, to make him supple and flexible, is exercise. To develop that straightness and flexibility is exercise. But to make him understand what we are telling him, and to stop him from doing what he wants to do, is education.

The firmer our position is, the straighter and the more still we sit, the less we interfere. But there is another very important element associated with this. What is it?

When I demonstrate this point in a lecture I usually ask for a volunteer. I ask him to concentrate. When I pinch him on the left arm he is to bring me a cup of coffee. If I pinch him on the right arm I want some sugar for my coffee. When I pinch him on the right hand I want whisky and soda. When I pinch him on the left hand I want some ice for my whisky.

Each time I pinch him in the same place he goes off to get what I want. When I pinch him on the right hand he brings me the scotch and soda straight away. What I try to demonstrate is very simple of course. If I press him or pinch him on the same spot all the time he is going to bring me the same thing all the time because that is what I have schooled him to do. If you press your horse on the same place every time, and for the same thing, it is amazing how quickly he will come marching up for scotch and soda, or for coffee, or whatever.

I can explain all this to you, and if you don't understand you can speak up and ask. But there is no way of discussing it with the horse. He can't ask you to repeat it, or say, 'What was that?'. You have to make it absolutely clear, and the better your position is the more consistent your aids will be. If your position is not under control, how on earth can you be sure that you are pushing him on the same place, in the same way, for the same thing, all the time?

But if you push him once, and you push twice, and you push him three times in the same way, you will be surprised how quickly he understands. Horses concentrate tremendously; they have a lot more concentration than we have. One day when I was riding Tina Wommelsdorf's Jackpot, something went *rattle* in the bush and he was away. He could hear something here and something there and so he looked around everywhere because that was what he felt like doing. He shied and I gave him a little kick in the ribs. I could feel him move as if inwardly saying, 'There is something over there and I would like to have a look, but I had better not'. I was on top of him and I could feel him as he tried to wriggle away and shy but he knew better because I was concentrating too. He knew that I was concentrating, and that if he did try to jump away I would be very quick with whatever was necessary to get his concentration back.

They concentrate if you ask. Every movement of your body should convey something to the horse, and if it doesn't convey anything because you are not moving, that means everything is good.

42

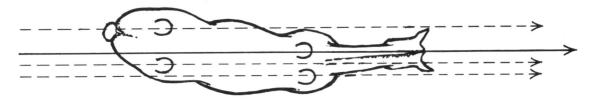

Diagram 1: A crooked horse

So, here we go. I say we want to canter. You move one leg back and the other leg pushes, because everything was motionless before. Away we go. The rider is still again. The horse canters and canters, but he listens, he listens, he listens. It is very hard. It takes a tremendous amount of work and development.

The horse's spine is on top of your line of movement. You try to achieve it but because of the horse's one-sidedness, because of the horse's length of balance with the weight, he finds it very hard to go on that line. Moreover, horses have a bag full of tricks. Sometimes I suspect that they use them deliberately, not just by accident. They really do use their heads and they seem to say, 'No! No! No! He is not looking!'. And away they go. They fall in with the quarters and they fall out with the quarters, they lug in and fall in with the shoulder. They can also fall out with the shoulder.

As one line, as shown in Diagram 2—that is the way the horse should go. As soon as he is moving in the way shown below, straight or flexed, you have achieved something, and that is what you want to achieve. You want one hindleg here and one hindleg there; one front leg here, one front leg there. The hindleg steps exactly on the same line as the front leg. As he does so he is stepping under his weight, plus your weight. He is stepping with both hindlegs under his weight.

While he does not distribute the weight evenly

Diagram 2: A straight horse

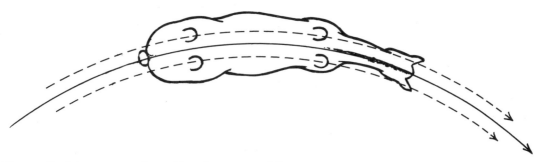

Diagram 3: A horse correctly positioned on a curved line

43

on four legs there will be a danger of his breaking down if you do too much. The other thing is that you will never develop the control necessary to have a really obedient horse, because you can't control that hindleg if it does not step under your weight.

This is something that you must have felt at least once in order to understand it. That is what we try to achieve. We try to achieve it on a big circle first, then we gradually make that circle smaller and smaller until we have a circle not bigger than 6 metres in diameter. No circle smaller than that is demanded on one track: anything smaller would be a movement on two tracks. You can picture it. A small bend only is needed when the turn is big. But the smaller the circle, the bigger the bend and the more flexion the horse has to have in his longitude, the more suppleness he must develop.

On the big turn you start off by asking for just a little; you ask for a little bit more flexion and a little bit more flexion. You do it in the same way as I do it with you. I say, 'Down with your heel'. If you bring it down a little bit I say, 'Yes, that is better'. I don't ask you straight away to come down to the maximum, because I know that you can't. Everything has to be developed gradually.

How do we develop it? So long as the horse goes forward in any old way at first that's good enough for me. But as soon as he understands and catches on I squeeze him a little bit. When he is willing to walk on, when he is willing to trot on, then we ask for more.

The freer the walk, the more he will overstep. You don't have a young horse collected; if you do, you have already broken some of the laws. The footprint of the front leg is shown below. The degree of free walk depends on how far he oversteps. He will overstep one or two hoof-widths. A good walker will overstep more. The more you collect him the more that footprint will come back until it is back on that front hoof print again.

He must overstep for a very simple reason — because his weight is moving. If I tilt my body I have to take a long step, because if I don't take a long step I will fall forward and hit my nose on the wall. I am going further, and therefore the support must reach under the weight.

The faster the pace, the more he over-reaches the foreprint. The shorter the pace, the more he must bend in his hocks and the less he will overstep because he can't. The weight then remains in the middle; and he can't overstep when the weight is there. But as he goes he must support his body. He must support his weight. Therefore, he has to step forward and overstep, because if he doesn't, he just does not go forward. It's all very simple.

In the beginning there is no need to worry about how much he oversteps. There is no need to worry so long as he goes when you say 'Go'. If, when you say 'Go' he says, 'Yes, I will go', you have taught him the most important lesson of his life. Never let him forget that one. If you say 'Go', and you *will* it, and maintain that picture in his mind — 'that means "Go"' — if you can develop it, and maintain it, you will be able to make him do everything. All you have to do is educate him so that he does the things he can do, when you want him to.

What do we have at our disposal to get our will over to the horse? We have our 'aids'. There are three main sets — weight, legs, and hands. Don't let me hear you say, 'Hands, legs, and then weight'. It is weight first. And why? Essentially it is a matter of balance; the horse has to balance your weight. Do not ever think that you can balance your horse. All you can do successfully (and it is done all the time) is to unbalance him. You cannot balance him.

Diagram 4: Lengthening the distance of strides

Your weight should go down into your saddle. If I look at you it should look as if all your weight is running down and out through your heels. Everything should be sinking down into the horse. If your weight is there, and motionless, you give him a chance to get his balance. Your weight does not bounce and move forward, or shift to the left or right, or just bounce, bounce, bounce up and down. Your weight moves down and rests, still and supple, on his back. That is the thing he has to balance himself under and that is why it is your most important aid. Moreover, it does not cost you anything, not the slightest bit of energy. All you have to do is just let your weight down, and nature will do the rest.

Most riders use their whole body to keep themselves tense, and so make sure that the weight does *not* go down. As soon as you relax—and I do not mean slump, but relax in your proper and balanced position—you have nothing to do. But that is usually the problem. It is very hard just to do nothing.

So there it is. You could not think of anything more simple—let go, and your weight goes down. If you do that you can never fall off the horse because the weight is there and it always pulls you down. The art—and you have to work hard at it—lies in developing the ability in your body to be supple, to relax in spite of the fact that what you are sitting on is bouncing you up and down. Your weight must rest in the saddle and move with all the horse's movements. No additional movement should be visible. There is only one movement, and that is the movement of the horse as he trots, as he canters—and that is also the movement of the rider. You watch the rider go past with the horse underneath, and as the horse goes up and down the rider goes up and down. But if, when cantering along, the rider bounces or waves his arms and elbows and goes up and down with his hands, that is 'additional movement'. All additional movements, even the smallest movements, help to unbalance the horse.

If I have a stick in the palm of my hand I can balance it easily if it is still, but as soon as it

moves I have to move my hand as well to support it, otherwise it will fall off. The horse has to adjust himself with every step to maintain himself on his four legs. Therefore, weight is the most important aid. Developed, it is the most powerful instrument you could think of.

I rode a fully schooled stallion about three weeks after I came to Vienna. We had to move all the horses from one side of the stable as one horse had developed symptoms of the strangles. These horses were moved out into the open near the Vienna Racecourse. On our first day out we were exercising the horses in an open field with an overhead railway line. A long goods train came along with a steam engine at the front and another at the back, making a hell of a noise. I was sitting on a stallion who hadn't seen a train for about twelve years, and he was fourteen years old at the time. Did he take off! I was hanging on, double bridle and all, for dear life. The Old Instructor, whose stallion it was, yelled at me, 'You are holding too much!'. I thought to myself, 'Well, if I don't hold him he is off; I have to hold him'. The next morning the goods train was on time—they always are when you don't need them. The stallion from the previous day started to run around and I could not do anything about it. The Old Instructor said, 'Here, stay here, check him'. He mounted up and you could really see that weight sink into that saddle. The stallion was bouncing on the spot, his nostrils flaring, and looked about to explode at any minute. To rub it in the Old Instructor said, 'I told you. You held him too much'. He threw the reins away and the stallion could not do a thing. He couldn't do a thing because he had to balance himself under that weight.

It might be hard to understand if you have not experienced it yourself, but that weight going down anchors him to the spot; he can't go if you don't let him go. It is important that you let your weight down. Don't forget it.

How long it takes to develop this ability depends on how much inborn natural suppleness you have. Some people have been born with so much suppleness that everything comes easily. Walking comes easily to everyone; it is natural. To the very few, sitting on a horse comes naturally, too. Everyone can learn to ride, but a real horseman is born so.

General von Seydlitz was one of the born ones. King Frederick blocked him in a manoeuvre in the middle of the bridge over the Oder. The King said, 'Now, you are my prisoner'. The General said, 'Not yet, your Majesty', and he turned around and jumped over the side of the bridge into the Oder. This was something few people could do, but he could do it. Sometimes I am under the impression that all people born in Australia are born horsemen. People born in Vienna are not all born musicians; some of them cannot even dance!

The more still you are, the easier it is for the horse to find his natural balance, which is effortless. Your lower leg is there to push the horse. The weight comes down and rests on his back, never interfering with the movement of the muscles moving through his back.

The lower legs, when they are closed, act on the side of the horse on the girth, and through the push the reflex action makes the lower leg move the hindfoot forward. This is the first thing the horse must learn. This is the first lesson you must try to teach him—that when you say 'Go' with your lower leg he actually goes forward. How he does it, at the beginning, doesn't matter. You refine it later on.

Why does he go forward? There is a very simple reason. All his muscles are there for the purpose of movement, not to carry a rider around. You must succeed in getting the horse to engage his whole system of locomotion, all his muscles, for the purpose of moving forward —whether to walk, trot, or canter. If he is fully engaged doing what he normally does without any interference, he cannot do anything else. He can't stop, because he is going. He can't turn to the right, rear up, or do anything else but go.

Some people can do a lot of things at the same time. Napoleon was in conference with his marshalls and had a talk with Josephine, and dictated some letters, all at the same time.

But when you think back through past experience you find out that if you try to do too many things at the same time, one of them will probably go wrong.

While you engage yourself, your whole body is engaged in walking forward. It is the same with me. While I walk up and down and swing my hands it is impossible for me to pick up a stick lying on the table. I cannot. While you engage the horse in moving forward he cannot do anything else. You force him into the right position without using any force—just by plainly letting him know from up there, 'Look, if I say go forward, that means go forward'. Then he engages himself in the forward movement. If he should want to look around, you just give him a reminder. If you keep that up, and if you are gradually more persistent with your defence, it becomes second nature.

Do not forget that he will do only the things you have taught him. If you have taught him to go forward when your legs say 'Go forward' he will do nothing else, because he has not learnt anything else. If you teach him to canter on, that is what he is going to do. That is the only thing he knows.

He cannot sit down and read books and then say, 'Well, Franz says you should sit straight, and so and so says you should come back with the body, and forward with the hip, and do this and that'. He only knows what you tell him. Take it for granted if you haven't experienced it for yourself. Horses have a fantastic memory which in itself proves that they have brains; otherwise they couldn't store any memories or experiences. I rode a horse in Adelaide in 1953 and 1954 and wasn't on his back again until 1970. He had been performing pretty well. In the meantime he had been ridden by the owner, by the child of the owner, and by the granddaughter of the owner. When I was there in 1970 the granddaughter tried desperately to canter on. The old fellow just had his ears back and would not. I said, 'Now, just let me sit on him for a few minutes'. I got on him. I picked up the reins. I put myself in the right position and from a standstill he cantered a few strides and did a flying change here and a flying change there. It was a bit wooden, granted, as he had not done it for a long time. But he knew. He knew after sixteen years. I wish that in sixteen years' time I could recognise all the people I see at a lecture. I wouldn't know all the faces, but a horse could probably do it.

The lower leg must say 'Go'. Your hands are there to guide the horse, to tell him to go straight on, turn right, turn left, and to stop. After you have mastered your initial difficulties and you have taught him to carry you and not buck you off, that is the most important thing. Everything else comes after.

When he has understood to turn right, and to turn left, and when he stops easily enough, then you can say, 'Now, look. I would like you a little bit more together. I would like you to engage your quarters a little bit more'. If you want to do this you have to use the reins, but you must use the reins in a passive way. By 'passive' I mean that your hands must be together with a supple wrist, and your driving aids put your horse to the bit. You are walking on a loose rein, you take up contact, and now you are pushing up to the bit. Your hands, your body, nothing moves. Here is the driving force of seat and legs pushing him together.

This is another use of your hands. Do not forget. Put your horse to the bit. Do not do it in accordance with an Australian expression I have heard many times, 'Pull his head in!'. This would cause the horse to put his head on his chest with the hindquarters dragging along. It is the same as dragging a wheelbarrow in front rather than pushing from behind.

When I say that we have weight as an aid—a most important one—it is true that the leg aids are there too, and the hands and actions of the reins are also an aid. Really it is not quite accurate to say that. We should find an expression which encompasses all of them. Our aids—weight, leg, and hand—are one whole thing. A rider can have a beautiful, supple position, the strongest legs on earth, and sensitive hands, and still not achieve anything if he cannot co-ordinate all three into one.

For if the legs do something and say, 'Come on, push', the hands have to do something even if that something is passive—doing nothing. The hands must know what the seat is doing and what the legs are doing. I say, 'Push him together; come on, put him on the rein, on the bit'; then with weight and legs, and hands close to the body, you are pushing from behind and not allowing the horse to run on without contact. Otherwise it is like a person carrying water to fill up a drum which has no bottom. If you want to collect him your hands must co-ordinate with your leg. It means, 'I push you this far and let you go here. I will push you a little bit more and let you go here, but I will restrict you in your frame'. The hands must be carefully co-ordinated with your riding aids because if they are not you will let him go too much, or you will hold him back too much, and you will finish by pulling his head in.

Co-ordination of your aids is most important. To do it automatically is a matter of experience —mainly a matter of how much you have developed your suppleness. While you are tense and stiff you will find it very hard to co-ordinate. By the time you get the message to relax, and have relaxed whatever aid you have given, it is already over. The quicker your reaction is, the quicker the horse will understand, and naturally if something is going wrong you can sense it. If he is going to throw himself on that left rein, he will make a big step as he comes on to that left rein. If you feel it coming, and you say 'No. Stay here', and you push, and he comes back— then you have prevented something from developing. Quickness of reaction. Experience. Ride, ride, ride! Have a lot of sticking plaster! Cry some tears of frustration. That's what I can promise you. As Churchill said in 1941, 'I promise you blood and tears, but Victory will be ours'. I promise you the same thing. Blood and tears and a lot of hard work, but victory will be yours.

The better you control your body and the more consistent you make your aids, the more quickly the horse will understand, as he *does* pay attention. The further you go with your education of him, the more you will get his attention, the better you will be. Frequently the horse concentrates more than the rider. That is why he puts it over the rider so often.

So, now we have the weight, the legs, and the hands. We can also use a dressage whip—not a long one for everyday riding, but a long one is useful for teaching high school movement, for tuition, and for helping him along a little bit. Otherwise it is too long.

You can use the whip or you can use spurs, but if it is a young horse forget the spurs to start with. (Even if the young rider is advanced in years, he is still termed 'young' as a rider.) When we first joined the army we were not allowed to go out with spurs on. It was the worst thing that could happen to us, as we were all very young and handsome in our uniforms, but we were not experienced. Everybody, especially the young girls, knew that as long as you did not have any spurs you were not much of a horseman. So we had to hide to put our spurs on and keep our eyes open so that if the Captain came along we could quickly take them off again.

There is a good reason for this because you should not have spurs on until you know what your lower legs are doing. If you have no control over the lower leg it means that you can kick the horse with the spurs at any time—and most of the time it is the wrong time. You must know when you have developed enough body control to use the spurs only when and how it is necessary, no more and no less. If it is too soon or too late it is useless. It only confuses the horse. The whip, on the other hand, is the most useful tool a horseman can have. The spurs are a reserve of the lower leg. If he doesn't answer the lower leg, then you can use the spurs with a little bit more pressure behind the girth and make him go forward. The whip does the same thing. You do not carry the whip to hit him over the head or punish him. When, and if, you have schooled him correctly you will have no reason to punish him. There is only one time when you can punish a horse, and that is after he has been ruined by some-body. Then you may be forced to punish him because he will not turn to the left, or turn to the right, or he will not go past his stable door, or he may show that he has developed other bad habits. You may say, 'Well now, you are no good to me if you will not turn to the left. So today is the day you are going to turn to the left'. Then you may have to use the stick in a more severe way, which is most unfortunate because it is not the horse's fault, but the rider's, for badly educating his horse and then letting him get away with it.

Habits are something that horses learn very fast. My first job here in Australia was at a wool store in Port Adelaide, South Australia, where I was working with a gang. I cannot repeat the first words of English that I learnt, but I still know those words. You learn bad things fast. So if the horse feels easier when turning to the left he will not want to turn to the right. And if you let him get away with it too many times and then say 'Turn right', the horse will think, 'Don't be funny; I have been turning left all the time', and he will be very annoyed about it. They can be annoyed and they can be stubborn; they can be very wilful, particularly if they have got away with doing it their way all the time. The rider can be in trouble. How big the trouble is will depend on the nature, intelligence, and personality of the horse, but it can be very big trouble.

Try to avoid a fight with the horse like a fire. Try to be diplomatic, avoid the fight, and if you get only an inch more than he is prepared to give, let it go for the time being and do not ask more than he is prepared to give; it will be the worst kind of education you can think of to ask something and then not get it at all.

If you say, 'Turn right', and then turn left and are able to get his nose only a little way, then jump off quickly. If you ask for more and he evades it, and if you can't bring him back and make him turn right, then you might just as well not sell him (think of the poor person who might buy him from you).

If you accept the fight you have to be prepared. It can be dangerous. If you have driven him that far, or someone has made him that way, be prepared to win or else die on the spot. Yes, it may sound a bit far-fetched, but don't go on if you haven't got the determination to wring his neck and make him do it or face being stamped into the ground. Something has to give. Otherwise do not try it or you are bound to lose your fight, and with the fight you lose the horse and the usefulness of that horse. That is why you should avoid the fight as much as possible. When I say that you have to be prepared to wring his neck, I do not mean that you would really do it. It is your inward preparedness to do it that matters. He will know it.

I have seen horses stop in front of obstacles in cross-country trials 24 hours before actually arriving at the jump. How did I see the horse stop? By seeing the rider approaching and evaluating that jump, and changing colour and thinking, 'I can never jump that'. In such a case the odds are that the horse is going to stop in front of that jump tomorrow—not because he cannot jump it, but because he senses that the rider is scared. The drive is not there. There is an uncertainty, and the horse can sense whether you mean business, whether you really want to go there, or whether you are uncertain. He can sense if you want to jump, if you have the determination to make him, in the same way in which he can sense whether you have the determination to make him turn here, or to make him go forward or whatever, when he does not want to do it. If you do not have it, avoid the fight. If you achieve only 1 millimetre, tomorrow you will probably get 2 millimetres and then 3 millimetres. This is very important—your realisation that the horse knows what you think. Whether you believe it or not, they do.

When you have yourself and your horse fully schooled, you just blink and he does it. You may think it is not possible, but it is. I rode my first performance in Vienna in the School doing a movement above the ground—the 'levade'. I was riding an old horse of Podjhasky's who was really fantastic. The Old Instructor said, 'Whatever you do, do not think that he will sit down,

because if you think too early, he is going to sit down'. I entered the School and was coming along the wall to the centre line and I was supposed to turn and do the levade in the middle of the School. As I was riding along the wall I was already thinking, 'I hope he doesn't sit down too soon'. That was where I was thinking it, and that is exactly where he sat down. That old horse had been doing that movement for years. He was a very old professor. He knew, 'Now I do my levade, now I walk away'. If you asked him to do it again he became very annoyed because he knew that he had already done it. This worried me more than anything else, because that old fellow knew more than I did, and I wondered, 'How do I get him to sit down once again?'. Well, he did sit down again, thank God, because if he had not I would have been in real trouble. As I came out the Old Instructor said, 'I told you not to think of it'. Whether it was a brainwave or subconscious tension, which it probably was, I *thought*, and it happened.

The same applies in the jumping field or hacking. Don't think, 'I hope he will canter on the right leg, or jump better'. No, forget about it; think positive. You are *going* to do it. He will know and sense your determination, and he will do it.

The tragedy is that you cannot spoil a useless horse, because there is nothing there to ruin. The only horses that are ruined are the good ones. We don't bother with the horse with no personality, or promise of jumping ability, or good paces. The horse that is going to be asked for more than he is capable of at present is the good horse that can jump, and shows promise.

Everyone and everything starts in kindergarten, then goes into the first and second classes, and so rises a step higher until he finishes up in the university, depending on how far he wants to go. No one ever thinks of skipping primary and high school and going straight into the university. Why? Because you could not pass your exams; you have not got the foundation behind you.

To me it just does not make sense to put a

horse into the jumping ring without that primary-school experience. When he does not jump the rider becomes very cross. We ask the horse to do more than we are capable of doing ourselves. When you ask too much of a good horse with personality and character, and treat him roughly, he will sit back and fight with you. If you are not careful you will have a real fight on your hands and he will go from bad to worse, to such a degree that it will be necessary to take him into a paddock and give him a bullet. That is where the best horses go most of the time.

At a school in Melbourne one year, the second group was working out behind my back. I heard a big crash while I was working with the first group. I turned around and saw the rider crawling out from a tangle of horse's and rider's legs. I said, 'What the hell are you doing? You were not supposed to jump. What were you doing jumping?'. It was not a big jump but still it was fair sized. The rider said, 'He was jumping so beautifully and now he won't jump any more.

That is why I tried him'. The horse still looked like a bit of a baby to me and I asked, 'How old is he? How much work has he done?'. Are you ready for it? The horse was only two-and-a-half years old; he had been broken in for only three months. And now comes the wonder: that horse had already jumped clear at three shows— actually jumped three rounds clear. And then came the jump off. The rider raced him against the clock because he did not want to miss out on a quid. He made a mistake and did not clear a jump, and he knocked his legs, and the next time he came out he did not want to jump. That horse would have developed into a gold-medal horse if he had been schooled properly or I would eat my hat. On top of that he was a good-looking horse.

Can you imagine that nature, that willing-ness, that natural balance, that intelligence? To be able to handle an Olympic course after being broken in only three months, and jumping clear! But he was finished. As I said earlier, it is only the good horses that are ruined.

SUMMARY

1. The reason for schooling a horse in dressage is to keep him serviceable for as long as possible. It is the systematic development of the mental and physical abilities of the horse. By training him to use himself correctly with the rider on his back we prevent him from breaking down.

2. We talk to the horse through his feeling and so we influence him by our position.

3. No wild horse breaks down. It is only our riding that causes this to happen. Dressage training aims at removing this risk.

4. The picture of the horse that we should see is one where all the power is developed in the hindlegs, driving forward through the spine, not the forelegs dragging the hindlegs after them.

5. When we train for any sport we strengthen the muscles we have to use. We do this through

exercise. This must be a slow, developing process. The horse develops at the same natural rate. He develops his mental and physical balance as he grows up. We must develop these with the rider on his back.

6. When we pick up a load we balance it to make it easier to carry. We ourselves must therefore be balanced when we sit on a horse, thereby making it easier for him to balance himself under the load. *We must sit still*.

7. The art of riding is the art of not interfering with the horse. To do this we must be able to sit still.

8. Xenophon says, 'Be kind to your horse. Do not be rough and tough with him. Try to show him'. We must all acknowledge the horse's right to a fair deal. You cannot explain to him. You must show him what you want and give him time to understand.

9. The rider must gradually develop the ability to avoid interference. That is the art of controlling the horse. If he is not interfered with he will carry himself as he would when loose in the paddock—that is, in the way he is designed to carry himself.

10. To avoid interference is a long, tough road for the rider, but there is no short cut. We are left-handed or right-handed and are therefore really one-sided. Horses also are one-sided. There is a lot of work in making two crooked bodies straight.

11. The rider must be the first to straighten out. The horse tends to hang on to the left rein and does not want to take the right rein. To develop straightness and flexibility is *exercise*. To make him understand what we want and to get him to do it our way and not the way he would like to do it, is *education*.

12. If the horse is to understand, we must give our aids consistently, and to do this we must be able to sit still. Every movement of the body should say something to the horse. If there is no movement, that tells him that all is well and that he is doing the right thing.

13. The horse's spine should be on top of the line you are riding—a smooth curve or a straight line. This is hard for him because of his natural crookedness. He avoids it by having his shoulders or quarters falling out of line. When he is straight, both hindlegs step in the line of his forelegs and so are stepping under his weight. When he does this we have really achieved much.

14. When he goes straight the weight is equally distributed over all his legs and so none is working overtime and there is no reason for him to break down. Also, when the rider can control the hindlegs he can control the whole horse.

15. We start on a wide curve which means little bend. That is all the horse can achieve at first. Then we ask for a little more bend, and still a little more. Everything must be developed gradually.

16. The freer the walk the more the horse must overstep. He must overstep because his weight is moving forward. The faster the pace, the more overstepping there is, to catch up with and support the weight. As you collect him the step becomes shorter and the hindfoot imprint comes back to the front imprint.

17. You say 'Go' and he goes. That is the most important lesson of his life. Never let him fail to obey. All schooling depends on the horse's accepting the forward driving aids. We have to educate him to do the things he can do naturally but when *we* want him to do them.

18. The aids are our means of communicating with the horse: weight, legs, and hands, in that order. The weight is well down in the saddle, and still. No work is required from the rider; he just lets gravity do his work. Then the horse can balance himself with his load.

19. The only movement is from the horse. There should be none from the rider's body unless he is giving an aid. He must go with the horse; any additional movement will unbalance it and spoil the gait. Letting the weight down

gives the rider control of the hindlegs and so of the horse's means of going forward. If the rider's body is supple it follows the movement of the horse and does not interfere with the muscles working along his back.

20. The lower leg acts on the side of the horse on the girth and the reflex action makes the horse move his hindleg forward. This is the first lesson he learns. At first it does not matter *how* he goes; we can refine his reaction later.

21. All his muscles exist to enable him to go forward. If you can get him to engage himself fully doing this, he cannot do anything else at the same time. If he is really going he cannot stop, rear, turn, or do anything else. So we let him know, 'If I say "Go forward" that means "Go forward"'. If we can keep him obedient to this all our troubles will be overcome.

22. If you have taught him to go when you use your legs he will always do so because he has not learnt anything else. He will only do the things you have taught him. Once it is learnt and understood, horses *never forget*. They may try to get out of it but they do not forget.

23. He has learnt to go when you use the lower leg and then to be guided by your hands. Then you can ask him to come together a little more, to engage his hindquarters a little more. You must use the reins to do this, but in a passive way. That is, your hands are there and your driving aids send the horse up to the bit. Weight, legs, and hands must co-ordinate. Each must know what the other is doing; you need the right amount of seat and legs to make him go, and the right amount of hands and reins to prevent it from all going out the front. And so

you shorten his frame and engage his hind-quarter more.

24. Co-ordination of aids is essential. It is a matter of experience, feel, and suppleness. The quicker your reaction is, the quicker the horse will learn and understand. You learn to sense that he is going to do something wrong, and so you apply the appropriate correction before it happens.

25. If the horse is inattentive the whip is used to smarten up his response to the aids. It is used mildly, as an aid. It is used only to punish, in order to correct a bad habit. He learns bad habits through being badly ridden, but if he will not turn to the right and he is firmly hit he will probably decide that it is wiser to obey.

26. In correcting a fault, try hard to avoid a fight because he may win. Accept the least concession and stop for the day. If you *do* engage in a fight, be determined to win and be prepared for real trouble. If your determination is really there he can sense it and will probably give in.

27. A horse will stop at a jump because the rider is afraid. Then the determination and drive are not there. The horse feels your thought through your body. When you and your horse are fully trained and schooled you merely have to think and he will do it.

28. In all the horse's education we must go slowly through the grades. Let him grow, develop, and learn slowly. Then he will understand and stay calm and responsive. Rush him, and he will become upset. Then he will jack up or break down because he is unbalanced and using his muscles wrongly.

CHAPTER FIVE

PSYCHOLOGY AND POSITION

If the rider just wants to go for a ride, then all he needs to worry about is not falling off. Nothing more. But the rider who wants to concentrate on showjumping or dressage needs much more—like the high diver who twists and turns before entering the water as against the person who jumps into it straight away. They both enter the water in the end, but one only just gets there in the most elementary way and the other shows how skill, practice, and body control can turn the dive into a thing of beauty.

Believing is not knowing. You cannot go against the laws of nature. Everything is created in the best way—like a young horse who is free and unspoilt by man. By nature a horse is free and balanced. When he jumps in his natural state he arches over the jump instead of jumping with a hollow back. He gets the maximum result with the minimum amount of effort, without the interference of the rider. This is the easiest way.

A horse jumping with a rounded back will last much longer than one jumping with a hollow back. He will land smoothly and gallop on. If he jumps with a hollow back, he will jar the tendons on landing and will tend to break down. So don't go against the laws of nature, but try to help them. In the School in Vienna

they used to watch the young foals and make a mental note of what they were naturally good at so that later on they would develop it. Always try to work *with* nature and not against it.

A horse should be balanced, obedient, and supple. A balanced horse is a more comfortable ride, will become fitter, and will have a longer life than a horse that is not balanced. A horse must be obedient because, if he is not, he will not be comfortable to ride.

A translation of 'dressage' is 'to train', which according to the dictionary means 'exercise, education, and discipline'. You can educate a horse because he has a certain amount of intelligence (sometimes too much). We must have an obedient horse so that he will carry out what we want him to do in an easy manner. He must not fight. If I say that I want to walk on a loose rein he must do so, and not fight. So we must educate him. He must submit himself freely. The more freely he submits himself the easier ride you will have and the longer he will last.

One of the reasons we school the horse is to make him last longer. The object of our schooling is to get everything out of the horse that he can give, but the minute he fights he uses his power, energy, and brains against us. If he can jump 1·5 metres with natural ability, and you have him schooled and educated so that he submits himself calmly and obediently to whatever you want him to do, he will jump 1·8 metres. There are a lot of horses about that are capable of jumping 1·8 metres. And a lot of them will never do so. Whether it is in Grand Prix dressage, showjumping, or three-day event riding, a horse that has not been educated will fight in many different ways—head up, overbent, tearing off, and so on. And as soon as he uses his energy to fight you he loses that energy from his performance.

There is no difference in the first stage of training between dressage, showjumping, or three-day event riding. The horse must be made balanced, on the bit, obedient, and supple. From then on, if he is educated, exercised, and disciplined, the particular training can follow. The same foundation is necessary in every horse. The dressage horse will have his special training and the others will go their different ways. I would not risk a dressage horse—except to prove a point—in a three-day event, because of all the work I had put into him to get him to that high standard. Grand Prix dressage is just what the high diver does; it is the result of hard work and complete body control of the person who does it. Grand Prix dressage is the result of complete body control on the part of the rider, who is then in complete control of the horse's body. Marshall Foch once said, 'War is easy in its conception, but difficult in its execution'—like modern art versus conventional art. Conventional art is easy to understand but difficult to execute; the other is difficult to understand but easy to execute.

When you walk, do you think about maintaining your balance? If you carry something, do you feel that it is comfortable? You are in balance because you have the reasoning to distribute the weight correctly and regain your correct balance—you don't stagger along uncomfortably with the load all on one side. You can adjust your weight and use the correct muscles.

Teaching a child to walk is unnecessary—it comes naturally. Nobody tells baby where to put his feet or how to walk because he would not understand anyway. Balance is something that the good God gave us all, if we are normal, and we cannot really explain how we know what to do. It is subconscious. We learn to crawl, then walk, then run, then climb trees, then drive a car. Nature has given us balance; we take it for granted. There is not one reason why we should be balanced and the horse should not be balanced to the same degree. Wherever you look, life is developed to meet the requirements of environment (fish in water, the horse on land). What conclusion does that leave us with? It means that by itself the horse is well-balanced and comfortable—*by itself.*

We are naturally balanced and so is the horse. Maintain that natural balance and teach him to go as free as he did before. The best way to do that is to sit still. If I put a bag of oats on a man's back and someone gives the corner a pull, it will unbalance the carrier. There is too much weight in one corner. The horse will never find his balance unless you say to yourself, 'I am going to sit still'. Then you won't fall on your nose. If you go against nature you pay the penalty.

Balance is equality of weight, so sit still. Balance makes a pleasant ride, and a horse will then live longer in working condition. If two people buy a car at the same time and the first one drives it at less than 60 kilometres an hour in the beginning and does everything correctly, and the other man does everything incorrectly, then the first man's car will outlast the other one by a long way. The same thing applies to a horse.

There is no reason why the horse should be different from us. If we carry something that upsets our natural balance, we adjust ourselves. Our power of reasoning is so good that we can work out how to adjust to the most comfortable way. If it pulls me back here, then I pull it forward to adjust it. A horse has no power of reasoning, unfortunately. If he had, he would push the rider into the right position. He cannot think, but we can. We must do it for the horse.

So many people look down when they ride a horse. But nobody looks down when they drive a car. A car has no brains, no life, only the life you give it when you press a button. Success or failure is up to the driver. That is the reason why we have more car accidents than horse accidents. If people drove their cars in the way they ride their horses, our hospitals would always be full. To make a success of our riding and training we must do the thinking for the horse and guide him. We must appreciate that the horse is one of God's creatures. We cannot go wrong if we appreciate this. You must not blame the horse when things go wrong. The rider is at fault, whether it is what you did today or yesterday, or what someone did three months ago, or someone else right back at the beginning. If things go wrong, then you must correct them in the proper way. If you cut a finger you do not bandage the finger next to it, nor do you change the near-front tyre if you have a puncture in the off-rear tyre. Whatever happens, and whatever goes wrong, there is a reason for it. Why are you sitting there? There must be a reason. If the horse is pulling, there is a reason.

A horse knows when he deserves a whack, or discipline, and he knows when it is unfairly given. The horse Coronation would not take sugar for three days after he had been hit for stumbling when it was not his fault. If you really try to work things out, much anger and heartburning will be saved . . . and much frustration. The horse knows when he is right or wrong. If you hit him to go forward, he knows. If you hit him when he trips through no fault of his own, he will be very hurt. Some people blow their top. They do a lot of damage. Look before you leap. Act according to the need.

A horse feels as we do—feels pain, has nerves, gets tired, stubborn, and upset. Realise this and it will pay in the long run. Try to be correct and as good as possible. If you lose your temper and punish him unjustly you may spoil a good horse. He will lose his confidence in you. You must have his confidence, so control your temper. Don't punish him when you are in a rage, because you may do more harm than good.

Absolute body control is necessary for the ballet dancer, diver, ice-skater, and Grand Prix rider. He has to have almost perfect body control. There is not much time to give the horse the aids. The rider must be relaxed and supple in the brain. It is the power station and everything is controlled from there. It is done subconsciously, but it is done. If the centre is not under your control what happens to the rest? You have to think. Your psychological approach has to be correct.

I can paint, but I am not a Rembrandt. If you only want to go for a ride, that is all right. If you want to educate your horse higher, he needs practice and experience. It is easy to get to the top, but very hard to stay on the top. The more you do, and the older you get, the more you try to improve. You will improve only if you improve your body control. The foundation schooling is essential even if you don't want to do Grand Prix. You cannot teach a horse our language. You teach him through his feelings. The psychological approach is important above all else—the know-how and the thinking ahead gained through perseverance and work. 'One-two-three-hup' is really only to restore the fading confidence of the rider and does not help the horse jump.

Horses have a fantastic memory. One of the Spanish Riding School stallions was out for eight years but when he came back he knew more than the rider. Because of the rider's inexperience, the horse had to guess what he wanted, but he still knew what to do. Horses do not forget the good things and they certainly don't forget the bad things. The bad things they always learn more quickly than the good things. The bad things are the comfortable ones. You are lazy, we all are lazy. If you were not, then I would be out of a job. The horse does not want to do anything but eat, frisk around, have a roll, rest, and eat again. What would we be without Mum and Dad saying, 'Don't do that', all the time and training us correctly? We could not live together. I have seen people running for their lives, all civilised thinking gone— running like a herd of cattle—no thought for babies in prams or people in the road. All education gone! Education makes life possible. We are supposed to submit ourselves freely (even to taxation demands), and not fight against discipline. The more freely a horse submits himself, the longer he will live.

The rider should sit as still as possible so that the horse has a chance to find his own balance. He will fight and resist because he feels uncomfortable if you are not still. He cannot tell you how to balance yourself. Don't give him the excuse. He feels it if you throw your weight from side to side, and he will become more and more upset. He will think, 'I will try to get away from him', and start running. If you hurt him he will try to run away.

To be completely still you must have control of your body and you must be quite clear in your mind as to how you must be in control of your body. The moment you have your body under control everything else comes, more or less. You have no hope of controlling a horse in an easy way if you cannot control yourself first, and yourself includes your head, your temper, and your different bodily parts. It is not only a matter of balance, but a matter of educating and schooling yourself and your horse.

The essence of dressage is to give the horse back his natural balance with the rider on top. If we want to teach him something we must have consistency. If you cannot understand, how can the horse understand? If you give the horse the same aids every time in the same way, the horse will soon understand. To school him quickly you must have consistency. If you cannot control the body you have no hope. You can only learn body control under the actual conditions—not reading at home on a kitchen stool. Try to think of the simplicity of the whole thing. Give the horse back his natural balance. By himself he is happy, relaxed, and balanced. If you really *want* to be a lawyer, half the work is already done. It is the same with body control. Some people are possessed of natural ability to make good riders.

The more natural ability the horse has himself, the less you have to do. A horse that is a free mover is very much better to work. Temperament plays a big part. A lot of bad temper is the result of previous bad treatment. Sometimes you can never undo it. You can get a horse to be a comfortable ride as long as he has not gone round the bend mentally. You must put him mentally at ease if you want a comfortable horse. He must not be stirred up.

If you want to jump down out of a tree and turn a somersault as you go, you do not start by jumping from a high tree the first time. You build yourself up for it step by step and then when everything is right under control you go higher and higher. You must start with a little bit, then a little bit more, then a little bit more. You are brought along gradually, as far as your natural ability will go, and as long as your ambition lasts. A child at primary school thinks the high-school boys are wonderful and clever, but when he goes to high school he thinks the university boys are wonderful. By progressing gradually you do not encounter any undue difficulties. You would never ask even a brilliant child of seven to sit for the School Certificate, yet people see a horse jump a high fence to get out, and they enter him in all the jumping events they can without gradually bringing him up to it. They say, 'Oh, he is just a natural jumper. Look at him jump out of that yard'. Six months later he breaks down. Use common sense. Don't expect a horse to be better than you are yourself. You would not do anything, physical or mental, without having properly prepared yourself. Nothing on God's earth has to put up with more injustice than the horse, and he must be the best of God's creatures.

If you gradually bring him on you are bound to have success. If his natural maximum ability is to jump 1·5 metres you can school him for a hundred years and he will not jump more than 1·5 metres. I wanted to be tall and handsome when I was young, but 170 centimetres was my natural limit and I can do nothing about it. There are things we cannot improve. We are unable to improve the conformation of the horse. We cannot improve his boldness or his heart. If he is naturally chicken-hearted, then he will always be chicken-hearted deep within himself, no matter how good you are; but by proper schooling we can get the best out of the horse.

If he has a straight shoulder you will never get a really good extended trot. The horse cannot do it. That is conformation. But what he has, you can develop to the last drop. Try to work your problems out. Find the facts and ride accordingly — with patience.

Let us go back to real nature. What is the horse's way of getting away from danger? Speed. He does not have to be fast to get his feed but he has to be fast to get away from other animals who would like to feed on him. Because he has to get away, nature has provided him with the means of getting away for survival. That is why we must ride the horse forward. The moment we hang on to his head we are defying nature's orders. If a lift breaks down, you can get down to the ground floor — and very quickly too — by jumping and not waiting for the lift to be repaired. But the point is that you will suffer the penalty for ignoring the law of gravity. It is your life that will suffer. The moment you cease to respect nature's laws and allow the whole of the horse's body to go forward, your penalty will be to lose the horse's true capabilities. It is very hard to prove, but common sense. We cannot run fast and survive when we are chased by preying animals, but we have the power of reasoning. Prehistoric man could dig a pit and get the monster to fall into it and hit him on the head to conquer him. To be safe, you must appreciate the laws of nature; if you do appreciate them, and act accordingly, you cannot go wrong. If you put the necessary work into your body.

Back to work. We know we must sit upright. Leg position — the knee close to the saddle and the leg just below the knee on the horse. The exercises you do will give you the ability to tune up your muscles and help you relax. We should try to make the horse as comfortable with the rider as he is without the rider. Have you ever seen a horse in his natural state prancing around when he is excited? He is beautiful to watch, full of natural rhythm and grace. Even an ugly horse looks beautiful when he is showing off.

If we want to go forward we have certain means of making him go. What are our aids? Weight, legs, hands, and voice. Don't say hands first. Hands are only second best. You can bet your sweet life that if a person says 'hands' first, his horse is not going forward. First is our weight. It is the most important and easiest aid to apply. To use your weight you don't have to do anything. Just sit down — there is your weight. Your horse should learn to carry your weight. The moment that weight is distributed in the right direction he will find it easy to regain his natural balance.

Can dressage improve his natural ability? It can cultivate it. You cannot go beyond what the horse has. If he is really excited, you cannot go beyond that. You can cultivate it and improve up to a certain point, but it is very dangerous to say that gymnastics can improve him to, or past, his natural limit. Normally he is lazy.

If he pulls, shakes his head, or runs away, something has gone wrong. He must have confidence in you and you must have confidence in him. When the rider says, 'Come on', he must come on, but don't ask too much too soon. A horse has an outstanding memory. He never forgets a thing, so teach him the right way the first time and he won't forget. Not even if you turn him out. He will remember it all when he comes in.

Sit firm and still so that you can apply the aids properly. If I pinch you in the same spot in the same place every day, the message gradually sinks in. If you ask a horse to canter by using different aids every day he can't possibly do it. The only way we can talk to him and teach him the language is through feel. So this is the way to turn left. Do it the same way every day, in the same place. Be firm, be still, and be balanced in order to be able to give the right aids.

Sit down as comfortably and as still as

Note position of hands—Franz Mairinger on Coronation

together, all three in co-ordination with one another. So you push him with weight and legs and the hands control him—co-ordination of all aids together.

Then you have the extensions of your legs with whip and spurs, and sometimes you can use your voice successfully. We can use the voice for calming him and the click of the tongue to make him go by throwing a scare into him, but that is brute force. Always carry a whip. You must have something to make sure that you are the boss. Use it to help the leg when necessary. If a young horse doesn't respond to the leg, use the whip behind the leg. That is the best spot.

To use your weight successfully you must have your body under control—relaxed and used in conjunction with legs and hands. The secret of working a horse successfully is body control to start with, then the co-ordination of body aids. If you cannot co-ordinate your aids, you are no good. That is why a lot of riders do not sit well at all, but they have a natural co-ordination and suppleness and can get the horse going kindly.

We should not really talk about aids with your weight, legs, and hands because they don't exist separately—only by co-ordination of all three together. You cannot use only one. The use of seat, legs, and hands can be passive or active. It is like a three-piece orchestra playing a waltz, rock-and-roll, and a Russian lullaby. All must be in tune, in the same time—then it is pleasant to listen to and pleasant to see. Your aids have to be tuned together. You can do it if you really learn body control.

If you want to get a horse into action, what do you do? Prepare yourself first. From the moment you prepare yourself your aids will be under your control. It is a very short moment, but necessary. Be calm in yourself, control your nerves, and make quite sure of what you are going to do. Sit down with the legs on the body, in the right place on the girth, and be ready for action. To go forward, increase pressure with both legs and keep your hands in the forward movement. And keep your hands

possible. Legs create impulsion. The front part of a horse is built to catch the impulsion from behind. A horse is naturally shy and has powers of great speed. Recognise it and keep him going forward. Keep the forward impulsion.

The legs maintain forward impulsion and help to bring his hindquarters under him. Hands steer and guide and control speed. Most riders use their hands only, leaving out the use of the weight and the legs. They must all be used

58

still. Weight just there, then take him with you. You must never be in front of the horse, never behind the movement, but you should always take him with you. Whether you start a walk from a halt, or jump a 1·8-metre fence, you should take him with you.

Keep the weight in the saddle. Don't kick with the heels; use the calf of the leg. If that doesn't work you can give a kick with the leg closed. Don't give a long squeeze with the calf; press and release, then press again. More and more, then kick if necessary. Don't try to use force, because you will automatically stiffen yourself, and then you will hold him, then he won't be able to go. So don't freeze. Think first, and make sure of what you want to do.

A fit three-day-event horse will give you everything that he has got—he is tuned and educated and should listen to you. That is the idea of dressage. A horse should take 10 minutes to work in if he is a fit three-day-event horse. Any horse that needs 3 to 4 hours of working-in will come on to a certain extent because he is so knocked up, but the rider may be knocked up first. We should have his strength, mental and physical, working for us, not thrown away and used against us. I want him working for me, not against me.

How do you sit on a horse? Open up your seat bones and get down as deep in the saddle as possible. The thigh should be as close to the saddle as possible and in a parallel line with the horse's shoulder. Sit up straight with shoulders back and down. Keep your head up and look between the horse's ears. Keep your hands down and in a forward position and keep them still. Keep your fingers closed and round the hands so that you can look into them. Your wrists must be supple, very supple, and elbows still and close to the body. The movement must come from your wrists, not your arms, so keep them still at your sides in a comfortable position and don't make them stiff. Heels must be down and toes in. You must be supple within the lower part of your body so that each part of you can work independently of the other. When you are sitting up straight and are deep down in

the saddle, and are supple in the body, and still, then you can feel your horse and apply the aids. The length of the stirrup should be between your ankle and the heel of your boot. The ankle should be supple. The knee should be close to the saddle. Most riders ride with an open leg.

You must listen to the sound of the horse's hoof beats. Riding should be like silent music; you should get the sound of your horse's hoof beats into your blood.

The rider's position should be such that he is in a balanced position without the horse. Using your imagination, try to think the horse away. The rider should be balanced in his position without the horse, and not falling on his backside or on his nose or something else. Whatever the length of stirrup, the rider should be balanced within himself. The hands have to be down, and (not just because I like the look of it) heels down. I couldn't care less where they are really, but if both heels are down it means that his

Franz Mairinger on Gay Pam. Outline of his excellent position. This was the key to his outstanding ability. Note deep seat, weight correctly placed and lower leg under him on the horse, with heels well down

weight is evenly distributed. What applies from the side-on view applies from the back view too. The rider is not hanging one way, or the other way. And from the front it is exactly the same. The rider's weight should be evenly distributed on the horse's back.

Having the heels down indicates that the rider is stretched, and as soon as he is stretched the collapse of one hip or the other is prevented. That is where the natural one-sidedness appears. As soon as you sit on a horse and have to sit straight, right-handers will find that they have a job to keep their right heel down—because the left shoulder is higher than the right and the right hip is collapsed because of the one-sidedness—and vice-versa for left-handers. As I said earlier, horses are inclined to be one-sided too. So we have two crooked ones, and together they don't make a straight one. So, one of the two has to straighten up first, and that's the one who knows what he wants to do and why. The rider has to straighten up. The rider has to sit straight with the weight evenly distributed on both seat bones. When you have been sitting on a horse for some time you may discover that you feel heavier on the left seat bone than on the right seat bone. But the body is resting, or should be resting, straight on top of the seat bones, not one way or the other way. The more evenly the weight is distributed, the easier it will be for the horse to adjust himself to that weight, and eventually to find his natural balance where he will trot and canter around and look as if he does everything himself.

It is the horse that has to balance the rider not the other way round. The rider can never balance the horse. You will probably find that a number of writers have suggested that the rider can do certain things, and so balance the horse. It cannot be done. It is mechanically and physically impossible. The load can never balance the support. It is the support that balances the load. The horse is no exception, but unfortunately because he has four legs and can run, and carry us around under all circumstances, we believe we are doing the right thing.

We should always look ahead and use a bit more common sense.

It is very hard, of course, to use common sense. Common sense will tell you to do something different and prevent you from putting the blame on the horse. First of all the rider has to be able to sit straight and still and not move, and if he has achieved that goal, then neither you nor any book has to tell him what he has to do with his weight. He will find out for himself.

Most books write about the finer points without stressing that you first have to learn to sit still and be supple. The 'finer points' will not work if your seat is not correct. Everything should be stretched, from the head to the hands to the lower leg. Everything should be still, and it should give you the impression that everything is sinking, sinking into the horse, and if you are not careful you are going to break and split in half. That is what you look for. You never get it, but you look for it. Everything is still and—a particular point of interest—the hands must be part of your position. This means that you go, and your hands go, in exactly the same way as your body does, and not as a separate unit.

Through the influence of your leg you want to drive the horse underneath your weight. You must have your hands next to your body, otherwise you will cut the wire and it won't go through any more. You have to push him. You have to keep the body and the hands together otherwise you can't put the hands at the horse's front with the back together (see page 64). This probably sounds double Dutch (I don't mean to say that I think you aren't clever enough to understand) but this is something that you really must have *felt* before you can grasp it. I know what I am trying to say. Feeling is a learnt process like everything else. No matter how much I explain how it *feels*, although you may understand, you still won't really know, because you haven't felt it. Not until you can say, 'Yes I have really *felt* it'.

You can observe, you can see a good deal, if you look for the harmony between horse and rider—harmony of movement, harmony of flowing transitions, and so on. You can have a fair idea whether the head is a unit in itself, and the hands are a separate unit in themselves. And if the hands are a unit in themselves and have no co-ordination with the body and the legs, you will just push the horse here and he will go out there, because you haven't anything to hold him together. It's very simple. You push him here, and if the hands are not part of your position you will not be able to hold them still. Your hands are going to move and so you push him here, and there he goes. And you push him here again, and it's like filling a barrel with no bottom. You can do it for the rest of the horse's life, or your life, and you will never succeed because as you push him together you can feel him rounding up, and in the early stages trying to sneak his way, coming out or coming in. If the rider's shoulders are not back and the elbows are not closed—I don't mean jammed, but in a supple way—you have no way of restraining the horse's resistance, because as soon as he jams his jaw the hands go slightly forward. And if he only goes *that far*, that is enough. You really have lost him.

So hands and body must be one, and when you say 'Go' the whole thing has to move together and not the hands separately, most of the time in front of the movement. Don't be in front of the movement, don't be behind the movement, take him with you. That's how it is. You must go with him. I also try to point out during schools that the rider should not stretch one way more than the other. The weight has to be evenly distributed. The important thing is that the rider should avoid one leg being shorter than the other because as the horse stiffens himself he will, through his lugging-in action, push you over here, make you collapse here, and either the one leg or the other leg is going to be shorter because you are losing the stretch in the other leg, and that happens, particularly in the turns. That is why the rider should stretch to the inside of the turn or half-pass, but not more, not putting more weight, not making that leg longer than the other one, otherwise

the weight distribution could be quite different. You might want the horse to stretch on the outside (in corners, circles, half-pass etc.) but often in trying this, the rider collapses his inside hip, which shortens the inside leg and pushes the weight on to the outside leg. Therefore you should stretch down with your inside leg but not make it longer than your outside leg; both legs must be equal. That is what it means to stretch to the inside, whether it is a simple turn or a half-pass or what have you. You can put a little more pressure on the stirrup. This does not mean that you actually make the leg stronger. You can apply more pressure just by leaning back on that inside seat bone or outside seat bone, but nobody can see it—it is all within the rider. Be careful that you are not misled into stretching down more to one side than the other.

Diagram 5: A rider with left hip collapsed, and left leg consequently shortened

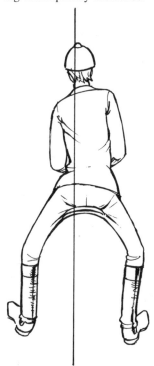

61

The firmness of the position and the correctness of the position is important for the well-being of the horse, to make it easy for the horse to find his natural balance, and to move and make use of his muscles and his body without interference. That is why we have to be firm and supple and still. The other reason is that only a firm, still, controlled position will produce consistent aids. If the rider does not control his position he cannot control his aids. It is impossible. If the rider doesn't know where his shoulders are, and doesn't know what the body does, what the hands do, how on earth can he speak the correct language to the horse? And the aids are the rider's language. The more clearly he expresses himself and the more consistently he expresses himself—always with the same words or with the same influence—the more quickly the horse will understand and the more quickly the horse will concentrate on the rider. If the rider is sitting still all the time, and then suddenly makes a movement, that means something. But if the rider's body moves all the time, the horse gets used to it and doesn't take any notice. You can kick him and push him. You really have to wake him up so that he realises that you are now kicking him for a particular reason; first of all you kicked him because you didn't know that you were doing it. Consistency of aids is just plain common sense.

We are not always aware of the simple fact that we are inclined to shove the blame on to the horse because he has a mind and will of his own. 'He doesn't understand.' 'He still doesn't want to do it.' I have heard of golf players having a fit of temper and breaking their golf clubs, but I really haven't heard anybody cursing the golf-ball for not running into the right hole. Yet I have heard a lot of riders cursing a horse for not jumping the right fence.

Always keep the hands in a forward position.

Most Australians say that the horse is on the bit when he pulls like a train. That is wrong. You should feel as if you have a rubber-band in your hand, slightly taut; then you can increase the pressure, you can give and take him. The important part is to push him forward under your weight, like a big fat man pushing a little fellow out of the yard. He will ask for the bit and come on by himself.

The hands must be closed. Don't let him take the rein when he wants to; you are the boss, so make him do what you want. Push him up with the legs. It is like an electric current from the legs, through the hands, to the mouth.

Now that you have him, what do you want to do? You must develop the feeling through practical experience. Any book will tell you, but that won't do you much good. You must try it yourself. You yourself must develop the feeling.

Some Exercises for the Rider

These exercises should first be done at the halt. Later they can be done at the walk and then at the sitting trot (keeping in rhythm with the horse).
1. Swing an arm backwards in a circle. Sit still and upright. Keep the head still and look forward. Look happy—take the agonised look off your face—smile. Keep the opposite shoulder and the head still. Then swing the other arm in the same way. Then swing both arms together, one after the other like a windmill.
2. Turn the ankles around in a circle towards the horse. There is no need to turn them out as they will probably go that way anyway.
3. Swing the legs backwards and forwards alternately (from the knee). Keep the thighs still.
4. Shake out the arms, then shake out the legs.

SUMMARY

1. Nature's way is always to get the maximum result from the minimum effort. The horse free, when walking, galloping, or jumping, uses his muscles to the very best advantage. For example, he rounds his back over the jump. In this way he lands ready to gallop on and the jar of landing is reduced to a minimum.

2. We cannot go against the laws of nature without doing some harm or at least losing some efficiency. If, by the rider's poor balance, he causes the horse to hollow his back over the jump, the horse will not be able to jump so high and the jar on his tendons on landing will be greatly increased. Result: before very long he will probably break down.

3. When we educate the horse we teach him to carry out his movements while carrying the weight of the rider as nearly as possible as he would if he were free. Thus, by not going against the laws of nature we can expect to have a sound horse for many years. So our first reason for schooling him is to prolong his years of usefulness.

4. To be a comfortable ride the horse must be obedient (educated), supple, and fit (exercise). The more freely he submits, the easier the ride he provides. He will also not be wasting energy, power, and brain power in fighting the rider.

5. The basic training of the horse does not vary, no matter what his ultimate use is to be. He must be made balanced, on the bit, obedient, and supple. From then on, any particular training can follow. The well-educated horse is the result of hard work and good body control on the part of his trainer.

6. Balance is equality of weight. Balance is a thing the good God gives to us and all animals. We cannot explain it. To keep our balance is a subconscious action.

We are naturally balanced and so is the horse. If we maintain our own balance when riding by sitting straight and still we will then be able to teach the horse to maintain his natural balance with as little adjustment as possible.

7. To sit still we must develop near-perfect body control, as must the ballet dancer or the ice skater. This control is developed only through a relaxed and supple mind. The psychological approach must be correct.

8. To make a success of riding and training, the rider must do the thinking for the horse, and guide him. We must not blame the horse if things go wrong. The rider is at fault—whether it is you today or yesterday or someone six months ago, it is still the rider. You must seek the cause and try gently but firmly and logically to correct it, whatever is going wrong. *Never* punish a horse for something that is not his fault . . . in fact, seldom punish a horse, just firmly put him right. He knows that he should go forward to your leg aids. If he does not respond, remind him with the whip, gently at first, but quite hard if he still dreams on.

9. A whip should always be carried to keep the horse responsive to light leg aids and to reprimand him if he is naughty—like swinging round to go home.

10. If you lose your temper and vent it on the horse you will give yourself endless problems because you will destroy his confidence in you. So, get off and walk until you have regained your composure. Remember that he has a terrific memory for the bad as well as the good. You cannot say to him, 'I am sorry, please forgive me. I will not do it again'. So do not put yourself back weeks by being unreasonable.

11. Proper schooling will get the best out of a horse. Some things, such as conformation, cannot be improved, but we can still get him to do his best.

12. What are our aids to make him go? Weight, legs, hands, and voice. First is the weight, the most important and the easiest to apply. You

63

don't need to do anything; just sit down and let gravity do its stuff. Then come the legs and lastly—and lightly—the hands.

13. Can dressage improve the horse's natural ability? It can cultivate it and improve it to a certain extent. But he cannot pass his natural limit.

14. Be firm, still, and balanced in order to give consistent aids. Prepare yourself and be calm in mind and body. Be quite sure of what you are going to do. All three aids must be co-ordinated. The weight takes the message through his back to his hindlegs. Sit the weight down in the saddle, with the legs on the horse's body in the right place on the girth. To go, increase the pressure from both legs, short and sharply inwards, keep your hands in the forward movement and keep them still. Take him with you; you must never be ahead of the movement.

15. Do not give a long squeeze. Press and release and press again if necessary. Do not get working too hard or you will stiffen. Use the whip behind the leg to say, 'Pay attention'.

16. How to sit on the horse: read carefully pages 59 to 60. The ankle must be supple. The knee and below the knee should be on the horse. The rider's position on the horse should be such that he is balanced without the horse, whatever the length of stirrup. The hands should be down and the heels down. If both heels are equally stretched down it means that the body is straight. Because of our crookedness this must be carefully watched.

17. As we said earlier, the rider is the one who must straighten himself first. He, the load, cannot balance the horse, the support. It must be the other way round. Therefore, the rider must sit still and straight and so allow the horse to balance himself and his load.

18. The hands must be part of the position, with the elbows closed, not jammed, and the shoulders back and down. Then, if the horse tries to get out of being pushed together, the rider can restrain his resistance. If the hands are not still and steady, because they are part of the position, the horse will get some rein and sneak out of it in some way. He is being asked for extra effort and he will get out of it if he has half a chance.

19. It is most important that you have your arms close to the body and hands together, otherwise the oneness from your back to the hands is lost. The oneness of your body with the correct use of the legs will enable you to influence—through the horse's back—the engagement of his hindquarters.

20. Don't be behind the movement, don't be ahead of the movement. Take him with you—hands and body as one unit.

21. The weight must be evenly distributed. In a turn, nature pushes you outwards. To overcome this you must have a little more stretch to the inside. This is to keep the weight even, not to put more on the inside. The legs must stay the same length. If the body is crooked one gets longer than the other.

22. To repeat, the correctness of the position is important for the well-being of the horse—to make it easy for him to find his balance, and to move and make use of his muscles and body without interference. Secondly, the position must be firm, straight, and established before the rider can be consistent in giving his aids. If there is a movement of any part of the body it should give a definite message to the horse. If the message is not clear we must not blame the horse for not understanding.

23. If the horse accepts the bit when you push him forward under your weight, it feels as if you have a rubber-band in your hand and it is slightly taut.

24. The hands must be closed. He must not be able to take the rein when he pleases.

25. Some exercises to loosen up the body.

CHAPTER SIX

SIMPLE MOVEMENTS AND THE AIDS

Now we come to the different aids for the different movements. First I must say a few words about the horse's gait. We should know how many gears he has. The horse can walk, trot, or canter. It can be a collected walk, medium walk, extended walk, or on a loose rein. Let us remember one thing: we cannot teach him anything. He can walk, he can trot, he can canter, he can jump, he can do everything naturally. We cannot teach him any of those things but we can educate and train him so that he performs them in the way we want. Your job is to get him to do what you want when you want it. Make him go as quickly or as slowly as you want him to. That is education more than anything else.

He should walk—near hind, near fore, off hind, off fore. It is 1, 2, 3, 4. This is one complete walk sequence and there must be rhythm within that sequence. The rider must maintain the rhythm. If you watch the horse, if you count the steps, then you will know if he loses the rhythm within the sequence. On top of this you have the rhythm of one sequence after the other. It's like music. The walk sequence is repeated, repeated, all the time until you ask for something else. The walk is the gait where clearness is most easily lost for the simple reason that there is no suspension during the walk. Suspension is where the horse is completely off the ground, where he is off the ground with one or other of the legs all the time, so you will find that 1, 2, 3, 4 can very easily change to 1, 2, 3, 4. The 1, 2 moves together and 3, 4 moves together, and the closer they move together the closer you come to an amble or running movement.

I was looking at a film from overseas with Tina Wommelsdorf one day and in it there was one horse that was not straight during his flying changes. Tina said, 'Look at him, he is at the Olympic Games and he is not straight. Why are you so fussy with my horse?'. Because he is going crooked does not mean that you can go crooked. If he had been straight he would have scored better in the test.

The same applies with the clearness of gait. You will see overseas competition, even at Olympic Games standard, where the walk is the poorest movement of them all, but that does not mean that we can do so too. On the contrary. Because of lack of concentration, or lack of realisation of its importance, people don't take enough notice of the walk. If we go there with a clear walk we are already a step ahead. The fact that we aren't going away with

Above: Collected walk. Rider, Ron Paterson

Below: Working trot. Franz Mairinger riding Gay Pam

Relaxed trot. Rider, Ron Paterson

the Olympic team this time, but perhaps some other time, is another thing in itself.

To walk on, prepare yourself first. Horse standing still. Both legs apply pressure on the sides at the same time. You are sitting straight, letting your weight down, applying pressure on the sides and inviting him to go forward. The knees must always stay close. About four fingers below the knee, use pressure. Use a little, use a little bit more. Your knees must stay close and your seat stays in the saddle. If the horse walks on, it means he has understood. Then you leave him alone. Don't nag with the legs. Tell him what to do and leave him alone. You want him to submit and he should work with pleasure for you. If I have to kick, kick, kick, it is more tiring than walking myself. Go with him and repeat your request if necessary.

Then the trot. The trot is 1, 2, and in between each diagonal is a moment of suspension where the horse is completely off the ground. To trot, use the same slight pressure. First you may have to do it roughly. Within three months you do it subconsciously. When he goes, let him alone. Don't niggle; keep still. If you niggle you will always have to niggle to keep him going, so keep still. He won't do it straight away, but in three months he will go.

When he starts to trot it is exactly the same. Both legs push him forward. You keep still and just maintain your position. Use your lower legs with your heels down and your knees close. Your hands are still. You want to get him on the bit—push together. How is he to know, if your hands go this way and that way all the time? Use common sense and don't be scared to say, 'It was *my* fault'.

The finer the aids are, the easier it is. As he

67

Working canter. Rider, Jim Delamont

learns the aids, the more finely you can apply them, and then you will have a comfortable ride. Take it easy and let him do the work. Sit still and enjoy the ride.

The canter is a movement in three beats, and you can lead on the near fore or you can lead on the off fore. If he leads on the near fore, the first leg on the ground to start the stride is the off hind, and then comes the diagonal—near hind and off fore—and then comes the near fore as the leading leg, and after that comes nothing. After that he is off the ground with all four legs—moment of suspension. And then here we go again 1, 2, 3; 1, 2, 3, but at first the footfall is so quick that you can't actually count quickly enough as you can count in the walk or trot. So you put your three into one count. My Old Instructor used to say, '1, 1, 1, 1'. Well, for the same reason I say 'Hop, hop, hop, hop'. It comes out the same. One stride as the other, no matter what he does.

I once asked a pupil, 'What leg are you cantering on?'. He looked down and then looked at me and said, 'He's galloping isn't he?'. We had a little lecture, and I explained to him what was what, and I said again, 'What leg are you cantering on?', and he said, 'On the off near, sir'. He just could not be wrong.

Now he can lead on the off fore, but if he leads on the near fore the first leg to move is the off hind one and then comes the diagonal— 2—and then comes 3, the leading front leg. For

68

one fraction of a moment his whole weight is supported by the off hind, then comes the diagonal and he is supported by three legs. He takes one away and he is supported on two legs. He puts another down and is supported by three legs. He takes the diagonal away and is supported by the near fore, then he is already moving his hindquarters forward for the next stride. That is the time when I say 'Put the fibre under your bottom'. When he brings his hindquarters forward, that is the time when he bounces you out of the saddle. That is the test. The seat should stay there. Then he takes the near fore away and is airborne for the moment of suspension.

We are cantering on the near fore—outside leg behind the girth, inside leg on the girth. Outside leg pushes his outside hind forward and develops the stride to lead on the near fore. There is no time between that at all—'Ho-hup'. If we are not supple and quick enough the horse will run away. Whatever we do with the horse, it is for the horse's gymnastics and nothing else. It is all gymnastic exercise and the horse will try to avoid it. He would be silly if he didn't. You must be generous enough to say, 'Well, this time you put it over me'. Every time you put it over him it is part of gymnastic exercise. Gradually you catch him a little bit more until he gets used to it, and then there won't be any reason to avoid it.

You apply the pressure where your leg is expected. Together, for walk or trot; outside behind girth, inside at girth for canter on. In that position you can keep your heels down. Press or squeeze and ease up. Don't squeeze, squeeze, squeeze. Stretch up and down: push, ease, push, ease. I prefer a whip to spurs. The spurs should be made to measure the rider and the horse. If you use spurs you are inclined to rely on them. What can you use when the horse is used to the spurs?

The canter is the most natural gait. If the horse hasn't a clue, do it in a corner. Sit up straight, weight to the inside, and take him with you.

If you watch a foal in the paddock you will see that he always changes his legs to keep his natural balance. So he should when you are riding him. Like the fat man in the yard. Sit down and take him with you into a corner on the leg you want to go. Don't look down; then there is no chance of your weight being on the wrong side. Your hands hold him together, the inside leg is the forward pushing always, with one exception and that is for shoulder-in. Use your weight to push him on. Weight can also be used to bend him. Flex him with the inside leg.

Ride to suit the job in hand. Stockriding is different—that is good for stock. A horse trained in that way is good for his job.

How do we check from a canter? Outside rein, inside leg. You block him with the outside rein, but not enough to pull his head to the outside and change the flexion. Block it and make the leading leg inactive to get the same result as before. We produce the canter stride by bringing the outside hind forward, because that is the leg the canter starts on, and if we block it (the outside hind) we reverse it. The outside rein increases the pressure without checking forward movement, and without altering flexion. Even if you feel the pressure on the outside rein he must not change the flexion or he may change legs. I want him to do flying changes sometimes so I must be careful here. You increase the pressure on the outside rein and with that increased pressure of outside rein through your seat, the inside leg takes him over straight away and holds him into a forward trot. You must not change the flexion. You must try to be very delicate.

The inside leg keeps him going forward. From outside rein to inside leg, you have to have the feeling and get co-ordination, and the finer you can get it the better. The pull goes into the body and through to the leg. Sit down. Rein first, then the leg. The horse should not shorten his stride—it should be as smooth as possible. The first steps after the transition are the most important. Don't let him run away, as it will take time to settle him down again. Whatever fault the horse has, catch him first, before he runs away.

How do you go back to a walk from your trot? All you have to do is to sit down with your weight in the saddle and stop the forward movement of your hands. Give the horse your weight and he will walk. You must have contact or else he will run away. If that is not enough at first, use both hands into your seat. But sit down first, then use your hands.

The weight goes down and we stretch out a bit more. You should get the same contact with both reins. You should take him with you, whether at the walk, trot, or canter, or jumping. You create that pressure by driving him up on the bit. You just stop following the movement. Don't pull him up or resistance can set in.

When the horse is galloping the stride goes 1, 2, 3, 4. Through the tremendous stretch he breaks the diagonal and makes four hoof beats instead of three—a lateral four-time movement at full stride. A gallop stride is 1, 2, 3, 4, but that does not come into dressage because he never goes fast enough. He can also get into the four beat, not by going fast but by going slow. By going slow, without any impulsion, he can come into a footfall that goes 1, 2, 3, 4.

When he jumps, before the take-off, he puts the leading leg there as he finishes his stride. Then comes the moment of suspension. In that moment of suspension he turns himself around the middle, brings his hindquarters under, and starts the normal stride. The normal stride is 1 immediately followed by 2, then he propels himself away, lets himself fly over the jump, and lands on the other side. He lands on the off fore, and by doing so completes a diagonal. He then completes the stride by putting the near fore down and takes it away for a moment of suspension before he actually starts his new stride with the off hind. He has all four legs off the ground, and that is where most of the crimes of jumping riders are committed—on his ability to prepare himself for the next jump. The rider forces him into a style of taking off which is unnatural. If this goes on for too long, horses start to turn until you can't hold them or you can't push them. They say, 'No thank you'.

Before long they stop altogether. Before long they start to go faster and then they rush. That rush is a stand back, stand back, stand back . . . and then one day they find that they are a little bit too far back and so they put in a short stride, to give the quarters a chance to come underneath. Putting the short one in becomes a habit and finally that short stride in front of the jump develops into a stop.

If he starts to stop there, then you can say goodbye. With the same tremendous force that he uses to throw himself over obstacles he can bring himself to a stop. He can turn that same force the other way round and put it into reverse before the jump. Then no power on earth can make him go, because he is too strong.

So when he jumps, the footfall for the jump is exactly the same as the footfall for the gallop. It is 1, 2, 3, 4, then the moment of suspension. With the walk the sequence must be clear and the same is true for the trot and for the canter 1, 2, 3, 1, 2, 3 (the count starts on the striking off hindleg). The rhythm within the sequence must be quite clear. The rhythm from one sequence to the other should also be clear. There should be rhythm, there should be evenness. As my Old Instructor often said, 'Your riding should be silent music'.

The clear footfall, walk, trot, or canter has to be maintained in all gaits. You have a working trot and canter; you have a medium walk, trot, and canter; you have a collected walk, trot, and canter; and you have extended walk, trot, and canter. It does not matter what type of gait you are using—whether you are collected, working, or extended—the rhythm must always be the same. Under no circumstances must the rhythm become quicker. It must always be exactly the same.

To illustrate what I mean: if you say that this is point A and this is point B and it is 60 kilometres from A to B along the first curved line; and if you have one line going this way and one line going that way, and one going another way, and all lines are 60 kilometres long; then if you let a car off here, or four cars off there, and they all travel at 60 kilometres an hour,

Franz Mairinger on Gay Pam

Above: Working trot, gaining more ground in each stride than the next picture. Diagonals are even, horse is going within his frame and with self carriage, the poll is the highest point

Below: Towards collected trot with stride shorter than at the working trot. Note poll remains the highest point

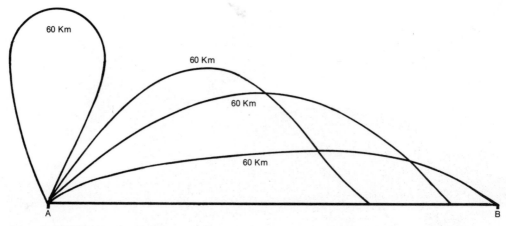

Diagram 6: Distance loops

who arrives at the destination first? They all arrive at the same time because it is the same distance.

In an extended movement the leg is carried forward. The higher the collection is the higher the leg movement up will be, until the highest collection is where it is only going up and down, which is the *piaffe*.

Whether he goes at working trot or collected trot or does piaffe or does an extended trot, the rhythm is always the same. With one little exception, and the little exception is in the extended trot, or the extended canter. It is 1, 2, 3, 4, 1, 2, 3, 4 if it is a walk. If it is a trot, 1, 2, 1, 2. It makes no difference. If your horse is going at the extended pace, and it is done properly, your count will be 1, 2, 3, 4. It will be longer. Contrary to what I tell you it is the same. But there is one little factor that drags the rhythm a bit. Because of the extension movement the period of suspension is longer. And because the period of suspension is longer, it puts a little bit extra on to your count.

We have to try to put in one line the difference between collected pace, working pace, and extended pace. The difference is only the length of the stride. The horse is making a shorter step or a longer step, but nothing else changes and this is important to know: there is no

difference. He just makes a longer or a shorter stride, but he must keep on going with impulsion or with energy.

We talk a lot about tempo and cadence. What is tempo and what is cadence? It is generally understood that tempo is the type of gait he is engaged in at that very moment—that the tempo is a bit short because he is going at a collected pace, or that it is better because he is going at an extended pace. He is going further, therefore the tempo is spread because he covers a better distance.

Cadence is something very difficult to put into words. In musical terms when you have cadence you have *vrom, vrom, vrom*. Every step is *vrom, vrom*; it is the cadence that gives it expression. Now we don't have the same thing in riding, otherwise we would say *vrom* with that near fore or what have you. Cadence is the expression within the sequence. You can have a walk or trot or canter which has rhythm. You can walk like this and have rhythm; but if you walk and have cadence, then you are going somewhere. It is life. It is the expression within the movement. It is something very hard to express in words. It is life. He has life and he is going somewhere. It is flair.

A very old saying is, 'Ride your horse forward and make him straight'. Ride him forward and

Straight canter on one track

sidedly. The rider is making the one-sidedness worse through his weight and other influences, creating impulsion and not letting it go in front. It has to go somewhere. If it doesn't go this way it has to go the other way.

Now 'straight' means that he is straight. The horse's spine is on top of the line that is the centre line, or whatever line it may be. The horse's spine is straight on top of that line, and there is the front leg and there is the hindleg, and the other one, and this is one track. The hindlegs follow exactly in the footfall of the front legs. At least, that is what we tend to say, but it is not really correct. It would be technically correct if we said that the forequarters moved exactly in front of the hindquarters— rather like a kangaroo, because as you know he can go on two legs. Everyone has seen a horse on his hindlegs, but I am quite sure that you have not seen a horse on his front legs, not in the same sense. I could show you a photo of Bill Roycroft where the horse is standing absolutely perpendicularly with Bill on top of him, and you would say that he is doing a handstand. Looking at the picture you would say that he has to go, but he didn't go. He will go up this way playfully, but he will not go up the other way.

He has to be on his forehand when he lands over the jump. I have seen a horse jump—not high, about as high as a table—and he took off with his hindquarters and landed on his hindquarters, which is of course the principle of the high school movement which is called the *courbette*, where he goes up with his forelegs and then he is on his hindlegs and then he goes hop, hop, hop, hop (depending on how good he is). Normally three or four leaps on the hindlegs is a very good one. I had one in the School which the Old Instructor said was the best horse in the history of the School. His average was eight leaps and his record was fourteen.

He doesn't need the forehand; he can move on the hindlegs. That is why it would be correct to say that he is moving the fore directly in front of the hindquarters. You can try that out, the straight movement, when you muck out the

make him straight. Why should you have to make him straight? If you said to me, 'Make that stick straight', I would say, 'Why?'. If you put the rider's weight on top of a horse and put the reins in his hands and give him a pair of spurs that tickle the horse right and left, you will probably have a horse that is going one-

boxes next time and take the load away in the wheelbarrow. You look ahead and you walk straight, and then you walk a bit crooked and you will soon see what the wheelbarrow is doing. You have a beautiful lugging-in wheelbarrow, doing exactly the same as your horse is doing.

The hindquarters or hindlegs are firmly connected to the spine by a big ball-and-socket joint. The hindquarters are connected to the shoulder through the spine. The push is transmitted through this structure. The forequarters are pushed forward and the horse steps straight forward. You can pick up very easily how that near hind is inclined to step in or out in some cases. If he steps out, the transmission of the power no longer takes place on a straight line, and then you have the horse lugging in. That is

the reason for the lugging in and that's the reason for a lot of other things, because he doesn't go straight forward. That's how it works mechanically. So, now you must ask yourself something else: is he straight?

If you try to give him the correct flexion and maintain your rhythm you will find that it is not as easy as it sounds. Maintain rhythm, maintain impulsion, and then every exercise you do will improve the horse's suppleness and obedience, understanding, balance, your influence, and comfort and ease of performance.

When I was in the School I was the pupil of Riding Master Polak. And Riding Master Lindenbauer was riding his stallion with one hand—his wonderful horse Conversano—and doing the piaffe, and the beautiful Spanish trot, and a pirouette on the spot, three times without

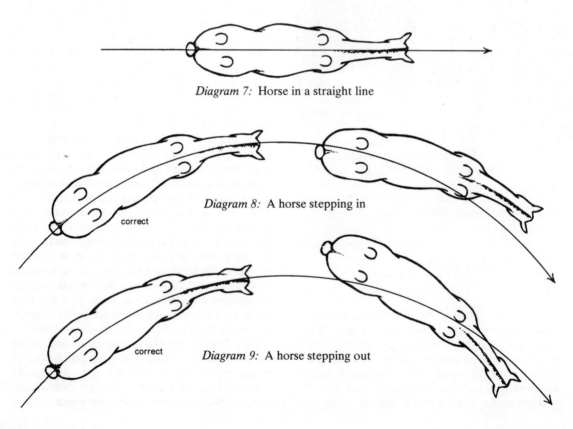

Diagram 7: Horse in a straight line

Diagram 8: A horse stepping in

correct

correct

Diagram 9: A horse stepping out

74

ever losing the slightest bit of rhythm. It looked glorious.

I said to Master Polak, 'Now doesn't he go well?', and he looked at me and said, 'That is nothing. I will show you'. Now the instructors were very good friends, but as instructors there was rivalry and friendly competition between them. They would correct each other even though they had been riding for thirty years. Then Polak brought out his stallion, which I had the pleasure of riding later on. He put the reins through his coat, just around the button, and hooked it up, folded his hands, and did exactly the same thing that Lindenbauer had done with one hand. This is of course the crowning achievement. What did he do it with? He did it with his weight, and only because his weight was going down with the horse stepping under it. This was a super-sensitive horse and it was the only horse he could do it with. When he said for the first time that I could ride him, my temperature shot up 10 degrees because he was a bubble. But he said, 'If you can sit on him you can ride him', and 10 minutes later he said, 'You look as if you can ride him better than I can'.

The concept of the whole thing is very easy. We try to reproduce the horse's natural balance with the rider on his back. He is made to go forward. He is not designed to carry extra weight. Why is he designed with four legs? To go forward and use the whole body to go forward, to gain ground, to go. What is the most important part of the horse? His back. No matter how strong he is everywhere else, it is no good if the horse stiffens and uses his muscles as a means of self-protection instead of as a means of going forward. Then he will lose his natural impulsion. He will only use his legs and run like a pig.

The back is the most important part of the horse so far as schooling is concerned. If you cannot sit comfortably, if he bounces you, then he is not using his back muscles properly. Some horses have a big movement and will swing you forward. He must be soft. In most cases the horse is fit but the rider is stiff. One has to give

first. The better he goes the more he stretches out and the more comfortable he will be. He must use his whole body with all four legs. All exercise, whatever we do, is gymnastic for the horse. It is done under a weight and the horse is doing things he does not want to do.

Everything is one-sided. Some of you write with your left hand, others are right-handed. We are not straight. Nothing is absolutely perfect on both sides. How can a girl carry a pitcher of water on her head? Because she stretches up straight to balance it. She cannot be stiff or one-sided if she is to carry it without spilling it. Our natural balance is not good enough to carry a pitcher. We must straighten first. A horse in his natural state is not straight. If we could fly over him we would see that he carries his hindquarters to the right. There are exceptions, just as there are with right- and left-handed people, but most horses are this way. We want him to do more than he does in his comfortable life, just feeding and galloping around. We want him to carry us on top. If he is to carry the rider successfully and look graceful we must make him straight. If you can do this no horse will stop. To which side does a horse usually run off at the fence? To the left. At that moment when he falls away with the shoulder you have no hope of controlling the hindquarters or making him go forward. He is really easier on the right rein because he curls that way. Every tiny bit you straighten or bend him is a little bit of gymnastic exercise. He will try to get away from it, and you cannot blame him. He would be silly if he did not try. First you have to straighten him out, have him relaxed, then you can start to work, collect him, bend him. Whatever you do is gymnastic exercise and, because it is, the horse is uncomfortable and he tries to get away. We must be masters of the situation and smile and try again. Start with a little bit.

You want to turn. It's like squeezing water from a sponge. Don't say 'Turn, turn, turn. Go on—turn'. Whatever you do with your horse, tell him to do it, then try to leave him alone. Indicate the direction, then ease up again. If he should want to go straight on, ask him to make another small turn. Hold him with the inside leg and take the rein out, and the moment he gives a bit, bring your hand in again. But that is only with a very green horse. Nobody can do it straight away. If we could, it would mean that the horse was already schooled. We have to try to go step by step by step.

Now we take him on a round line. The horse's spine should be on top of the line, and the hoof-fall is again with the hindquarters following the forequarters or forequarters in front of the hindquarters. If the horse is stepping in (see Diagram 8) you can say that he is falling in with the hindquarters. By the same token you can say that he is falling out with the shoulder (see Diagram 8).

If the horse is going as in Diagram 8, you will say that he is falling out with the hindquarters; if the horse is going as in Diagram 9 you will say that he is falling in with the shoulder. Principally it is always the same thing. You try to make him straight and he says, 'I am a lot more comfortable if I go crooked'. It is just as if you tell me that I must write with my left hand. As soon as you aren't looking I will put my pen in my right hand—because it is a lot easier, it's natural. As soon as the rider takes his eyes and legs, or his concentration, away from trying to keep the horse straight, he will go crooked. He will either fall in or fall out. Whichever way it is, he is putting himself in the crooked position which he likes to be in. Just as I like to write with my right hand. Everybody has some little thing which they like to do their way.

The ideal straight position is what you must aim for—because without that straightness and without that flexibility there is no foundation for collection. If the horse is not really flexible and straight, you can never collect him. You can collect him to some extent, but if you put your glasses on you will see that as soon as he starts to collect himself to a certain degree he will veer off the track with the hindquarters or the forehand, which is about the same thing. The more you try to collect him the more you are going to lose impulsion, and the more

crooked the horse will be, until you finish up trying to do piaffe. And if you try long enough the horse will lie down and snore because he is dying from lack of impulsion because the foundation for it is not there.

You will recall what I said before about the horse stepping under the rider's weight, and the rider's lower leg completely controlling the horse's hindquarters or individual hindleg. That is the foundation for collection.

Lindenbauer said, 'If you can ride a proper turn you can do everything else—for everything and anything'. When he said this to me I just could not imagine that a simple turn could have so much importance and I must admit that I didn't believe him. I did not tell him that; I was not game enough. Deep down I could not really see how a simple turn could have such a bearing on piaffe and flying changes. But he was right. If you can do a correct turn you are prepared for doing everything else. The 'everything else' is only a higher degree of suppleness and balance but the foundation is that proper turn.

If you are hanging on one side he just can't flex away from that rein because if he did he would stumble and fall over. He has more sense than to do that. So he steps under the weight that is hanging on one side all the time, and you desperately try to flex him away from that side where your weight is hanging. But until you wake up to the fact that your weight is not distributed evenly, you will work and work and get nowhere.

Every turn is an exercise, so bend him in the ribs. He won't like it, but make him do it the right way. All he will want to do is to swing his hindquarters out or else fall in with his shoulder. Increase the pressure with the inside leg to stop his shoulder from falling in and have the outside leg behind the girth to stop his hindquarters from falling out. And keep the seat straight. When he turns where you want him to go, ease up and he will go. Sit still and he will find his balance. At the moment he turns, ease up the pressure. The hindlegs should follow the front legs. The most common fault is that he will fall in with his shoulder. That means that you have no inside leg. You must push him out with the inside leg; he won't want to. If you can ride correctly through a corner you can do anything. You have him under control. It is most important to prepare yourself for everything you do. Get the feeling and concentrate. Always try to be consistent. Don't try for perfection straight away; you can polish it up later. The inside leg pushes him out and keeps him going forward, so keep him going forward. You are the boss.

The bigger the circle is, the less flexion and the less strain there will be, and the less he will try to get away. If you can keep him on a big circle then you can make the circle smaller. You will some day end up with pirouettes but you don't start with them. Ride your horse forward and make him straight. You can ride him forward on a round line. You must not accept whatever he offers—that is no good. If someone brings a box of chocolates, be careful! If the horse offers you a trot, trot, trot, it is no, no, no. He must go with rhythm. Some horses offer you all sorts. The moment you take it you give everything away. It's a matter of education. You tell him what to do. The whole schooling is based on plain nature. That is the conception—that you should have him as comfortable as possible, that you make him straighter and more supple.

Right through the whole line of schooling use your common sense. Routine will let you carry out all sorts of things without having to think. But if you school a horse you must think all the time. You must observe and translate your observations and find reactions and counter measures. If you have trouble of any sort let him have the rein and let him go on, and then you can slow him back again, but don't get stuck into collected work. No rider can ride him fast until under control. Don't let him just race. You can ride him slowly, properly, if you have been riding him fast forward when you want it.

Most riders are under the impression that the horse is easier on the right rein because he is invariably softer on the right rein, but really he is bringing his hindquarters in, falling away with the shoulder to the left. Our aim is to make the horse straight. Why won't the horse go straight? How does he avoid the rider? You must co-ordinate your aids to ride him at your pace, on your line, the whole time. He avoids by:

- trying to run away;
- falling in with his shoulder;
- falling out with his hindquarters;
- slowing down.

Despite these, the rider must maintain his centrally seated position on top of the horse, inside leg long and active (effectively). Beware of neck reining. Use more inside leg. By stretching down with the inside heel and pushing the inside leg down, you will eventually prevent his falling in. The inside-leg control of the horse is the essence of all work. Try it on a stationary horse. Pull the right rein; what does he do? Pull the left rein; what does he do? Invariably he will fall in or step in with the shoulder. He won't turn his head. Anticipate a falling-in turn by stretching out with inside leg before the turn and don't allow him to fall in. At walk, trot, and canter, the horse's whole body should follow the rein.

In bad cases of falling in, the outside rein may be used to assist the return to a normal position on the track, and then the inside rein relaxed to allow the inside leg to do the job. Shoulder control is the first essential in controlled movement. Other factors follow from there.

We will finish with the circle and then go on to the turn. You can do a quarter of a big circle or a quarter of a smaller circle, but never smaller than 6 metres in diameter. It is the smallest circle that high-school dressage permits (that is, a circle on one track). Everything we have talked about so far has been on one track. Our first aim is to keep him on one track on the circle. First make the circle on a big track, then you can make it smaller and smaller but never too soon, and never smaller than 6 metres. The corner of the school is a turn of a quarter of a circle.

The rider's position is all-important. Equal weight on each seat bone is the aim, otherwise a falling to one side or the other will be probable. That is the one thing you must think of. That is the goal of every rider who is concentrating on the horse and trying to make the horse do things. Before you work or try to do anything with the horse, check on your position; then work the horse for as long as you can maintain position. The horse is all right. As soon as you lose position the horse is lost, and so are you.

Theoretically, if we could sit perfectly and never move, we could break him in today and in six months he could do Grand Prix. It's hard to believe, but if we could sit still and never move, that's how quickly we could progress. But we do move, and we realise that we have moved. And at the same time as the movement, comes the realisation that we have lost the horse. That we have lost the flexion, that we have lost impulsion, that we have lost the type of movement that we were doing at the time. Concentrate on position; this is a most important thing. It is just common sense—you are the load and if you are not still then the horse cannot do it.

Fundamentally we do not want anything more from the horse than to be straight, for he is inclined to be crooked. So we try to make him straight and with the straightness we develop the suppleness and flexibility within which you can relax the horse. By relaxing and engaging the hindquarters more you will eventually get your short paces and your piaffe and canter pirouettes, flying changes, and so on.

This is the foundation. If that is not there it is like building your house on sand, and the first time you collect the horse you will see that the sand is all rolling away, and then if you are serious about it you will have to start from scratch. It is a lot better to start from scratch when you start in the first place, and not try to be quick, quick, quick. You cannot ask him for flying changes before he is ready, and 'before he is ready' means before you can keep him straight and before you can flex him here and flex him there with ease. If you can do that

then collection will come easily. It goes back to what the Old Instructor said, that I *had* to do it. I believed it and I did it, and because I did it I know he was right.

If one of *my* pupils ever says, 'My Old Instructor said this and that', then I will not have lived for nothing. I will have left something when I have gone.

The most common fault of riders is quite unreasonable. What is that fault? *We do not look where we are going.* If you want to go from here to there, and you want to make use of that line to make your horse go forward and to make him straight, then you must look. It is so important. There is so much in that look. Let me point you in a given direction. Look in that direction, then I will blindfold you and away you go. See what happens. I have done it so many times. The horse should go straight from one point to another. He starts straight and then moves off the line. At first you are concentrating, you still have that picture in your mind, but then something takes over and makes you forget. It is the same process as the man lost in the bush who walks in circles. Our one-sidedness takes over. If you are right-handed you can bet your sweet life that you will be going to the right. If you are a true left-hander you will be going to the left. I have seen it happen so many times.

As long as we walk or drive a car we look at what we are doing, and because there is no known process we are not conscious of what is going on. How are actions computerised? We are looking and all the connections are made without our knowing it. One muscle is co-ordinated with the other and one leg moves after the other. But to turn that off, shut your eyes, and your one-sidedness takes over and you wander. If you do not look forward it is the same as shutting your eyes. If you look forward and say, 'This is my goal', then you have your goal. Now, if you can't make yourself go straight when you don't look, how on earth can you make your horse go straight? If you look forward and your horse starts to wobble around to the right, what is he telling you? You look immediately, you feel, you sense that you have moved off your direction, and because you can feel it coming, you act or react. The horse is saying, 'If you want me on that line you have got to use more right leg'. If he wobbles to the left then you have to use more left leg. By just looking, your reactions will be right.

If you don't look then you just won't know that you are not on your line and you won't know what you should do. You can wobble one way or another but you won't get the finer point; you will not make the horse straight. You can't make him supple going around the corners unless you are consciously drawing a line in your mind. Take a rake and mark it on the ground, or put out a few drums or pieces of paper so that you have something to go by. You have to ride him on your line at all times.

You can't get him straight right away. That is impossible because he is not supple enough. He just does not understand, and is not responsive enough. Try every time to get him in position with his spine on the correct line. That is in one step a gymnastic exercise.

It's easier for the horse to go to his natural one-sidedness than to go straight. As soon as you straighten him out you can then start your gymnastic exercise. If you push your horse together and he has to stretch from the neck right through to his hocks, oh how he will try to get away from that!

The line principle—and you have to try to understand it—is that every line you put him on, and try to keep him on, is gymnastic exercise for him. Do not be surprised if it takes a bit of doing. If gymnastic exercise was something we did every day, the army intake would be 100 per cent admitted and not 54 per cent rejected. Everyone would be a lot fitter.

Every line you put him on is gymnastic exercise until he can do it with ease. It is then just everyday work. There is no strain at all. Only then can we say to him, 'Can you bend a little bit more?'. The horse cannot collect until he is supple and can do what is required without strain.

I once knew a girl in Adelaide who could turn herself into knots and could pass under a limbo stick only 38 centimetres above the ground. But put her on a horse and you have never seen anything so terrible! Which proves that the mind controls the body. When she got on the horse all that suppleness disappeared and turned into woodenness.

Do not try to make a small turn until the horse can turn with ease on one track. It is the same as a circle. Do not try it until he can go straight forward at any ordinary pace, accepting the bit. If you do he will automatically fight, resist. You must look upon every single move as gymnastic exercise, and if you do so you cannot go wrong.

If you take the time to make the horse really go forward, to get him really straight and to make him really supple, then you can start to worry about other things.

To get your horse on the lines and to make him straight is harder work and takes longer than to teach him all sideways movement, flying changes, piaffe, all movements. It is harder because it is the foundation. If he can flex himself with balance and suppleness and accepts the rider's aids and the bit, the rest is only a little more gymnastic exercise. We come back to what my Old Instructor said, 'If you can ride a proper turn you can do anything else'.

What is necessary for a turn? It has been worked out that there are 3982 ways of riding through the turn wrongly. That means that you must avoid 3982 ways, in order to get the one right way, because that right one is your goal.

We have a large turn and to start off with the horse must be on one track. We have one leg following the other completely on one track, hindquarters not to either side but exactly following in the footsteps of the front leg. While he is on the bit he maintains his rhythm and impulsion as he goes for the turn. He is flexed to the inside, and the rider's weight is evenly distributed. That's why he can do it. The rider's inside leg is in absolute command of forward impulsion; the inside rein flexes him with ease and he accepts it. The outside rein, outside seat, and outside leg control the hindquarters so that they do not fall away and are on the track. What more do you want? The inside leg drives him forward. He accepts your weight and carries you with balance; therefore he does not try to rush, does not try to fall back, fall away, toss his head, or anything else.

Your horse's head should be in one position and never move. When you stand still, walk, trot, canter, gallop, canter, trot, walk, and halt, it should never change or move. Then he is stepping into the bit, accepting it, and is flexing. But so long as you can feel and see that your horse's nose goes out there or down there, or turns to one side or the other, so long as there is something going on with his head, it proves that he is not stepping forward into the bit. He has not learnt to accept the bit, because he has not learnt to be supple enough, because his rider has not spent enough time trying to make him go on that line.

SUMMARY

1. We have said that we do not teach the horse anything. We educate him to do his natural movements when and in what manner *we* want. We teach him the different aids for the different movements.

Walk   Even four-time with no period of suspension. There must be rhythm within this sequence and each sequence is repeated and repeated in rhythm.

Aids: Prepare yourself, check your position, with the horse standing still. Your weight is in the saddle. With the knees closed, apply pressure with both legs just below the knee. The hands are still. Tell him what to do and leave him alone. If he does not respond, repeat a little more strongly and if necessary use the whip.

2. **Trot**   He moves the diagonals together with a period of suspension between steps.

Aids: As for the walk, but a little more definite. Teach him to obey light aids. The finer the aids are, the easier and more comfortable the ride will be.

3. **Canter**   A three-time movement. Near fore leading the order . . . off hind, near hind and off fore together, near fore, period of suspension.

Aids: Near fore leading. Outside leg (right) behind the girth lightly. Only a little back. The knee must stay on and the heel down. Followed immediately by the inside leg, on the girth, more strongly. The inside leg at any time or any gait says, 'Go on'. Press, ease up but keep the legs there. Do not look down. Sit up and straight and take him with you.

4. *To Check From the Canter:*   Outside rein increases pressure but not to pull his head out or change the flexion. Inside leg takes over and holds him forward into the trot. The first steps after a transition are most important. He must go smoothly into a true trot. He should not shorten the stride of his canter. There must be co-ordination from the check with the outside rein to the forward with the inside leg.

5. *From Trot to Walk:*   Put the weight down into the saddle, and stretch a little more. Stop

the forward movement of the hands. Have contact but do not pull.

6. **Gallop** In four time. Near fore leading. Off hind, near hind, off fore, near fore. Through the great stretch he breaks the diagonal to give the four time. A very slow canter can also give a four-time beat through lack of impulsion.

7. **Jump** The footfalls are as for the gallop. He crosses the jump between 2 and 3. The order, near fore leading, is . . . off hind, near hind (here he propels himself up and over the jump by the tremendous bending and straightening of the hindquarters and hindlegs). He lands on the off fore, then the near fore, the moment of suspension, and off to the normal gallop or canter stride. The rider must sit still, especially during the period of suspension before the jump. Many horses are upset by the movements of the rider at this moment. The discomfort and unnecessary effort caused by this interference often cause the horse to stop or rush.

8. The rhythm within the sequence, and the rhythm from one sequence to the next, should never change in any one gait.

Each gait can be collected—working, medium, or extended. Ideally, the beat at any of these should be the same. As the metronome goes tick—tick—tick, never changing its beat, so should the footfalls of any one gait remain in the same time and rhythm, whether it be collected, working, medium, or extended. The beat should never quicken. The slight exception to this rule is at the extended trot and canter; the period of suspension is longer and so the count comes a little slower.

9. In these three types of gait the only difference is that he takes a longer or shorter stride, but he must keep going with impulsion.

10. Tempo means the correct speed for the particular movement the horse is doing. It must always remain even. Cadence is the expression, the life within the movement.

11. 'Ride him forward and make him straight.' Straight means that the horse's spine is on top of the line he is following, be it straight or curved. He is on one track, the hind feet following exactly in the path of the forelegs, or to be more technically correct, the forelegs move exactly in front of the hindlegs. The hindlegs are the important ones for they are the engine. He can stand on them in the rear or the levade and he can go forward on them as in the courbette. One stallion at Vienna could do fourteen hops. A horse cannot stand on his forelegs.

He must be straight in his body to go on a straight line. If the hindlegs step straight forward the forehand will be pushed straight forward. If his quarters are to one side the whole horse is crooked. So you have another problem. Is he straight?

12. When the horse's spine is exactly over a curved line he is said to be correctly flexed. If you can maintain rhythm, impulsion, and correct flexion, every exercise you perform will improve the horse's suppleness, obedience, understanding, and balance. It will also improve your influence, comfort, and ease of performance.

13. The horse's body is designed to go forward using everything he has. If the rider makes him uncomfortable and he stiffens his back in self-protection he is *not* using all his muscles to go forward, so he loses his natural impulsion. The back is the most important part of the horse so far as schooling is concerned. The muscles must not stiffen. We give him gymnastic exercises to teach him to remain supple under weight.

14. All animals are one-sided in some way, just as we are left-handed or right-handed. The horse is not straight. Most carry the hindquarters a little to the right, though a few do it the other way. They mostly run off a jump to the left because of this right curve. To carry the rider and use all muscles equally on both sides and so remain sound, he must be made straight. Every small degree to which you can straighten or bend him is a gymnastic exercise and will gradually make it easier for him. He

will try to get out of the extra effort, and will often succeed. But you must smile and try again.

15. Whatever you do with your horse, tell him to do it and leave him alone. Indicate, then ease off, and repeat if needed. To turn, don't go on pulling the rein. If the very green horse turns too quickly he will fall in. Hold him with the inside leg and take the outside rein out. The moment he gives a bit, bring the hand in. In time he will learn to turn on your line, not falling in or out with shoulder or hindquarters. He resists being put straight or flexed correctly because he is more comfortable when he is crooked—just as you would resist being made to write with the other hand.

As soon as the rider loses concentration and position, the horse will put himself back where he is comfortable. Until the horse is flexible and straight it is impossible to collect him to anything but a small degree. The foundation must be there to maintain impulsion.

16. 'If you can ride a proper corner you will be able to do everything else.' To do a correct corner he must be straight, flexed, and going with impulsion. These are the foundations for everything. Everything is just a higher degree of suppleness and balance. He steps forward under your weight. If your weight is crooked he will step forward crookedly because he must balance the load. Prepare yourself carefully for what you plan to do. To stop him from falling in with the shoulder, press with the inside leg to keep him forward. Have the outside leg behind the girth to prevent the hindquarters from falling out.

The bigger the circle is the less the flexion will be, so start with 20 metres or more. Do not make the circle smaller until he is going well on the larger one, and decrease very slowly.

17. Horses often offer all kinds of things such as a canter start when they feel the leg behind the girth for a turn, etc. You must not accept anything for which you have not asked. If you do you give everything away. You must always be the boss. Being consistent in this is simply education, common sense, and nature. Through all schooling you must think, and use your common sense. Translate what is happening and find counter measures. If you have trouble, let him go long and start again.

18. He feels softer on the right rein but really he is falling in with the quarters and falling out with the shoulder. This fits in with his crookedness and so he does not go up to the right rein. He may avoid this by trying to run away. To try to correct this the rider must maintain his central position on top of the horse; the inside leg is long and active.

Do not neck rein but use more inside leg to prevent him from falling in. The inside leg control is the essence of all work. Before a turn, anticipate his falling in by having him on the inside leg. As in No. 15 of this summary, correct if necessary with the open outside rein to get him back on the track, but do not hold him with it. Work on circles and turns but do not make them too tight. A 6-metre circle is the smallest that even the best horse can do correctly.

19. As I am always explaining, the rider's position is all-important. It must remain balanced, straight, and still. If things go wrong it is probably the result of faults in the rider's position. If we could sit completely still it would be so very easy to train the horse. But we move, and if we realise this and know that we have lost the horse as a result—that is, we have lost his flexion, tempo, or impulsion, or something—then we are slowly gaining in feel, and so will also gain in the feel of maintaining the position. This is the foundation, when *through our position* we can have the horse straight, supple, and flexible. Then he will be relaxed and we can get him to engage his hindquarters more and more, and so attain collection and the more advanced movements.

[*This is the essence of the teaching that Franz Mairinger has given us*—Kay Irving]

20. We must look where we are going. If you

try to walk with your eyes shut you will only keep straight for a short way, then your crookedness will take over and most right-handed people will curve to the right. This is why someone who is lost walks in circles. So, when you ride the horse you cannot ride him straight if you do not look where you want to go. Also, head up and looking ahead keeps the body position in control. If you are looking forward you will know immediately if the horse wobbles and will instantly bring the required leg into action to straighten him on the line. This is a gymnastic exercise to improve him.

21. To get your horse on your line, to have him straight and supple, is harder work and takes longer than all the advanced movements. They come easily provided that you have laid this foundation soundly. 'If you can ride a turn correctly you can do all else.' What is a correct turn? Read and study carefully the paragraph on page 79, from 'We have a large turn . . .' to '. . . toss his head, or anything else'.

22. His head should be in one position and never move, whatever the gait. If his head is moving or his nose tipping he is not stepping forward to the bit. He is not yet supple enough. The rider has not yet spent enough time on the foundation.

CHAPTER SEVEN

COLLECTION AND FURTHER MOVEMENTS

Collection is the degree of engagement of the horse's hindquarters. You collect him by pushing him towards the bit.

There are various paces, and we have to go from one pace to the other, or one gait to the other. If we start off from a halt it must be obvious at what gait the horse needs the most impulsion—when he is standing still. The impulsion is there. All you have to do is turn on the ignition. He has to be standing square at the halt. He has to be standing square, weight evenly distributed on all four legs, and not carrying more weight on the forehand than he does on the hindquarters. If he does, there is no doubt that the horse will break down before his working life is over—because of what I said earlier, and what old Roy Stewart said, 'Horses are made to be horses' and not made for man. If the horse had been made for man he probably would have had the legs of an elephant to make sure that he didn't break down. As it is, if you look at a horse's leg you will see that there is really nothing to it, just a bit of bone. Just compare that colossal weight and that little bit of bone and a few tendons which are capable of supporting it, of withstanding that colossal point of impact over a jump, and doing it for years and years. It's really amazing. For the

whole engine works according to the Lord's design, and He didn't design it for the horse to go with a hollow back. He designed it so that the horse could collect himself.

There is a notion that was put forward hundreds of years ago, and, incredibly, it is traceable from 1765 to a book I read in about 1967. As I said earlier, the notion is that the horse is by nature over-balanced, by nature carries more weight on the forehand than he does on the quarters. The reasoning is not correct. This reasoning is based on the belief that the head, neck, and shoulders (forehand part) are heavier than the hindquarters. In a way it may be true enough. We even made some rough tests. We drew a chalk line along the ribs and we put one end on the weighbridge and then the other end. Very roughly, it appeared that the forehand was heavier than the hindquarters by about 27 to 36 kilograms. But the good Lord did not design a monument. If He had designed a monument He would have made it out of bronze or something like that. He designed something that moves, and as soon as the horse starts to move by himself he does the very thing we have tried for years to make him do. What is that very thing that he does? He collects himself and he balances himself and distributes the weight evenly on all four legs. He carries as much weight on the hindlegs as on the forehand. And if we don't make him go forward when we are on top, we are going to let him break down. We are going to break him down because the forelegs are going to carry more weight than they have been meant to carry.

Another wrong idea is that the rider, by sitting (leaning) backwards or sitting further back in the saddle, transfers his weight automatically back on to the hindquarters, thereby shifting the point of balance and taking weight from the forehand of the horse. There is nothing more stupid than that belief. It would be all right if the rider had been born on the horse. But our doing this will only result in making it impossible for the horse to move, to use his muscles in the natural way that he should, and will consequently put more weight on the forehand than he had before. Lifting him up with the snaffle and bridling him with the curb and using a lot of lever actions is a load of rubbish, yet it still happens.

I was reading a book once, and after about three pages something struck me. There was something wrong. 'Go back', I thought. The writer was talking about a capriole. A capriole is where the horse jumps straight into the air and, when he reaches the apex of his jump, fires out with both hindlegs, kicks out. It was developed in the past as a war tactic. If surrounded by attacking foot soldiers, just one capriole, a half-pirouette, and then *choo* straight through the hole and away you go. Now, if he jumps up straight and he kicks up when he is level it is really easy after you get the hang of it. There's really nothing to it. But if he jumps up and starts to land, starts to go down, and then kicks up, it can be very uncomfortable. To prevent the horse from doing that, it is suggested that as you jump up you give the horse a little arrêt (pull) with the left rein to stop him from going down (and that is where I sort of lit up three pages later and saw that there was something wrong). Now, you tend to read this and

not take any notice. But if you could do that—if, when the horse is starting to go down, you could give him a little arrêt, and keep him up there—that would turn on the anti-gravity belt, and we haven't found that yet. It's impossible, it's physically impossible. If the force of gravity has taken over and the horse is going down, no power on earth is going to hold him up there. But still the book says that if you give him a little arrêt he will stay there. As you read it through, unless you are very careful, you are likely to take it as the gospel. It is not. Men walking on the moon proved that gravity is there too, and they had to develop a tremendous amount of thrust in the rocket to overcome the gravity.

Say you have collected him. He is balanced. He is balanced on all four legs, collected to a degree, ready for anything. He is ready to walk on, ready to trot on, ready to canter on, ready to rein back, or ready to do piaffe if you so desire. He is evenly distributed on all four legs.

Now while we are on that point there is a notion in the horse world that the horse's head

Collected trot

85

has to come down. That it is better for the horse to be down than up. Very debatable. The position of the head should not change. It should not go up and should not go down and the horse should be stepping into the bit. By stepping into the bit he is engaging himself with the hindquarters; he is stepping through on to the bit.

There is a German expression, *durchlaessigkeit*, which cannot be translated. The word suggests that glass is transparent, that the light goes through it; the same expression suggests that the horse is transparent and the aids are flowing through. It means exactly the same thing. As the light goes without any resistance through the glass, so the aids go without any resistance through the horse. From your hands into the horse's hindquarters, and from his hindquarters forward into your hands, without any resistance.

So now he is stepping into the bit, he is transparent to your aids, or he is letting the aids through. He is supple, he is balanced, he is not resisting anywhere. Now this is the desired head position (see Diagram 10). It is, of course, the Grand Prix position. And that is the frame for piaffe and passage. The head can be as shown in Position 1, Diagram 10, or the top photograph on page 71, which is the working frame, or it can be as shown in Diagram 10, Position 2 (the collected frame), or extended forward as shown in the photograph on page 88, into the extended frame. A degree of head movement is an indication of resistance to the aids, a resistance at being pushed together, and as such it is a fault. We move him on and say 1, 2, 3, 4. Without visible influence from the rider the horse should walk on without changing his general outline, without changing the general appearance. That of course includes the head position. He doesn't change that; he doesn't drop it. We stand him up square and the way he looks is the way he keeps on looking. He moves the legs, nothing else. He does not toss his head up and down or anything else. From that position, walk, trot; complete the transition from the halt into the walk, and the same

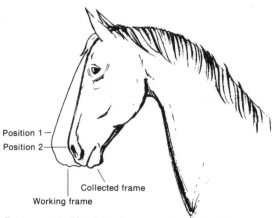

Position 1 —
Position 2 —
Collected frame
Working frame

Diagram 10: Working frame and collected frame

applies from the walk into trot, and the same applies from the trot into canter. In the moment of canter off you will find that the head position appears to change, but it is not a movement in the head itself. The movement is determined by his preparation for the canter, and that changes his whole position, and with his whole position of course his head position changes slightly too. But within the horse it does not change. The whole position of the horse changes in the moment of strike-off because he comes under. From a halt, that is important, from a halt into a clear walk—meaning that the first steps should be a clear walking step followed immediately by the second, third, and fourth, and not some shuffling around or a half job around. A clear step forward on to the bit.

In a higher dressage test he would go from a standstill immediately into a clear trot or a clear canter without any fuss—without any additional movement except for those which are necessary to develop the walk, trot, and canter. From a clear walk 1, 2, 3, 4, 1, 2, 3, 4 he would go immediately into a clear trot (I always count the trot 1, 2, 1, 2) and from a clear trot into a clear canter without any extra leg movement. The trueness of gait is the important thing. On that everything else rests. If the walk has gone, or the trot or canter has gone, you

86

finish up with a circus horse—which is not enough for us. Circus is an art in itself and has really nothing to do with practical training. There is no gymnastic exercise involved in circus, or hardly any.

From the clearness of gait (that is so important) there follows the straightness and flexibility, and then comes the collection. Clear walk, into a clear trot, into a clear canter, back into a clear trot, into a clear walk, into a clear halt. They are the complete transitions from one gait into another.

Now we have half transitions when we take him from one gait or one particular part of a gait, through a collected walk or collected trot, into an extended trot or extended canter. Now when we extend the pace, something that was pointed out before has to take place. Firstly you have him in the frame of working trot or collected trot, and then you want him to extend his pace. You have to let the nose or the whole front end, neck and head, drop forward a little, but a little longer and lower. He has to stretch after the bit a little in order to give him room to stretch out forward.

If this is the ground here (line A–B in Diagram 12) and the horse's front leg is pointing to B, he has to put his foot down exactly where he points it and not anywhere else. You will often see horses come out to point C—very impressive if you only look at the front legs. If you look at the hindlegs too, and make a unit out of it (that's something that takes experience), you will see that the front legs and the hindlegs as they move are parallel (lines D1 and D2). The general impression should be that the top part of the front leg, above the knee, and the lower part of the hindleg, below the hock, have to be so near to parallel that they work as a unit. They have to, because if they are not they don't distribute the weight evenly; the one that comes later on has to carry more weight than the other one.

You will see horses that go to point C. Just to look at, it seems very impressive, but what if you put it to the test? There's a German expression that says a horse never steps over

Diagram 11: Flicking front leg in extended trot

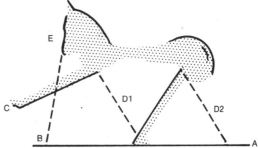

Diagram 12: A horse, showing various lines from head to footfalls

his nose, meaning that if his head is at point E, and the line of his nose goes down E–B, he is not going to put his foot in front of B. He cannot step over the line of his nose. If you put this horse to the test, the head position wouldn't really be too bad, but you see that the leg at C is cut off. Now that leg has to come back for mechanical reasons. If you measure the length of the diagonal, the length of step of the supporting diagonal, then you will see it is nearly half as much again. Obviously he can't keep going like that. He has to bring his leg back, because if he doesn't bring that leg back, he has to start to canter or he has to break in half. He is not going to break in half and so he has to canter. He cannot keep trotting with one diagonal being longer than the other. That is impossible. He cannot adjust the length of the diagonal on the ground because that is what his weight is

Extended trot, longer frame with maximum length of stride gaining tremendous ground in each stride. Horse remains balanced, without becoming heavier on the forehand, as is so often seen with the poll no longer being the highest point. Franz Mairinger riding Gay Pam

resting on. He can only adjust the length of the diagonal off the ground. You can see how, as he throws his leg forward, the hoof by the force of momentum flips up to point C and he has to bring the leg back to the corresponding length of the other diagonal, because otherwise he is not trotting. The horse's back is stiff, he does not go forward enough; therefore, the floating effect of the extension is not there.

In correct extension (see the photograph above) the rhythm is still the same, plus that little bit extra, because he is off the ground for longer. In the extended canter it is exactly the

same, with the lengthening of head and neck and the same rhythm, and a little bit longer again, being longer off the ground because he is going forward more. The period of suspension is longer than if he were going shorter. He definitely must lengthen that stride. Just as we have to go a certain distance with forty steps instead of fifty, so he has thirty strides or twenty strides instead of twenty-five. So we have long strides and at the same time he always has to be straight too. You will notice that horses are reasonably straight when going at ordinary pace, but as soon as they start to extend the

88

pace the hindquarters come in, indicating that they are not going forward as much as they should. The horse must remain straight. He must remain straight no matter what he does, no matter where he is; when he is on the bit and when he is not on the bit.

There are so many terms and one term is related to the next. You cannot say that the horse is truly on the bit and that he is crooked, because if he is truly on the bit he can't be crooked. We get him on the bit, we have ridden him forward, he is obedient to our leg, and he is carrying our weight with ease, then we have to concentrate and make sure that he is straight. If he balances your weight and goes forward and is on the bit, you can forget about the straightness because he *is* straight, otherwise he wouldn't be on the bit and he wouldn't go forward, and he wouldn't carry you with joy and ease.

He must accept both reins in the same way. The rider should have as much pressure on the right rein as he does on the left rein. The horse is inclined to give you nothing, or little, on the right rein, and a lot on the left rein. If the pressure is transmitted more to the left, he will lean on that left rein. You have to make him straight, and as you try to make him straight he will automatically even up and accept the influence of your right leg. The right leg makes him go forward as well as the left leg. He is going to step through and give you that feeling of tension on the right rein as much as on the left rein. It is a matter of schooling really that you can keep him on the right rein and then with a slight action of the left rein take that little bit too much off and ease up and hold him forward and level him off that way. But he has to accept both reins in the same way—and then it feels as if you have a stick in front of you and that stick is pushing along all the time—and you sit there comfortably and he steps into the bit at every step. He will only do that if he is going forward and if he is straight. So if he is on the bit and accepts your leg he is straight.

He is on the bit if he accepts it, goes lively, does not resent it, and does not resist, fight, or try to get rid of it in any way—not by going against it, not by dropping behind it, not by tilting the nose one way or the other, or shifting his jaw this way and jamming himself like that. He is straight. He is supple in his neck. He is going forward with energy. He does not go up and down. His contact with the reins is constant, he is not coming more or less on one side with one and not more or less on the other side with the other one. Constantly he accepts the contact and goes forward into the bit, towards the bit. The rider will have that position achieved whether he is at halt, walk, trot, canter, halt, rein-back, canter, because he is letting his aids through weight into the hindquarters and from the hindquarters forward into the rider's hands or into the horse's mouth.

Most of the resistance you can pick up in the horse's head with the horse resisting the bit. Sometimes the horse resists the bit itself, but most of the time he resists it because he is resisting the rider's driving influences or correcting influences. It works like this—the rider pushes him with weight and legs and he says, 'That's too much work', and so he tries to step out near hind to get rid of that gymnastic exercise. The rider pushes him with his left leg and then he tries to go out again, and if the rider doesn't let him out near hind then he goes out off hind. Then he could go wide, he could go crooked, he could do anything, or just lose impulsion, stop going with verve, and crawl along. This is the degree of the gymnastic exercise that has to go into the horse—you must have him on a long rein to start with and then you must push him a little bit more and he still keeps going, still accepts. Then you push him a bit more and then you have him . . . and there is piaffe, but that takes a little bit longer.

Apart from riding you may need to do some gymnastic exercise. It will take a long time before your body submits to the command that comes from your brain. You may set your mind and say, 'I want to be like Margot Fonteyn'. (She practises 8 hours a day, I'm told, but if you try to get there you may have to practise 10 hours a day.) It takes time before your body gives and submits and develops the necessary suppleness. It takes a long time before your body submits to the understanding that comes from your head and the command that you have to sit straight for various reasons. Exactly the same thing applies with your horse. It takes a while before the horse develops the understanding and the ability and the suppleness by which he can be pushed together and stay together and still keep going, maintain his impulsion, and his flair and balance. That takes time. The trouble is that too many people don't have time, and by not having time they actually take a lot longer than if they had taken time in the first place.

Before the second World War a famous surgeon was the first man to operate inside the chest. One day, when he was in a hurry to get to an emergency operation, he said to his chauffeur, 'Go slow. I am in a hurry'. That goes for driving and it goes for training your horse too. Take your time because you are in a hurry. There is no way at all that you can cheat nature. Even if we think we do, we are penalised for it by the horse's not giving us his complete capabilities. Or we try to push him, we overface him. Then he usually starts to jack up and we have to go right back and try to undo everything that has been done to the horse, try to make him forget everything and start from the beginning. Then you are already in trouble. It is a lot easier to put something new into his head, something he doesn't know, than it is to take something out and then put something new in. That is very hard.

Don't forget that horses are intelligent creatures. If they didn't have any intelligence we could not school them at all. The reason why they don't react in the same way as we would react under similar circumstances is very simple. They are horses and we are people. They have to react differently. We couldn't teach a horse anything if he couldn't remember. Because he can remember, he must have a brain. He can certainly remember a lot better than I can . . . a lot better.

In all movements on one track, whether it is a straight line or a round line, whether it is a circle or four circles together, across the diagonal or down the centre line, they are all on one track. He has to be straight, from the nose to the tail. That is what we have to look for. At the same time he has to maintain his impulsion, his rhythm, one step or one sequence like the other, regardless of what he does. He has to come here 1, 2, 3, 4, 1, 2, 3, 4, regardless of what he does, whether he does something on a circle, through the turn, or on a serpentine. He must always maintain the same rhythmic pace. Shoulder-in, half-pass, he should never change rhythm. Horses either try to rush through it, or they try to fall in with the shoulder, or they try to fall out with the quarters, or they slow down. And if all that still doesn't work they will think of something else. If they maintain that rhythm, 1, 2, 3, 4, and impulsion, there is nothing else that can go wrong for the very simple reason, as I keep repeating, that the horse is made to be a horse. All of his muscles are there for the purpose of moving, and he should apply all of them for the forward movement. If he does, then he can't do anything else. He can't toss his head. He can't fall in, he can't fall out, he can't do a thing but 1, 2, 3, 4. If I am walking, my body is completely engaged in the exercise. I can't kick someone on the shins; I'd have to interrupt my walking to do that. As long as I am walking I am completely engaged in moving and I cannot do anything else. While the horse is engaging himself completely for the walk or trot or canter, he cannot do anything else either. It's as clear as daylight. Every time you get him right, every time you are successful in forcing him to use himself completely for the forward movement, even if it is only one step, you have gymnastic exercise. We have done one step of gymnastic exercise. Clear gait, rhythm, impulsion, straightness, flexibility.

There is one movement that always causes some misunderstanding. It is the contra canter. Contra canter is really an ordinary canter. If you are going around to the left and you are leading with the near fore you have an ordinary canter. If you go around to the right, leading on the near fore, then you have a contra canter. But in the canter itself nothing changes at all.

You have to be clear as to how the horse should be flexed. The horse is always flexed towards the leading leg; if it is the near fore, the horse is flexed to the left. He should look where he is going, but contra is an exception where he does not look where he is going. He is flexed to the left, towards the leading leg or towards the inside leg and that turns over again. The inside leg is where the horse is flexed. He is bent around the inside leg. The fact that he goes to the right and canters on the left or vice versa does not make any difference.

One book states that the inside leg is the leg towards the inside of the school. Now the inside leg has nothing to do with the school. You can be in the Gobi Desert and you still have an inside leg and an outside leg. On the Never Never or the Nullarbor you still have an inside leg or an outside leg, without any school.

Stick to the fact that flexion is towards the leading leg and that is where the inside leg is too. The inside leg is what the horse is bent around. That is the inside leg. And the supporting leg is the outside leg, regardless of where you are in the school. The horse should still be on one track. You will observe that some riders

try to make it too good and go too far into the turn. If you go too far into the turn and with too sharp a contra canter, then it is impossible for the horse to stay on one track. He has to swing his quarters.

The back has to be bent enough so that, in spite of the fact that the horse himself is slightly flexed to the left, the track itself is still on that round line and does not swing away with the quarter. Particularly not swing the quarters out. He still has to be on one track, not falling in or falling out. Flexion is to the leading leg, and there should be no change in rhythm. He comes here or there, hop, hop, hop, hop. No matter what he does, and no matter where he is, the rhythm has to be maintained. Impulsion and rhythm have to be the same. As soon as he gives that up it is a sign that he has stopped engaging himself and is falling in on the forehand, leaning on the hand, and so on.

In the free walk the horse should go in a relaxed way out of the rider's hands and stretch forward, and as he stretches forward he increases the length of stride—not faster, not slower, no rush. If he is stretched and you still have contact you have him on a long rein; and if you let it drop you have him on a loose rein.

One thing that is not quite clear is on which diagonal the rider should rise to the trot. To

Free walk

my knowledge there is nothing in the F.E.I. Book that says you have to rise on this or that diagonal. For schooling purposes, if you are going around to the left you sit down on the diagonal: near hind off fore. That is the diagonal you should sit down on. If you go around to the right you should sit down on the diagonal: off hind near fore. If you change direction you also change diagonal at the same time. At the same instant when you change flexion you change your diagonal. When rising you stay on one diagonal and you keep on going around; and then you change direction, and as you change direction you must change to the other diagonal. If you go around to the left and you sit down on the other diagonal then it is all right. There is no rule that says you must not. But you must change diagonal when you change direction. So in my way of speaking you would be riding on the wrong diagonal all the time. That is something you have to watch.

Some people will ride on only one diagonal, and the diagonal is the one the horse offers them. If you are unfortunate enough to have to ride a horse like that, and you try to get him on the other diagonal, you won't have a hope. The horse just makes a step and a sort of wiggle and a wriggle, and without your knowing he changes. 'Aha!' you say, 'I am on the wrong diagonal. I must change it again.' The correct comment from a judge's point of view would not be, 'Rising on the wrong diagonal'. It would be, 'Did not change diagonal'.

What is a turn on the forehand? Personally I don't approve of it at all because we want the horse to take as much weight on the hindlegs as he carries on the forelegs, and he cannot in this movement. If you put a horse on a weighbridge he averages 36 kilograms heavier in the front than in the back (that is only approximately, because he can't be cut in half, and because he is standing still). When he goes forward he naturally carries as much on the hindquarters because he balances himself. I have never seen a wild horse broken down, have you? If he did not balance himself he would break down in the tendons by carrying too much weight in

front, and wild animals would have eaten him and there would be no horses today at all. It is the front tendons that go when the horse breaks down. Too much weight and stiffness is the cause.

In the turn on the forehand, all we do is push the weight on the forehand. We give him a kick and make him drag the hind part round. It probably originated in the army when a major would line up all the riders. One would be standing crooked, and he would make him push the horse around straight so that the whole row would be standing in line. In the Spanish Riding School the turn on the forehand is not practised because it is not a classical movement. I don't know of any old book on riding that says anything about a turn on the forehand. Every classical movement means gymnastic exercise, which means he must use his hindquarters. There just might be some value in the turn on the forehand from the point of view of teaching a child rider the value of using his legs.

First we must have a proper halt on all four legs. An absolute must is the straight line of the rider with the straight line through the horse. The shoulder, hips, and seat bones should be absolutely horizontal so that the line is at right angles to the straight line of the horse. Before you do anything else try to think of that position. When that position is right we can start to do the exercise, but your aids must never alter that position. You have him straight. You have as much contact on your right rein as you have on your left. If you have not got it, your position is not quite right. You maintain your position and then your outside leg goes behind the girth with the heel down, applying pressure and making the quarters go sideways. The ideal is for the horse to maintain his walking rhythm, just as he would if walking forward. I don't agree that the horse should pivot. The horse must always maintain his easy rhythm at walk, trot, and canter, and he cannot keep one leg glued to the ground and hop along on the other three. Once the horse understands that you want him to move his hindquarters over he likes it. It is what he wants to do, being lazy—

that is, not go forward. He will do it very willingly. Then, when we teach him the pirouette, he might do one good step in front and then start to swing his hindquarters over. He does not like the pirouette so much; it is gymnastic exercise. We can do it out of a movement when we do the half-pirouette, at the trot (piaffe), and at the canter.

As he should not be able to walk on three legs he should maintain his walking rhythm. He should pick up his front legs and mark time as he goes round. Apply repeated pressure and, if he does not answer, use a whip. Make him stand, take another step, make him stand, in order to prevent him from rushing round. In case the horse should not show any response at all what do you do? Indicate the turn, ease up, and push. If you pull his head to the right, his hindquarters will fall away to the left. The more you pull to the right, the more you have to hold with the outside leg to prevent him from falling away. He will not mind this because it is not gymnastics, and there is no stretch required. It suits him well.

How much supporting leg should you use? None at all. If he falls with the shoulder that way or goes to step back, you push him or nudge him back again. Then use the outside leg behind the girth again; but do not use both together. Your supporting leg is always in contact.

If I want to retire with something in the bank, then first I must put something into it. If the rider wants to have a comfortable ride, then the rider has to put something into it: contact with hand through seat and legs. The rider sits correctly in passive contact 'with the gun pointed'. If he uses his legs only, what happens? Does the horse do anything? The reflex action activates his back, but when he pushes his body together the rein will be hanging slack. Without co-ordination of the rider's hands to take up the slack, it is not much good. As he comes up in answer to your leg you should take up the slack. If I could put you on my horse I could show you, but I cannot tell you how to feel. It is like turning on a switch and seeing the

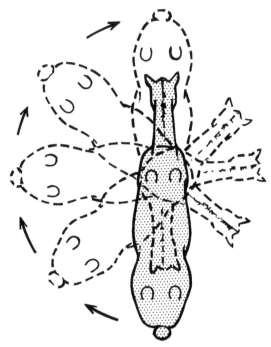

Diagram 13: A turn on the forehand

light. Feeling is everything. The Spanish Riding School has been going for 400 years. The old instructor teaches the young horse, and that horse when old and experienced teaches the young instructor. When the instructor is old he teaches another young horse, and so it goes on.

Development from the novice dressage horse to the Olympic horse should take not less than three years. And it is the same with the jumping horse.

I have attacked the turn on the forehand. It is not a gymnastic exercise. All the horse has to do is to move away when the rider pushes. We have the turn on the forehand and the half-pirouette, which is a turn made from a movement. You will have a lot of difficulties when you try this, no doubt because it *is* gymnastic exercise. It is a collecting exercise, and a very good one. You will have the hindquarters under control (and gymnastic exercise increases your control over the hindquarters by making the

93

horse more supple). You have more control over the horse's engine or his power to go forward.

A half-pirouette is a movement where forehand and hindquarters move on two different tracks. The forehand moves around the hindquarters in a half-circle. The ideal, which we try to achieve, is that as the horse comes up he is walking 1, 2, 3, 4. He maintains his walk 1, 2, 3, 4 and then, marking time with the inside hindleg 1, 2, 3, 4, the outside hindleg moves around the inside hindleg. In other words, the inside hindleg is moving up and down in the same spot, in the same rhythm. That would be ideal—perfection—if at the same time the horse were flexed properly.

The important thing is that the horse maintains his walk. That is number one. Number two is that the rider shows control over the hindquarters to a degree. In the beginning the horse avoids that exercise because it is difficult. The horse has to be rounded, on the bit, together, has to keep going. Therefore he has to bend a lot more. He has to be more flexible in his joints. That is the reason for the exercise— more flexibility, and with that greater flexibility, more suppleness. Naturally we increase our control over the hindquarters, over the engine.

Now it would be silly to try to make that small turn immediately, because it is too difficult. If you go springboard diving and you want to go to the Olympic Games, you have to do a double somersault and a corkscrew as one of the exercises; you don't start by practising double somersaults and corkscrews. If you did you would probably give it up after the first try because the water can be very hard. You start with the simple exercises and gradually increase your suppleness and then you start the head dive and you try a somersault or something like that. Gradually you start to build up. Well, here you build up that suppleness by letting the hindquarters go on a bigger half-circle (but still the forehand has to move around, the hindquarters must definitely make a smaller circle than the forehand); that is the start of the movement, and at the same time the horse

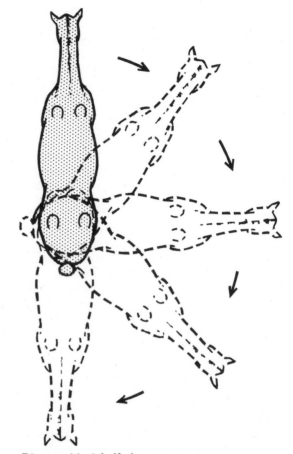

Diagram 14: A half pirouette

must maintain his rhythm. Then you can increase the demand and make the circle smaller, smaller, smaller. If you have a half-pirouette to judge then it is for you to assess the value of the exercise and find out if it is going to help him on his way, if he is on the right track, or if the major importance of the exercise has already gone because the horse has not maintained his impulsion, lost his rhythm, because he has pivoted or is swinging his quarters.

Most riders make the mistake of coming up here and then starting the half-pirouette without having checked the forward movement. They start the turn without having checked the for-

94

ward movement. He starts to go 1, 2, 3, 4, 1, 2, 3, 4, and so on, now I have checked my forward movement, maintained my impulsion. If you don't check your forward movement the exercise turns out like this, and the next instant the hindquarters are falling away. What I am trying to point out is that he is going this way, this way, this way and you have to stop him from going this way, check him with the outside rein, keep him going with the inside leg, and then you will have the hindquarters under control and they will make a smaller circle than the forehand.

How big that first half-circle is doesn't make any difference, so long as it is definitely smaller than the circle of the forehand. The hindquarters must not move against the rider's leg. If the rider's leg is here and you try to make that half-pirouette then the horse must not push that leg away—i.e., the rider's outside leg. He must keep the outside hindleg moving forward in the direction of the turn. He must not push against the outside leg and swing the quarters, because as soon as he swings the quarters you have lost the very thing that you are after—more control of the hindquarters and, with more control, more suppleness and more collection. Firstly you seek to maintain his rhythm and secondly to prevent him from falling away with his quarters, so that he does not step to the side. This is quite easily picked up, as he comes along the side here all you have to do is keep your eyes on the horse's legs. You will see them start off and then the quarters will swing away. You can see it quite clearly as he steps away, and as soon as he steps away, against the rider's leg, it means that he is getting away from the correcting influence. If you are judging, down goes the knife. You have to cut him back, because if you don't the rider will think he is good and will keep on doing it that way without realising it. In some cases it is hard to feel that the horse is stepping away. He has to come up rounded on the bit and maintaining a good 1, 2, 3, 4 walk. Check the forward movement, maintain his rhythm. In perfection it would be inside hindleg moving up and down in the same spot and outside hindleg moving around the inside leg in the same rhythm and properly flexed into the direction of the pirouette.

Horses are inclined to offer you a turn on the forehand instead. You start off a half-pirouette, make one or two steps, and then he stops with the forehand and swings the quarters. That is why I don't like the turn on the forehand because horses like to do that movement themselves, because there is no strain, no gymnastic exercise at all. That is why you have to be very careful that the horse doesn't do a turn on the forehand when you ask for a turn on the hindquarters.

He is flexed in the direction he is going. The inside leg maintains impulsion, the rider is sitting straight and not towards one side or the other, and the outside leg is behind the girth. It is behind the girth to prevent the hindquarters from swinging away, but not by pressing against the outside of the horse, merely by being present. The leg is there watching, and if he tries to go wrong then you can be active and say, 'You are not supposed to push my leg away'. Because if you try to hold him there with the leg by force, with power, you won't have a ghost of a chance. It can't be done for the simple reason that you are sitting on top of him. It is mechanically impossible. You are sitting on top of him, and if he should make up his mind to go this way, how on earth can you hold him there? You would have to have a sky-hook and hold him back. You can only keep him there by educating him that he has to respect your outside leg, that he must not swing against it. If he does swing against it, give him a push. He must not swing away with the hindquarters because as soon as he does that the whole thing is down the drain. It is less of a fault if the half-pirouette is carried out on a big half-circle than if he loses rhythm, or pivots altogether. He must not pivot.

Try to remember what I said about that stepping out or back. He must go forward. That is where a lot of riders fall down. They lead him in with the inside rein and he starts an ordinary turn, not prepared at all, and then the outside leg tries to keep him there but by that time it is already too late and he is stepping to the side. Even if he doesn't step to the side he is just making a complete plain turn.

The forward movement has to be checked with the outside rein. That does not mean that he should look to the other way. Flexion is maintained with the inside rein. The inside leg keeps him going and the outside leg is behind the girth and prevents the hindquarters from falling away. The rider should sit straight. That is something you have to watch for, because often it will explain why things have not gone right, why the horse was falling away with the quarters. The simple reason is that as the horse comes up, stepping straight, the rider's position is correct. But when the rider starts to lead him with the inside rein, he is twisting and does this and that with his position. Automatically the support of that outside leg is gone, and the horse is too. Watch the rider's position. He should maintain that position right around, never changing, always square on. But because riders are busybodies, eager beavers, they try to do a bit more and twist themselves out of position. Lift the outside leg off the horse and the outside seat will come off the saddle. Then the powerful influence of the outside leg is practically nil.

In dressage tests all movements are carried out when the rider is on the marker. So if it says half-pirouette at 'A', you start the half-pirouette when the rider is at 'A'. If it says halt, you halt when the rider is there. If it is trot, you trot when the rider is on the marker. You do whatever is required, when the rider is on the marker.

SUMMARY

1. Collection is the degree of engagement of the hindquarters. The horse must stand square with the weight equally distributed over all four legs. He does not carry more weight on the forehand. As soon as he moves, his hindlegs step under him to do their share of the work. His legs are so slender that it is amazing that they can work as they do. However, he does not break down because according to the Lord's design he collects himself—that is, he uses his hindquarters. Now, when we put the rider on top, we upset his natural balance—the weight being naturally balanced over the four legs. Our schooling aims to activate the action of the hindquarters so that the hindlegs take over their share of the extra work caused by the weight. As he is more and more collected he becomes lighter in front, his supple back allowing the hindlegs to step well under the weight at every stride.

There are many old theories that are quite contrary to the laws of nature and so must be false. An example is the belief that the load is able to balance the support.

2. The aids must go through the horse without resistance—from your back and seat, through the back of the horse to his hindquarters, which

bring him forward into your hands. This will give him the desired head position because his head and neck are part of his balance and he uses them to balance himself. From the square halt he should move off without changing his general outline into a clear walk. At all transitions he should go immediately into the new pace, which must be full and true. His only movements are those necessary to develop the pace required. He must perform complete transitions: halt, walk, trot, canter, trot, walk, halt.

3. *Half-Transitions* We have to take the horse from one type of a given pace to another type of the same pace—that is, collected trot to extended trot. To go into an extended pace the horse needs his whole front end, head and neck, to drop forward a little as he stretches after the bit. This gives him room to stretch out forward. He must put his foot on the ground exactly where it is pointing. He must not fling it out full stretch and then put it down on the ground. At the trot the diagonal pairs of legs must remain parallel, otherwise the weight is not equally distributed. Also it is wasted effort as he cannot put his foot to the ground in front of his nose. If he flings it out it must wait until the nose catches up. The rhythm should not have altered except that he is longer off the ground. The extended canter is similar. He must lengthen the stride, not go more quickly, and he must be straight. He may be straight at the working paces but when he is asked to extend, the quarters come in. This shows that he is not going forward as much as he should.

4. If he is truly on the bit he cannot be crooked. If he balances your weight and goes forward on the bit you will know that he is straight. He must accept both reins equally. The horse's inclination is to give you little on the right rein and much on the left. He does not accept the right rein. Schooling aims to make him even. If he is on the bit he goes in a lively manner. He does not fight or drop behind the bit or tilt his nose. If he is straight he is supple in the neck and his contact with the reins is constant and even. The horse will go through all transitions smoothly because the aids are going smoothly into the hindquarters, which take him forward on to the bit. When the horse resists the bit he is really resisting the driving aids or correcting influence. He resists with his head as he tries to get out of the gymnastic exercise being asked of his body. With his body he tries to fall out or in here or there, etc. When he accepts the work being asked he is still and calm.

5. Apart from riding you need to do some gymnastic exercises yourself. It will take a long time before your body will submit easily to the commands from the brain to sit straight and still. The horse must also have time to understand and develop ability and suppleness so that he can be pushed together and stay together and still keep his impulsion, and so on.

We must take time or in the end it will take much longer because it is easy to put something new into his head but it is very hard to take out something he has learnt. He is intelligent and can learn. And, above all, he can and does remember.

6. In all movements on one track—straight lines, curves, or turns—the horse's whole body is on the line and so he is straight. He must also maintain his impulsion and rhythm. If he does all this, nothing can go wrong because all his mind and muscles are fully engaged. To do something else—say, kick up or shy—he must cease going as above. So if he keeps going as you wish, he just can't do anything else. Every time you get him right, even for a few steps, you are improving him and it will be easier to get him right next time.

7. *Counter Canter* This is going to the left with the off fore leading. The canter does not change. The horse is flexed towards the leading leg. The leg towards which he is flexed is always the inside leg. At the counter canter he is still on one track, so you must not ask for too tight a turn or it will be impossible for him to stay on one track. He will be forced to swing his quarters out because of the unnatural lead. The rhythm and impulsion must remain the same.

8. *The Free Walk* The horse should go relaxed

out of the rider's hands and should stretch forward and down. He increases the length of stride. If it is with a long rein there must just be contact. With a loose rein there is no contact.

9. *Diagonals* The rider should change from one to the other and work both sides equally. On a left-rein turn, sit on the off fore and near hind; on a right turn, sit on the near fore and off hind. There is no rule that says which way to do it but the rule says that you must change. The above way helps to engage his inside hindleg. All riders find that their natural crookedness makes them more comfortable on one particular diagonal and the more they ride on one, the harder it becomes to change. It is absolutely necessary to ride as much on one as on the other if the rider is to sit straight.

10. *Turn on the Forehand* The author does not approve of this movement:

- It puts more weight on the forehand and we school to make the weight equal on fore and hind.
- It does not require the horse to go forward.
- It is not a classical movement.

To Effect the Turn The horse is standing square and straight. Check your position. The outside leg goes behind the girth and applies pressure, making the quarters move sideways. The horse must maintain the normal walk sequence, moving all four feet in rhythm. He should not pivot on the inside foreleg but it should mark time in its place in the sequence. The right leg on the girth is supporting—that is, in contact—but do not use both legs at the same time. He will do this easily because it is not a gymnastic exercise; he does not have to use his hindquarters more.

11. The rider must put everything into whatever he does; he must use all his body correctly. If he uses his legs only, and the reins are hanging loose, the horse is not brought together because of the lack of co-ordination. It is a matter of feeling.

In the 400 years of the Spanish Riding School the old instructor teaches the young horse. That horse when he is old and experienced teaches the young instructor. When that instructor is old he teaches the young horse . . . and so it goes on. From novice dressage to Grand Prix should take about three years.

12. *The Half-Pirouette* This is a gymnastic exercise and you will find it difficult because the horse will not want to make the effort. It is a good collecting exercise to give you more control over the hindquarters, the engine. It is a movement on two tracks, forehand and hindquarters on different tracks. The forehand moves round the hindquarters in a half-circle.

From the collected walk, check the forward movement with the outside rein. He must maintain the sequence and rhythm of the walk, marking time with the inside hindleg while the outside hindleg moves round it. The horse is flexed as the forehand moves round. He finds this difficult because he has to be more flexible in his joints. With the exercise we increase his suppleness and so our control of his hindquarters.

At first let the hindlegs go on a small circle while the forelegs go on a larger one, and try only a quarter turn. Gradually decrease the size of the circles until he marks time with the inside hindleg. The important points are that he maintains impulsion and rhythm and does not fall out with the hindquarters.

Horses are inclined to offer a turn on the forehand. They start correctly, then swing the quarters out because it is easier. This is yet another argument against teaching the turn on the forehand. To the right, he is flexed to the right. The right leg maintains impulsion, the rider sitting straight. The left leg is behind the girth to *prevent* the quarters from swinging, not pressing as if to move the quarters away. The leg is there, watching. He must be schooled not to push the leg away.

It is less of a fault if he covers a big half-circle than if he loses impulsion, or pivots.

CHAPTER EIGHT

WORK ON TWO TRACKS

My Old Instructor said, 'If you can ride a proper corner you can do everything else'. A proper turn is the foundation for everything else. The horse is supposed to maintain his rhythm and impulsion. That means that he is accepting the rider's leg, he is accepting the bit, he is flexed, he is on one track, the inside leg controlling forward impulsion, the outside leg and outside rein assisting with flexion and maintaining proper position, the outside seat and outside leg preventing the hindquarters from falling away. You have him forced around your inside leg, he is going into your rein, he is accepting both sides of the reins, he is carrying you, he is working. Everything is there. There is not a single bit of stiff flesh in that whole body. Now that is a simple turn. He carries you with ease.

If you want to do more, if you want to do a shoulder-in, you need to have flexion around that inside leg. But the inside leg says go forward. The outside leg is behind the girth, and you sit still and straight and the horse feels you there. The outside leg prevents him from falling out, the outside rein prevents him from going forward in the direction he is facing but indicates *this way* the degree of flexion and direction. The inside leg is exactly the same as we have in a corner, but we have a bit more. The inside

leg not only says 'Keep going forward' it also says 'Go sideways'.

The more flexion you have in the shoulder-in, the more danger there is that he will slip away with the shoulder-in altogether. Then you have to bend more or you straighten the body of the horse and only the neck is in, and then there is no shoulder-in, there is no exercise any more. Have a slight bend in his body, not a pronounced one, because the next thing will be that the forehand will straighten and all you will have is a horse which is flexed to the left with the neck alone not straight. But that is not exercise. You don't want to make the neck supple, the neck is supple enough. If you have too much flexion you lose that connection—outside rein, outside seat, outside leg. You can only maintain that with a minimum degree of flexion. As soon as there is too much bend in the horse's neck you lose that contact, and as soon as you lose it you lose the ability to hold him up with the outside rein and outside leg. That will happen, but you have to be aware of it. If it does happen, forget about it, straighten him up, ride him forward, get him on the bit and try again. If you succeed it is another step forward.

The shoulder-in is a sideways movement, where the forehand is off the track and the

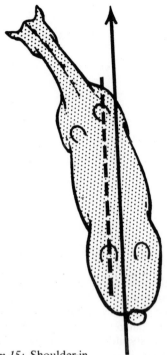

Diagram 15: Shoulder-in

in a passive way. Now what else is there? There is one little bit extra. That inside leg not only keeps him going forward as soon as he has established that shoulder-in position; there is a little bit more pressure which says, 'Keep going forward and now sideways, sideways'.

If you can't ride through a corner, or a circle, properly you can't do it. Most horses will cheat and put their heads in but not their shoulders. I have said before that a horse always looks in the direction in which he is moving—with one exception and that is for shoulder-in. He is flexed to the right and moves to the left (or vice versa). It is the only exercise when he looks in the opposite direction. The outside leg maintains the impulsion. Wake him up before the corner, keep him going around it, and then the inside leg will take him sideways and the outside leg will keep him going on the line. This is the only exercise where the outside leg keeps him going. It is a strange thing but a fact. Keep him sideways with the inside leg and prevent antici-pation. He starts all right but he will want to sneak back. Don't ask too much; first try one or two steps, then straighten him up, then three, then five or six. Don't try too much at first or else he will sneak back before you want him to, and that is difficult to counteract. So keep the control. His front legs cross over, his hindlegs don't. It is a good gymnastic exercise. Use the same aids as for a corner—the inside leg on the girth and the outside leg behind the girth. The only thing this time is that the outside leg keeps him going.

With any exercise that is exercise, the more you do the better it is. That does not mean you start off with shoulder-in, and you go shoulder-in, shoulder-in, shoulder-in. Whatever you do, do it for short periods. Don't extend it for too long because if you do it properly the horse is really working, and he will get really tired. Not only will he try to get away, because it is hard work for him and because his muscles get tired, but when he gets away you have done a lot of damage. The end of the lesson is as important as the lesson itself. The lesson does not mean an hour's work. A lesson is three steps shoulder-

hindquarters go on the track. It is a two-track movement (do not confuse it with a three-track movement). Some hair splitters talk about three tracks and four tracks. That's rubbish and to be disregarded. If the forehand is on a separate track it is one track, and if the hindquarters are on another track it is two track.

Now the forehand is going on one track and the hindquarters on another. What do you need to achieve this kind of movement? The horse has to be flexed to the inside. The inside leg has to be able to maintain forward impulsion. The outside leg has to have control to prevent the hindquarters from falling away from the track—outside rein in contact with the seat, and the leg assisting flexion and tempo.

Now so far there is nothing different. It is exactly the same thing: the horse is flexed around your inside leg with the inside rein; your outside rein is restricting forward move-ment, your outside leg controlling the quarters in, and at the end of three steps or whatever, end it. How you end it is as important as the three steps. The three steps are very important for his physical suppleness, and the end of it is very important for his head—for his mental exercise. You say he is good, he does it, and you finish. You finish before anything goes wrong. Leave him with a good impression. You shouldn't finish after you have pulled him up. You should finish when he is going well.

As I said to somebody once, 'Well, he is going well. Get off him. Finish'. He said, 'Why should I? I worked for a whole hour to get him where I have him now, and now I should give up? Now I want to work him'. And I replied, 'No, you worked him for an hour to get him where you got him. That is why you should finish—because you got him there'.

A friend of mine once said, 'You sit down to roast pork [Roast pork is my favourite] and when you say, "Oh! Isn't it glorious, roast pork?", that is when you should finish, because you are going to look forward to the next roast pork'. You finish when it really feels good. You have the security of knowing that next time you will get him again, and then he will taste a lot better, and you can do a little more before you have to finish up again. But if you work him, and get him going, and because he gives a little more you keep on working—doing shoulder-in, and collection, plus this and that—he gets tired, and then he starts to fight, and then he succeeds in getting the better of you, and then you have taught him a marvellous lesson he probably won't forget either! That he does not really have to work if he does not want to. That is the last thing you want to teach him. Horses are clever, clever enough in looking after themselves. They are cunning, very cunning.

Work for something, achieve it, and then finish. Even if it is only one step, finish. Give him a little rest and try again, and you will get him where you had him a lot more quickly. Because that finish says, 'Yes, that is how I want you'. As he gives, finish. As he gives and goes the way you want him, stop. He will put

two and two together very quickly. Every time he gives, he stops work. But he doesn't realise that as he gives he has to make two steps, and the next time three steps, and then four steps, but he is going to start to live happily with it. Don't overdo it after you have got him to give. As soon as he does what you want him to do, end the lesson. Don't overdo anything. Xenophon said 2400 years ago, 'Too much of anything is not good for man or horse'. He was quite a philosopher.

You can turn him sour very quickly. That happened to me in the School. I had a young stallion that could do everything but a flying change at every stride. In four weeks there was to be a performance, and I wanted to have that stallion, because he was the youngest and most advanced of that year. I wanted to say that my horse was doing every step of the high school, including the flying change every stride, and I wanted to push that flying change at every stride into him before that first performance. And do you know what happened to me? After a week—work and try—I couldn't do a single flying change. I had to forget it altogether and not do any flying changes for a week, and then I gradually built him up and he came good. He just went sour. They get sour very quickly, and the better they work the more quickly they will get sour if you work them too long. Don't make them sour.

When I was a young boy I loved pineapple. When Hitler came to Austria you couldn't get pineapple because there was no money for importing it. So when I went to Switzerland in 1948 I ate and ate pineapple for six weeks. I ate nothing but pineapple and cream and ice-cream. Now if you say, 'Do you want a pineapple?', I answer, 'No, thank you', because I had too much of it.

The next exercise is a similar one but the other way round. First we had the shoulder-in, now we have the hindquarters-in. The forehand stays on the track and the hindquarters come off the track. Again this is the minimum and in most cases the maximum.

You will probably notice something here that

is a little bit different from the other one. Now you have more flexion, more bend in the body, because it is a different exercise. The forehand stays on the track and the hindquarters come off the track. Because of that position the hindquarters are stepping across and the forehand is going straight on.

If it is done correctly, what you would aim for is a situation where the head and neck are straight and the horse is bent under your seat around that inside leg. This is giving him more suppleness through his ribs, through his whole body, and it exercises that inside hindleg again in a different way. It builds up the influence of your inside leg to a tremendous degree, and at the same time increases the influence of your outside leg. The inside leg pushes the horse forward and maintains impulsion. The outside leg behind the girth controls the hindquarters. The outside rein and outside seat help to maintain flexion. You do a little more. You sit square, no shifting of your position, and you sit so that the inside leg holds him forward—not really meaning that you push him more but you have to be more careful with that inside leg to keep him going, because instead of stepping forward he will try to step sideways. Just step sideways, instead of under your weight and forward.

You will have to be more careful with that inside leg, but as you succeed that inside leg is developing power without using any power. That leg will be so powerful that the inside leg will just be there. The outside leg does not just control the hindquarters and prevent him from falling away as in the corner or shoulder-in. It says, 'Come in, hindquarters', and then the outside leg says, 'Stay'. You do a little more, not much more—a few steps and straight on, a few steps and straight on, and never go through the turn hindquarters-in. Always straighten him out before the turn, have him straight, and then ride him through the turn. Don't ride him through the turn hindquarters-in in case he doesn't know he could sneak through the corner that way. He will know because it is a lot harder to do it the right way, and he will resist

Diagram 16: Traverse

more flexion and more bend. Going through the turn he will try to sneak through and step to the side, and you might be teaching him something that he didn't know before. Always straighten him out and then execute the turn.

Outside leg takes him in and inside legs holds there and takes him forward. A few steps and you will probably find that horses will work with less resistance on that left rein. Even considering that they are inclined to hang on, there will be less resistance than there will be on the right rein. You will find it more difficult to do shoulder-in on the right rein, but easier on the left. You will find that hindquarters-in is easier on the left rein, harder on the right rein. You must put the hindquarters on your track. Don't let him put the hindquarters where he wants to. Inside leg must always be on the girth, outside leg a little bit further back, but you still must be able to keep your heels down.

Experience has shown that people who have to work hard to achieve something, to get somewhere, go further in the long run than the ones for whom everything comes easily. The one who has to work for that suppleness goes further in the long run—if, of course, he has the determination to do it. Now, if someone wants to do Grand Prix, or really to get a horse to the finest point, and if he is not fortunate enough to be a born horseman, then he has to work for it. And the born ones as a rule are overtaken by the ones who have to work hard to achieve it. Only a few people who are born to it have everything else to go with it, and if you run across one who has, then you haven't got a hope because no matter how much you work you will not be quite as good as the one that has been born to it and works hard. But you overtake a lot who have been born to it and don't work. Because it comes naturally, they don't take any notice of it. They go so far, but as soon as they have to do something more they give up, because the first part came very easily.

There was a young fellow in the School, and I have never seen anything as supple as he was, as natural as he was. He was sixteen years old, had never sat on a horse, and I started him off with the lunging rein. All I had to say was that his head had to be there, and his shoulders had to be there, and his leg had to be here, and his lower leg was to hang down and the horse had to be there, and that's where he stayed, regardless of whether the horse started to move. He just stayed there. His natural suppleness was fantastic, but he lasted only about nine months in the School. He had everything that the School was looking for in a horseman, bar one thing. Suppleness of the body is not enough. You have to have a little more to go with it, and he was so supple all round that the suppleness even went to his head. He was supple there too. Too soft. In three months he was riding on a School stallion. Three months! And he had

never been on a horse before. He just couldn't, he just didn't go on. He had enough of one thing but he didn't have enough of the other.

The next movement is a half-pass. The half-pass is a forward and sideways movement. Never forget that. Forward and sideways, not sideways and forward. Some books suggest that there is a half-pass and a full-pass. A full-pass is impossible, it is a circus act, but you can't carry it out on scientific lines. Try to do a full-pass yourself. Try to put your foot across and then put it back here—across and back on the line—and then bring that one and put that one across and back on the line. It is an awkward movement. The horse can do it too, but as soon as he does he loses any forward impulsion, any energy of the hindquarters. He is just dragging himself to the side. That is the movement that has been practised in the army and in the cavalry. How you got from one place to the other didn't make any difference so long as everyone was lined up as the major rode past. There is no full-pass, and if you make a full-pass it is a dragging sideways. It is not classed as a movement because it is not collected. Anything you do you must look upon as gymnastic exercise to produce more collection, more suppleness, more flexibility, and within more control. Finer control.

Now, the half-pass. The horse comes to the turn here and then he goes with a slight flexion. There is a slight flexion in his body. He is looking in the direction in which he is going. The rider is sitting straight, and the horse should go more or less parallel to the side to start off with. But the horse goes forward and sideways. And whatever you do, whether you ride a straight line or a round line or through the turn, half-pirouette, hindquarters-in, shoulder-in, or half-pass, the horse must maintain his rhythm. As soon as you lose the rhythm, as soon as he slows down or goes faster, there is no more exercise because he is avoiding it by going slower or faster.

My Old Instructor always said, 'The best preparation for anything is to ride properly through the turn'. So the better you ride through

103

the turn [Remember we said that there are 3982 ways of riding through the turn the wrong way, and we try to miss them all and get the right one] the more you are perfectly prepared for whatever comes after, whether it is shoulder-in or whatever.

What is the first thing for the rider to do to start the half-pass? The first preparation is to look where you want to go; that look will tell you that you have to start here. You have to check here, and you have to flex that much, you have to have that much, and now you take him sideways and keep going. And if you have prepared him for the turn, and everything is right, he will go correctly.

My Old Instructor, Gottlieb Polak, put me on a horse and said, 'If you can sit on him you can ride him'. I had been riding him for about 10 minutes and he said—born in Czechoslovakia he never learnt German or English—'Now look at him, he rides him better than I do'. And I had to buy a new hat. We got on fine together.

Now I come to the turn. Now sit straight and look at the 'X', and he will go with impulsion and rhythm. You must look before you do anything else. You look, and say, 'That is my direction', and then you flex the horse. You make the horse look in his direction, or your direction, flex him, and then you lead him. This is a safety measure—it is just as if you were starting shoulder-in—you take him away, and as he comes away you take him sideways with the other leg. If you don't lead him away with the shoulder first (riders are inclined to be eager beavers and say, 'Oh! The half-pass; outside leg'), then he will do a half-pass leading with the hindquarters. Now he must always lead with the shoulder. Even if he is parallel he will still look as if he is leading with the shoulder, simply because of the sideways movement.

If he trots, now he trots with the inside leg going forwards and sideways; it is that leg that is obvious for you to look at, obvious to the viewer that it goes from under him and steps in a forward sideways line. That sideways movement of that front leg will be obvious, even if

he is completely parallel to the wall. That leg is moving sideways while the other leg is under him.

You can't see the leg that is stepping under the body, and therefore the inside one will be the obvious one you pick up as he goes sideways. And the same goes for the canter. As he comes sideways that is the leading leg, even if he is completely parallel, which technically speaking he should be. It must be that one which you can see moving sideways in front. If you can pick up the hindleg moving sideways then there is already trouble because the horse is going against the rider's inside leg.

So we have been looking. We have been flexing him. We started off slightly with the shoulder and then we took him sideways. What is necessary for the rider? The inside leg must be able to say, 'Go forward'. The inside leg has to be able to flex him, outside rein contact blocks the forward movement and transfers it into forward sideways. The inside rein is there all the time. It prevents him from going straight on and falling against the rider's inside leg because you transfer the impulsion to the side. It does not mean that you are not really parallel. It does not mean that you pull him on that outside rein. That rein just stays there with you.

The inside leg has to hold him forward and flexes him, inside rein shows him the way; outside rein controls the forward movement. The outside leg controls the hindquarters, prevents the hindquarters from falling out, and a little bit more. As you come to the turn, you are not saying to the hindquarters with that outside leg 'Stay here'. You have gone through your preparations, you finish your count-down, and now comes zero hour, and here we go sideways. That is the little extra job for that outside leg. Not just 'Stay here', but 'Now we are going sideways'.

Look forward, and the inside leg has to take him forward. I said that the first thing you have to do is look. Why do you have to look? Because if you don't look you don't know how much inside rein you have to use for flexion in

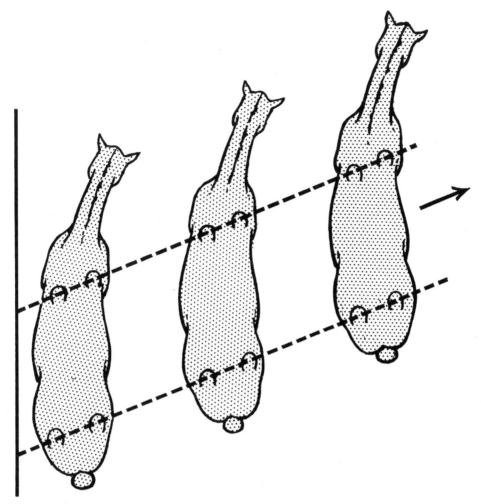

Diagram 17: Half-pass—quarters are gradually leading (a bad fault)

that direction. You don't know how much inside leg you have to use to keep him going in that direction. You don't know how much outside leg you have to use to keep him going sideways enough to reach a certain point. If you put it around the other way and say you have to get to point 'B', well you have to reach 'B' here. You have to get there. If you don't look you just don't know.

It is exactly the same as if you didn't look when driving a car. If you don't look you don't know if you have to straighten up or not; if you have to turn the wheel; when to take the foot off the accelerator and when to put it on. You have to look, and that look is transferred into action, that much action and exactly that much action, no more and no less. You have to look, otherwise you just go sideways and you finish up going with the hindquarters in front of the forehand. You finish up anywhere, and in most cases if you are supposed to finish here you probably finish short of your marker, because the horse is going against the inside leg and is not going forward. Now the inside leg is there and holding him forward, and the outside leg says, 'Go sideways'. You have an exercise that goes down the centre, and then half-pass, straight on, canter, flexion, half-pass, canter, flexion, half-pass, canter, flexion, and straight on. Three strides or 3 metres—it makes no difference. The inside leg is holding him forward. It is more easily picked up when he is cantering. The horse may have to canter right one stride, two strides, and three strides, and as he finishes the stride the rider's inside leg turns into the outside leg and says, 'Canter left'. Outside rein becomes inside rein and gives him the flexion. You look, and there he goes forward again.

It is that inside leg which catches the sideways movement; it becomes the new outside leg and transfers the movement to the opposite direction. The more comfortably you sit the more you are with the horse. You still have a lot of time to sit up straight and bring that leg back, and at the same instant you change the flexion and you hold him forward—it is so smooth. We come back to the same principle that we had in the first place. You have to sit, and the rider must not change his position. Riders tend to lift the outside seat more quickly than the other because they place too much importance on that outside leg, especially as they try to squeeze him with it.

You must maintain your impulsion as he trots, 1, 2, 1, 2, one step the same as the other, not slower and not faster. The spectator should not see that the rider is working; it should look as if the horse would do it by himself.

I remember some years ago a horse was doing the half-pass, and the half-pass was falling sideways against the inside leg. The rider was working terribly hard, and because the rider was working hard the horse didn't have to work and the horse went with short steps. The more still you sit the more easily the horse can balance himself, the clearer your aids are, and the more powerful they will be. Every movement

of your body unbalances the horse to a degree. The horse is in danger of falling on his nose, so he has to put special effort into maintaining his balance and that special effort of course comes off his impulsion. The more collection you have, the more still you must sit. If you unbalance him, the first thing he will do is to lose impulsion and then start to crawl. As soon as he starts to crawl, don't do it any more—because you are not collecting him, you are not making him work with the hindquarters, and as soon as you don't make him work with his hindquarters any more there is no exercise, there is no going any higher. Finish!

The horse must maintain the same rhythm. If you lose your rhythm the best thing to do is to forget the half-pass. Ride him straight forward, push him, make him level, take him to the next turn, and start again. The first time you have him prepared, make one step and then two steps, and then ride him straight forward. Go somewhere else and prepare him. Make one step, two steps, and then three steps, and ride him straight forward. That straight-forward section is most important, because the one thing you can lose more easily than any other is the ability to drive him forward with the influence of the inside leg.

As soon as the horse has caught on, you can go across a quarter of the arena and finally across the whole arena, but in most cases you don't have to go across the arena. The most important thing is to maintain impulsion. Sit straight and comfortably and keep him going. The less you move and the less you interfere, the more quickly he will understand. There is no Einstein's theory of relativity about this, it is not as difficult as that. Every rider can do it if he wants to, but it takes a lot of work to be able to do a little and achieve a lot, and I can't think of any other situation where you can achieve more by doing less. The less you do, the more comfortable you are, the more you will achieve.

I watched the Old Instructor Lindenbauer when I was a young fellow and he was sixty. He had a young stallion and he was a really hard nut. Lindenbauer was sitting there and doing sitting trot for an hour with that stallion, determined not to put up with his waywardness. I started to sweat just watching him. After an hour Lindenbauer just stepped off and that was all. I said to myself, 'Goodness me, I am forty years younger and I could not do it'. And I couldn't have done it either, for the simple reason that I was still using a lot more power to sit there than he was. He was sitting there by that principle and it didn't cost him a grain of energy. All he had to do was keep the horse going now and again and just keep him there. He didn't need any extra effort to sit there.

It is not necessary to be able to swim to stop yourself from drowning because if you can relax yourself in the water you will float. If you can't relax you will sink. Likewise, when on the horse, if your body is tense you will fall off more easily. Your control of the horse is at all times dependent on your body control.

The Old Instructor was right. If you can ride a proper turn, then you are prepared for anything else. If it is not right, you will be struggling more and more until one day you will meet your Waterloo and then you won't be able to go any further. Then you must try to erase from the horse's mind everything that you have put into it and start afresh. It is very easy to erase a blackboard but very hard to rub out what has already settled in a horse's head.

SUMMARY

1. *Shoulder-In* This is a sideways movement on two tracks. The forehand is off the track and the hindquarters are on the track. The front legs cross over, the hindlegs do not. It is a good gymnastic exercise. The horse is flexed round the inside leg but not too much. This is the only movement where he is bent the opposite way from the way he is going. He must not have too much position off the track. The inside hind following the outside front is enough. This gives rise to the term 'three tracks'. There is no such thing. Either the forehand and hindquarters are on the same track—a one-track movement, or they are on different tracks—a two-track movement. The horse does not have a third part to make a third track.

2. The best preparation for the shoulder-in, as for almost everything, is a well-ridden corner.

The horse is straight, moving with impulsion and is flexed round the inside leg. After the corner is completed and we have the horse on the long side we take his forehand one more step on the circle to take the forehand off the track. Then the outside rein restricts the forward movement. The outside leg controls the hindquarters from falling out and helps to maintain the impulsion. The inside leg not only keeps him forward but as soon as the shoulder-in position is established there is a little extra pressure from it which says, 'Keep going forward and also sideways'. The outside leg maintains the impulsion and this is the only movement where it does this. The tempo, rhythm, and outline must remain unchanged.

3. There must not be too much flexion, only a slight bend in the body. With too much flexion

just the neck may bend, which is no exercise. Also the connection of outside rein, outside seat, and outside leg will be lost. This can only be maintained with a minimum of flexion. The horse must be accepting the rider's legs and he must be accepting the bit. If you lose the above connection, straighten up and start again.

4. If you cannot ride a proper corner you cannot ride a good shoulder-in. You must be able to maintain his impulsion, rhythm, and flexion.

5. Never continue long on the one exercise. If you work and work and then he does it well for one or two steps—end the lesson. Let him stop for a spell or even finish altogether. Next time it may be three steps done correctly. In this way the horse does not get tired muscles from the gymnastic exercise and he comes to understand that, 'If I do as he asks, even if it is a muscular effort, he will give me a rest'.

Never overdo the schooling. Good work tires the muscles and if you keep it up he will become very uncomfortable and so will resist in some way. Stop while all is well. The next day do a little more. You can turn him sour very easily by doing too much for too long. He may jack up and refuse to do even the simple things for you, because you have made his muscles ache and overtaxed his brain.

6. *Traverse, Hindquarters In or Head to the Wall* The forehand stays on the track and the forelegs do not cross. The hindquarters come off the track and the hindlegs *do* cross. Head and neck are straight and he is bent under your seat. He now looks the way he is going. This exercise gives him more suppleness in the ribs and it builds up the influence of the legs.

The inside leg pushes him forward and maintains impulsion. But watch carefully because he will prefer to step sideways instead of forwards under the weight. The rider must sit still and square. The outside leg is not so passive for it has to say, 'Come in hindquarters and stay there'. You do a little more, but not much.

7. Do a few steps and then straighten him and ride forward. Always straighten before the turn because if you take him round this way he will find it easier than a proper corner. Then when you want a correct turn he may say, 'Oh, no. This other way is easier. It is less effort'. These two movements are usually easier on the left rein than on the right because he has more contact on the left rein and does not go up to the right rein willingly. You must put the hindquarters on your track, not where *he* wants.

8. People who have to work hard to achieve something often go further than those to whom it all comes easily. The former must have determination and application or they would not work so hard. The latter have never had to work hard and when they come to something that takes effort they often give up. You have to have what it takes on top, as well as physically.

9. *The Half-Pass* As always, the best preparation is the well-ridden corner. Everything is right. The horse is looking where he is going, with slight flexion. The rider is sitting square and still. Now you have to look before you do anything. So take him through the corner and look at X. You make the horse flex and look towards X. Then you lead him *as if* you were about to do shoulder in, but you take him sideways. If we do not lead him away with the shoulder first, he may go with hindquarters leading, which is incorrect. The rider's inside leg must be able to say, 'Go forward', and flex him. The outside rein checks the forward movement and turns it into the sideways one.

The inside rein is continually there. It transfers the impulsion to the side. You do not pull him with the outside rein; it just stays there with you. The outside leg has to say a little more than just, 'Don't fall out'. It has to say, 'Sideways', but it must not say too much or the quarters will lead. The outside knee must stay on and the heel down.

10. You have to look where you want to go so that you know what aids must be increased or decreased to get you there. It is just the same as if you are driving a car or riding a bike. If

you want to half-pass to X you must keep looking at X to be sure that that is where you are going.

11. In a certain exercise you take him so many strides half-pass from the centre line, then twice as many back the other way across the centre line, etc. For the change of direction the rider sits straight. The inside leg and rein become the outside leg and rein. The flexion is changed and off the horse goes the other way. The rider must not change his position. It is a mistake to use the outside leg too strongly. This lifts the outside seat bone and so loses the control of the outside hindleg.

12. Impulsion and rhythm must be maintained at all times and especially at the change of direction. The more still the rider can sit, the clearer the aids are, the more powerful and meaningful they will be. Every movement of the rider's body upsets the horse's balance to a degree and the effort to regain his balance comes off his impulsion. The greater collection he is asking, the steadier the rider must sit. If he loses impulsion all collection is gone.

In the half-pass he must maintain impulsion and rhythm. If he loses either, forget the half-pass and ride firmly forward. Take him through a turn and try again. The straight forward is so important, to keep the influence of the inside leg. Sit straight and comfortable and keep him going. It takes a lot to be able to do a little and achieve a lot. *Where else can you achieve more by doing less?*

The less you do, the more comfortable you are and the more you achieve. The more experienced you are the less work you do. Just sit and let gravity do its stuff.

CHAPTER NINE

ADVANCED MOVEMENTS

Now we come to flying changes.

You should be on a straight line, with a straight horse. If the horse is not straight and not tuned up he will wobble along that centre line like the Loch Ness monster. As he comes along here you should be able to count—hop, hop, hop, hop. It should never change. You have to aim for perfection.

Somebody once said, while looking at a film, 'But look, he is at the Olympic Games and he is crooked. Why do you have to fuss and try to make my horse straight?'. Just because someone is crooked at the Olympic Games does not mean that you should do the same. If you go there and are straight, what can they do with you? They can hate you. They can resolve to give you nought when you come in. But if you come in and you are straight you will force them to give you the point. Be like Neale Lavis when he went to England. One judge said to the other, 'What are we going to do with him? He doesn't do anything wrong'. That's the way we have to do a test.

Nobody is going to look for the good points in any Australian rider who goes overseas, particularly in dressage, until such time as we get an Australian judge sitting in the tent. He may be likely to look for the good points. But judges don't normally look for your good points, they look for your bad points. So you have to present the horse and come down the centre line straight.

We start with a simple flying change. In the simple flying change we canter 1, 2, 3, suspension. The horse can change the leg only when he is off the ground. So, when he has that leg off the ground, he changes this leg position into that. The aid is simple. When you canter to the left, the outside leg is behind the girth, flexion left; all you do is keep it there and all you say is, 'Canter left'.

Before you try to do it make sure that the horse understands your aids to perfection. The best way to check whether he does or not, and whether he is straight enough to do so, is to go cantering, hop, hop, hop, and then to go straight, smoothly, clearly, back into a walk 1, 2, 3, 4. You have to say, 'Canter right' or 'Canter left', and on a straight line or a circle, and he has to stay like a light switch. When he can do that then you can try.

At first try a serpentine. Do a half-circle, and in the moment of change, sit up and simply change the coming outside leg backwards. Keep the other leg on the horse in a normal position to hold him forward, and in the same instant,

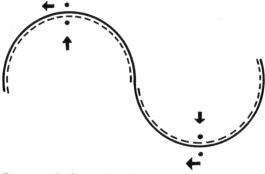

Diagram 18: Serpentine loop

smoothly, you change the flexion say from right to left as in Diagram 18. Be careful. Most riders pull back when they change flexion and as soon as you pull back you muddle up the flying change and make it impossible. A lot of riders throw their weight around in the flying change but that won't lead to flying changes at every stride. It only gets them from one leg to another.

In the moment of changing direction you change the flexion and you change the outside leg. The straighter you sit the better. A common fault is that the rider changes that coming outside leg backwards and lifts that outside seat. Here comes the horse. The rider is sitting straight and the weight stays down. He is flexed to the left. The inside leg holds him forward and what happens? The inside leg moves back and says, 'Canter right', and in the same instant you change the flexion from left to right and that leg takes over and says 'Go forward'. But the seat has to stay there otherwise you interfere in one way or another; because the moment of suspension is a tremendously delicate moment of balance for the horse, if you move a little too much or at the wrong time you will unbalance him and the first thing he will do is to put that nearest foot to the ground, and it is very seldom the right one. When he is cantering to the left and you unbalance him, he might change in the front but still canter with the wrong one behind. Then he is disunited, and he might do two or three steps, and then come through with the hindleg.

But he has to change in one go. And as you look at the horse it appears to the eye that the two legs, the near hind and near fore, are coming together. It is one movement. But if you keep your eye on that near hind you will see that it comes to the ground a little earlier than that near fore. Now he puts it down, and you can see that the near fore is coming to the ground a little later.

When he changes, the off hind near fore diagonal has to come forward because that is the diagonal and the off fore is the coming leading leg. But the two legs here will look as if they come in one go. If one leg moves and the other one doesn't come through, flowing through, the movement is no good and you will see that he is disunited afterwards.

The inside leg goes back in exactly the same way as the outside leg goes forward. That indicates the direction of the canter. The seat stays in the saddle, and in the same instant there is a smooth change of flexion. You have to look where you want to go again, otherwise he may tend to throw himself over and fall in with the shoulder if you don't hold him forward. He has to go straight forward. He has to change through under your body and stay straight, and the changing stride is the same as any other stride. There is no change in rhythm. He really has to be supple. The change has to go right through. He gives throughout his length, not hanging on, and flexing around the inside leg. He keeps going straight on.

The less commotion there is during the flying change, the better it is. He must change when you say so. Your timing has to be on the dot. There is really only one blink of the eyelid when you have to be there. You can't be a little too late or too early, because the moment when he can change is so short. If you come too late or too early he can't do it.

He has to be able to canter on from a walk. He has to be able to change the leg when you say so, regardless of where you are. If you are really careful and take your time, and develop that ability to change no matter where you are, you will find that you can do it by counting 1, 2,

111

3, 4, 5, 6. That is the best count to start with. It can be more but never less. Change him—six strides—change him. And if he does it twice, let him have a rest. Don't try to get those flying changes with every stride, otherwise you will end up as I did and he won't do a single flying change.

You do it on the long side and then you try it on the diagonal, and then if you have no trouble make five strides. Give him a week or two and ask him for four strides, and another week and you can make it three strides; another week and you can make it two strides, and then be careful. When the foundation is right every stride will be no trouble. Because it is such a tremendous exercise you have to stay supple or you can't do it. You start off after you have done it at every two strides, then you come and say (and you are cantering on the right), 'Change', 'Change', and then go straight on in the canter. Hop, hop, keep going, make sure that he doesn't get excited and then you can perhaps try it again—hop, hop. If he does it the first time I would suggest that you don't try it again the same day.

The next day, try it again, and he will be quite happy doing it, and then try a second one, and the third day try a third one. And it shouldn't take you longer than four weeks (always taking for granted that the foundation is right). He has to go forward, he has to maintain impulsion, and he has to be straight. If he changes the leg and doesn't go forward it is useless. If he doesn't go forward it is no good. But again there is that exercise, the necessity of giving here and giving there and being supple through the whole body. The suppleness makes him a better horse. You have to keep your seat on the saddle, and you have to sit straight, and your inside leg has to be able to say, 'Stay straight', and your outside leg says, 'Go forward'.

Now we are nearly ready for the Grand Prix.

Piaffe is a trot on the spot, and with 990 horses you teach this on the hand first—side reins (but don't make him too short), cavesson, and then a lead rein on the cavesson.

To begin with you have a wall or a solid fence where he can't run away. When teaching piaffe you have to have something you can lean on, where he can't get away from you. If you don't, he will walk around the whole paddock as Gay Pam did with me for half an hour until my dog came to the rescue. Then she was all right.

You take him on the lead and then you just bring him in, walk him on the lead, and halt. And as you halt, you put yourself in front of him and then you step to the side or his shoulder, and walk on. As you walk on you can touch him with the stick. The whip should not be too long. You should touch him where your leg is normally because that already means 'Go', but don't touch him on the hindlegs to start with (you never do).

Walk on, halt. Walk–halt. Trot on, halt. Walk on, trot–halt. Trot–halt. And that period becomes shorter and shorter. You say, 'Trot on, halt', 'Trot on, halt', and then you say, 'Trot–halt', and give him a hard check. Don't stop him completely though. Touch him and keep him going shorter. Most horses come fairly quickly on the hand. Normally they get the idea in a fortnight, and in most cases it is consolidated in four weeks—that is, he does the piaffe on the hand, still going forward. Your aim is that he will trot on the spot. He is still going forward, he is going shorter but still gaining ground to the fore, and that is reduced more and more until he is trotting on the spot. It is important that you finish as soon as he shows the first diagonal steps shorter. If he does something wrong, correct him immediately; if he does something right, reward him immediately.

Don't say, 'He is doing it fine', and keep him going and going, or you will have a case of 'pineapple' as I did. He will go up the wall. As soon as he shows that he has the idea, try it again. You have to be relaxed within yourself. This is really not quite as easy as it sounds, and not everybody is good at the work in the hand. I've seen very good riders who were pretty useless at it; they lacked judgment.

It takes a lot of experience, a lot of patience, and you have to be fit. You have to run along with him, and sometimes you have to run a bit more than you should. And you should not try to hold him when you sit on top because you will finish up running second. You will find quickly enough that you have no hope of holding him on the short rein, but you can hold him quite easily, if you feel that you just have that contact. Now you push him, and as he tries to go a bit more, take him and keep going, take him and check him and keep going. But as soon as you try to pull him hanging on he is gone.

I had a stallion in the School who was really doing piaffe on the hand. There is a special section of the performance when that type of work is shown, and he was really good. You just threw the rein over his neck and walked beside him, and he went like a steam engine right around the School.

Major Sandford, who was really responsible for my coming to Australia, was in the School for two years. What determination! When he came to the School he was sixty-seven and he had been chasing kangaroos and lions and what have you. When he wasn't chasing wild animals he was riding in a hunt quite happily, with his feet stuck forward. He spent two years in the School and he did it. He didn't say anything but I know he suffered. In spite of his age he just went on the lunging rein like everyone else. If you want to do it you have to do it: in two years he did it. He was determined, and he worked. Now he wanted to learn how to do that piaffe on the hand, and so I explained everything to him. I handed him the reins and I turned round and walked away and he was in the middle of the School. As soon as he picked up the reins the stallion refused to perform—just like that. I took him back again, got him going perfectly, and kept going with my hand on the rein. But as soon as Major Sandford picked up the rein the stallion refused again. The stallion knew. He thought, 'You don't have enough knowledge to make me work, so goodbye'. He would not work then, but he did after a while. Major Sandford

had disturbed that fine understanding of the rein and that forward movement by taking him a bit hard. He was interfering, unbalancing, or just annoying the stallion, and *whoosh* away he went. It took quite a few days until Major Sandford was able to make even a few steps—because the stallion had brains.

As soon as the horse has established on the hand the knowledge and ability for piaffe (ability, because he has to bend much more—similar to that half-pirouette walking), he has to make shorter steps, and because of those shorter steps he has to bend more through all his joints and in the haunches. He has to give more, therefore you try to take your weight off. Make sure that there is no interference whatever. Give him the idea, and when he can do it you put a dummy on him (it is not a dummy, it's a live rider, but he has to act like a dummy; he just sits there, he doesn't do anything). All that has to be done after that is to consolidate. Piaffe is there. Consolidate the transition from trot to piaffe, from piaffe to trot. And again, granted that everything is right in the first place, it shouldn't be a problem. But it is very difficult all the same.

The transition into piaffe is more difficult than piaffe into trot, because what you have to do is have him trotting—working trot, or you can make a transition from an extended trot into a piaffe. He goes forward, forward, shorter, shorter and he should not miss a beat or change his beat. He should go 1, 2, 3, 4, 1, 2, 3, 4, 1, 2, 3, 4. This is very difficult. The more finely the horse is tuned up, the better. You have to push him, drive him under so that he trots on the spot. If you still have to use a lot of power to push him when you get there you will never get the transition right. He has already been tuned up so that a little less push is needed to collect him than was used in the earlier stages just to get him moving on at a walk. Otherwise you will not be able to maintain that delicate balance. As the horse comes and goes sit dead straight and still, stretch down, influencing him through position. He is together, and as you trot and you sit up close with your legs, you

113

keep him going, keep him going, you go forward, forward, forward, and then you sit down, and then you let him go forward again. He comes backwards and forwards into your hands without holding on. It is very difficult and therefore seldom seen — in most cases the riders are eager beavers who started advanced work before true suppleness had been developed. If it has not been developed down to a fine art the stiffness that remains will show. You may have seen the film of Filatow, the Russian who won a gold medal in Rome, doing piaffe. You can see that every now and then there is a funny step with the off-hind. This is a lack of suppleness developed from the early stages. But in Rome in the actual tests Filatow did very good transitions from passage to piaffe and vice versa.

What is necessary? It is necessary that the horse is straight to start with and that the rider is sitting square, with both seat bones staying there and the weight continually flowing down into the saddle. It is necessary that you have contact with both reins, and that both reins are equally responsible for the forward movement and keep him straight. At the same time as you bring him back it is that stretching and pushing influence of the rider's position that brings the hindquarters forward underneath, and the hands must keep him straight. But you have to sit dead straight because if the weight shifts just a little bit the horse can't and won't step under his body as his balance is disturbed. Because your weight distribution is uneven he can't step as he should. So the essentials are your position, even weight distribution, control of hands that have to be supple and soft, the whole body functioning as a unit. Then the following connection should flow through:

- from the hands through the mouth,
- through the reins, into the body,
- through the seat into the hindquarters.

If he does not let your aids through, if he is not supple enough and submissive enough to accept it, it is not good, particularly not with the transitions. You might have him doing piaffe but if you try to do transitions you won't have a hope.

Many people say that at the School they put the horse in the pillars and then take a big whip and just hit him until he does piaffe. Now if you think that's how it's done, have a try; when you have got a horse to do proper piaffe and proper transitions by having been taught that way, let me know. You will probably have to contact my grandson and let him know because that's how long it will take you. It will take you longer than that. The pillars are there because they are part of the performance. But the horse is not put into the pillars before he can piaffe on the spot on the hand. If you can do it there, then you can put him in the pillars and the pillars sometimes can be of help in teaching him movements above the ground. He is not tied into the jolly thing and hit from behind until in desperation he does piaffe — because, although the stallions are not very big (they are only about 15 to 15·2 hands), they would walk away with the pillars if you did that. People talk a lot without knowing anything about it.

Piaffe is a trot on the spot. The more even it is, the more flow of rhythm, the less interference or interruption there is.

Now we have the next step, and after that you can nominate for the Olympic Games. This is the Spanish trot. There is no Spanish walk in the classical school. There is one in the circus, where the horse does the trot — incorrectly named the Spanish walk — and goes forward with the forelegs but the hindlegs go with short steps and no elevation.

The Spanish trot (passage) is a highly elevated trot, carried forward, where he halts, floats, and halts, and floats forward. You can see it particularly with stallions. I had a gelding in the paddock and he did the most beautiful trot by himself. You couldn't ride an ordinary walk on him, but by himself he did a most beautiful Spanish trot, really together and rounded. It floated. The hindquarters really have to be engaged. If you see a picture of the Spanish trot and the floating leg, that hindleg, is off the ground and the hock of the floating leg is behind the leg on the ground, then that Spanish trot is no good because the horse is not stepping

Above: Piaffe

Below: Passage

through. He is doing a bit of a Spanish walk trot. He is not really coming through enough with the hindquarters, not carrying enough with the hindquarters. Like all other movements, the Spanish trot is a natural movement which you can see the horse doing freely in the open. Horses can do capriole, courbette, flying changes—and they do piaffe too.

Never teach him the Spanish trot before he can do piaffe, because if you do you will probably never get him to do a proper piaffe. If you should succeed you will never get a decent transition out of him because every time he will resist. Piaffe has to come first and then the Spanish trot is developed out of it. What you do is to drive him—as if you were doing an extended trot—out of the piaffe but don't let him go. You stretch out and let him go forward but as he starts to go you say, 'Stay here'. Instead of saying, 'Go forward, trot', you go forward and go with him. You say 'Go', and as he goes you go with him, but only so far. You keep on pushing and let him go that far and that far. If the piaffe is right and everything else is right that first step will be glorious.

It is no problem if he accepts the forward driving aids and the constraining aids. If he lets the aids through forwards, backwards, and forwards, you will have him together from the driving aids to the restraining aids, and here you push him. He goes together but you only let him go that far. In most cases horses just love it and you have to be careful that they don't do too much or do it when you don't want them to. The first indication is that he goes into the bit. And because he can't go forward there comes the higher elevation of the trot. Come back, walk, stop, pat, let him walk, gather him up, piaffe, piaffe, piaffe, everything is right, stretch out and hold him forward, and there is the step again, and check him and walk. Do that two or three times on the first day. That's plenty. The next day do it three or four times. Plenty again. After that it is a matter of feeling. You get the feeling that when you say 'Go' he really does go. You get a sense of security, of certainty within yourself. You feel you can

drive him, take him up, and make him go. There are three steps and you keep him going, and there is another step. The next day you can do it still a few more times; after three weeks he can go down the whole long side.

You try something, you get the taste of it, you 'taste blood' as they say, and then you can't leave off. You want to have a bit more and then you try a bit more and then you sit down and say, 'I am a fool; I have to work so hard to get it'. The more you do, the more you realise how much more there is in it. You start off, and after the first year of serious work you say, 'Goodness me, last year I thought I could ride; now I know that I don't know a thing, but I know a lot more than I did last year'. And the year after that you will say the same thing, and so it goes on until the day you die. There is always something to learn.

To know is like sitting in a dark room. You don't know it is dark and it doesn't worry you. But as soon as you light a match you know how dark it was before. Now that match is a little knowledge. And the bigger the flame is, the more light you have, the more darkness is pushed back, the bigger is the horizon of your knowledge. But it also makes you realise how much more darkness there is further on.

After my test to ride in the Cavalry School in Hanover, my Old Instructor and I had a cup of coffee together in the canteen. We were talking about horses, naturally, and I said to Mr Polak, 'You wouldn't have any worry about schooling horses or anything?'. And he answered, 'Oh, no. You finish one horse and then you think that the next one has to be a little bit more sensitive and a bit straighter still, and a bit finer on the hands, and still a bit more this and that'. He was still seeking more darkness because he had a little bit of light.

This is Grand Prix. Everything above that is schools above the ground—exercises where the horse is in the air. To develop a really good Spanish trot that seat has to be glued there. And by glued there I don't mean that you have to be pressing yourself into it (which you never should do anyway). All you do is let your weight down and keep it there. Don't press it down. No, that seat has to *be* there. The horse has to be sensitive to the legs. Naturally he has to be straight, and he has to be on the bit, and he has to let your aids through transitions forwards and transitions backwards. And as you make the transition forward there is the transition, the half transition, to a sort of half-halt, but you keep him going and there he goes. But your seat has to be here otherwise he can't do it. The horse can't maintain his balance and float like this while you bounce on his back.

The better that preparation has been, the more easily everything will come. If the foundation is there it is only a matter of taking your driving aids a little further and giving a slightly finer polish to that half-halt. As you drive him, check him, don't let him go; but in the next instant you do let him go.

I don't think I have to reiterate that you have to have your body under control, otherwise you have no hope. As General Buerkner said when he came to England, 'I can't help. Your position is not right'. And if your position is not right, if you can't sit there, if you can't apply the aids properly, then, no matter how much I tell you, or anybody else tells you, it's just useless.

The capriole and the levade are both movements starting from piaffe. In the capriole the horse goes piaffe, piaffe, piaffe, then straight up into the air, and as he reaches the apex of his jump he kicks out with both hindlegs. It was developed in the past when a knight was surrounded by foot soldiers. He made a capriole and scattered everything around him. Then he did a half-pirouette and *poof* he was gone. It is a natural movement. You can see horses, particularly young horses, doing it in the paddock with no artificial aids at all. But no rider with any sense will try to teach capriole to a horse that has never shown a natural desire to get off the ground.

When the stallions come to the School and they are there on the lunging rein you check them in and you start to ride. If you see one bouncing about on his hindlegs and kicking up

well, you keep it in mind as you go along. 'Yes,' you say. 'He shows some promise, some aptitude to do schools above the ground.' Some of the horses never get off the ground—like that wonderful horse Mr Lindenbauer schooled in one year. He never did anything but Grand Prix but he did that to perfection. He used that stallion in 1934 when he worked on the programme for the test for the 1936 Olympics. That's when they had that horse as a sort of guinea pig. He went through all the movements for the F.E.I. Committee, but he would never go up above the ground. That was just unknown to him. He was a very good horse and it was not necessary for him to do anything above the ground. That has to be in the horse.

You could see that with the stallion that knocked me in the head. He was never anything but on his hindlegs. He would have made a wonderful courbette, where he comes shorter, shorter, shorter, and then he comes up in a levade, after which, he comes a little bit higher and then he jumps. He must jump or leap with both hindlegs. It is a very sensational exercise to ride. You ride him just the same way as for trot on, halt, trot on, halt. The same principle. You get him up, you ask him to come up. In most cases all the schools above the ground are schooled without the rider first. You put the rider on afterwards.

When I did my first courbette the first thing I did was to slide off the horse's back and hang on to his tail. First you take him and then, when he is up, you have him on the bit in the same way as if he were on the ground. Then you say 'Go' and at the same time you take off and let him go with your hands. Then you check him and then you say 'Go', and 'Go', and 'Go', and you push him and check him, push him and check him, in just the same way as if you were on the ground.

I had a stallion in the School for seven years. I am reminded of him after seeing a picture of the levade and Prince Eugene—a monument in the square of Vienna, what we would call a war memorial. It is a memorial to Prince Eugene who was the rescuer of Vienna when it was surrounded by the Turks. Mr Fernkorn was the artist who made the monument. Mr Polak and I usually met in the underground on our way to the School, and we walked many times across the square, past that monument. And Mr Polak said, 'Yes, Fernkorn had it easy; he did that levade sixty years ago and it's still standing there, and we have to do it every day, every day, every day. Yet in a sense it also takes an artist to make the horse do that and produce it over and over again'. He had a point there. Normally four leaps on the hindlegs is the average. But that good stallion of mine had an average of between four and eight and his record was fourteen. Fourteen leaps on his hindlegs! He was a big stallion, 16·2 hands, and very beautiful. He looked absolutely magnificent. I never saw him doing it because I was always on top of him, but when he came up everybody said he was just so powerful. And he was beautiful to ride. He went up higher than some other stallions, and that's why he could maintain his balance longer. But because he was so high it took some getting used to without pulling him over. He did go over once in Hamburg. He took off, went up, and crashed, and I shot forward over his neck.

Levade is nothing but a piaffe carried on, carried on. You start to collect as for the piaffe and you keep on collecting and collecting and collecting, and then the horse comes further and further down with the hindlegs. As he goes further and further down he moves the support more and more, and his gravity and the rider's gravity, until the support is so far underneath that he does not need to come any more. You can feel him. You can see the tremendous stretch that is going through his body and that suppleness has to be there. There can't be any stiffness. He is rounded everywhere. Sometimes we may think that we can afford a little movement with the body and get away with it. When you do the levade there is no getting away with it. The rider does nothing with his body. He does not move backwards to transfer weight backwards or forwards. All he does is to keep on sitting this way and letting his weight down.

The lower legs are close and keep him going, and keep him going, and keep him going. The rider's position has not changed at all, but the horse's hindquarters are coming underneath, underneath, and underneath, and you see that the approximate plumb line from the rider's and horse's weight is going right down between his hindlegs, and in most cases as he comes down and down, he goes wider, wider, wider with the hindlegs. It gives him a wider stance to balance himself.

The courbette is exactly the same thing, developed from the levade, except that the horse comes up higher. And then he jumps on the hindlegs—both legs together—hop, hop, hop.

In the capriole, he is doing piaffe, and then he comes straight up and kicks out. Once you have got used to it, it is really nothing. What you have to get used to is not really the jump. He does piaffe, piaffe, piaffe, and just before he takes off it feels as if he is bending down, and *boom* he bounces off. Now if you are a fraction stiff and your weight is not flowing there, coming down, you will stay there. And you will certainly know about it when he comes up! As I have said, it is quite simple if he does it properly. And 'properly' means that he goes up and reaches the apex of his leap, and then he fires out, and comes down. He goes up and down on the same spot. But if he goes up and starts to come down, and then kicks out—that can be very uncomfortable.

You can see perfect caprioles in the paddock. I once had a little black horse called Dolkeg. When you let him out on Sunday morning in his little yard he would do ten perfect caprioles one after the other—all perfect, just bounce, bounce, bounce like a rubber ball, up and down. He would have been a tremendous horse to teach capriole. He would have done it at the drop of a hat. But some other horses you can't get off the ground whatever you do. You can make some of them get up, but the impression is a sort of strangled one. That ease and joy and life and fun in the movement just isn't there.

I rode two horses for a performance when

General Patton took the School under his protection. I was just riding one of them around in the School in Upper Austria, when suddenly, *boom*, he made a capriole. I didn't do anything. I didn't hit him. And then, *boom*, another capriole. It was not until then that I caught sight of the Old Instructor. It was an old building, and little bits of broken building material were lying around. I just saw the Old Instructor picking up a little pebble and throwing it. All he did was to toss it on to the horse's hindquarters, and *bang*.

You encourage the horse to collect up, and if he shows an inclination to do so all you have to do is to give him a little touch on the hindquarters, and *bang* there you go. The Old Instructor tossed a little pebble on the stallion's backside and away he went.

We have a few other movements. I have a strong suspicion that one of the old instructors 120 years ago was trying to make a capriole when the horse jumped up but he didn't kick out. So they called it a croupade. Because it was a capriole that didn't come good they gave it a new name. The croupade and the ballotade are jumps up. If the stallion keeps his legs under his body it is a ballotade. And if he jumps up and sort of shows his legs as if he wanted to kick, then that's a croupade. It was never done in the School while I was there. Nor was the mêzair, which is a levade that really didn't come true. It is really the same thing, only done in a canter motion. The horse collects himself completely, right down, and he comes up and does it, and comes down, makes a stride, and does the same thing again. I must say that I have never seen it nor have I done it. There was no horse in the School doing a mêzair and they never really tried to do it either. It was either a levade, or a capriole or a courbette. We never tried for any of the others.

Well, when am I going to see you all doing Grand Prix?

Long rein work—Oberbereiter Lindenbauer

SUMMARY

Flying Changes

First, the horse must be straight. The horse can change the leading leg only when he is off the ground in the moment of suspension—the fourth silent beat of the canter. You should not try the flying change until the horse will go canter, canter and come smoothly back to the walk, clearly and softly with no trot steps. Then he must go clearly into a canter right or left without any trot steps, change of outline, etc. Then he will be ready for a try. Try the first time in a serpentine. In the moment of change of direction when the horse is in the air you change the flexion, say from right to left, by bringing the right leg to the backward position. It is the new outside leg. Do not consciously move the left leg. The change of flexion will bring it into place. It holds the horse forward. The reins must allow him to move smoothly into the new lead. The rider must sit absolutely still. If you move your weight it will unbalance the horse and he will put the nearest foot to the ground to regain his balance—and this is seldom the correct one. He may then be disunited for a few strides. To be correct he has to change smoothly through in one go from the back to the front. You must look where you are going to keep him on your line. Your change of aids must be on the dot, when he is in the air, or just as he takes to the air. He cannot do it if your timing is wrong.

When he will change the leg whenever you ask, try a certain number of strides between changes, say six strides, then change again. If he does it twice, leave it for now. Next day, if there is no trouble, try five strides and after a week or two try for four. It is a tremendous exercise. The rider must stay supple and still or it cannot be done. After some time you get back to every two strides. Lastly comes every stride—hop, hop. If he does it, do no more that day. It is quite a long time before you try hop, hop, hop. It could take you four weeks.

Remember that he must go smoothly forward, not check and hop. You must be supple and still.

Next in the text comes piaffe. I don't think that any reader who has taken his horse up to this stage will need a summary.

120

CHAPTER TEN

DRESSAGE

There is no need to try to explain or translate the meaning of the French word *dressage*. Books have been published about it, articles and long explanations written, but the word is still a mystery and misunderstood. I suppose it always will be. The best we can do, is either to accept it or try to find another more suitable word, an English word, to replace it.

I could not think of a better substitute than 'to train', because it means 'to educate, to instruct, to form by exercise and discipline'. The sooner the word 'dressage' disappears the better. There is already one dressage test called 'Trained Pony Test', and I am sure that all tests will soon be called 'Trained Horse Tests', graded from Novice to the Olympic Test.

It is only a very short time since dressage started in Australia and the reaction of the Australian has been true to form, very conservative, very suspicious. It is rather amusing to hear people say, 'What's the good of the new fancy Continental style of riding? Let's stick to our good old Australian style. It was good enough for Grandfather; it must be good enough for us'. They forget that when Grandfather was young there were no cars, no TV, and many other modern things were missing. But that is beside the point. The point is that the so-called

new style of riding, the idea of a dressage or trained horse, is much older than most people realise. In fact it is nearly 2500 years old and goes back to the old Greeks. That is why the Continent calls the art of riding 'classical high school' because it goes back to the classical age. If something can survive for 2500 years it must have great values, great inner virtues, great advantages, or the riders of long ago would have abandoned the whole idea and we would not even know that it ever existed. Men were always business-like, and nobody would play around with something without getting a good return for his work and effort.

Before we go into more detail about dressage, let's get one thing straight. Different people have different reasons for riding a horse, and of course different ways or styles of riding, just as there are different card games, different ways of cooking an egg, or whatever example you might prefer. The stockman developed his style because that style is most suitable for his purpose. So did the jockey, and the jumping rider or polo player. By reading articles in magazines and by talking and listening I have discovered that some people complain that the Australian is giving away his good style of riding. Now what is the true Australian style? I have made a point of asking countless numbers of people what they thought was the Australian style of riding. In 90 per cent of cases the answer was the style of the stockman, the camp drafter. That is the Australian style, and I quite agree and admire them for their skill. In one article the author wrote, 'Why alter our style, our Australian style? Our riders have been successful on the race track, in the jumping ring and cross-country, and have proved to be better than the continental riders'. So they did, but the style in which the Australian riders were so successful overseas was vastly different from the style of the stockman—for different reasons, in different ways. They did not prove that the Australian style of riding is the best, but they proved that the Australian rider can adjust himself to any style and be as good in it as in his own.

Now back to dressage, and what in my opinion has kept it alive for such a long time. Most certainly not the soft talk of some riding instructors who wanted to make a living out of it (especially the ones one always sees in boots and breeches but never on a horse). No, there is certainly more to it than that.

It can be contracted into two words—common sense. Common sense will make us appreciate the wisdom of nature or creation. Common sense will tell us that a horse has much more physical power than we have; it will also make us realise that force never lasts and certainly does not create co-operation. Common sense should tell us that we get nothing for nothing in this life, and it should force us to think. 'Look before you leap' is an old English proverb.

What does dressage have to do with the wisdom of nature and the various laws of nature? If you look at the different forms of life—mammals, birds, reptiles, insects, fish, and plants—you will discover that they are equipped with the best means for survival both individually and for their kind. The group or class that interests us most is the mammals, because to that group belong human beings and also our horses. What are our means of survival? Strength? Speed? Certainly not. It is the power

of reason, the ability to find facts and draw logical conclusions, or in other words more highly developed brains without which the man from long ago would not have had a chance. If we have survived by using our brains, and the flies survive in spite of D.D.T. on account of their fertility, horses survived the battle for life because of their speed. The horse does not have to chase after his feed, because grass does not run away. But other mammals try to kill the horse, and that is why the horse had to be fast—to get away from danger. All his speed would be useless if it were not combined with shyness and an extraordinary sense of hearing and smell. Do not get cross with your horse if he should shy. Do not forget that it is natural—the trigger for his speed. Do not punish him for something he can't help doing, but show him that there is no real danger. If nature meant him to go forward then we must not try to know more than nature or our Creator—and that is the most important fact in our realisation of nature's wisdom. A dressage horse must go forward because nature developed him for this purpose.

Gravity is a law of nature and because of it we use the lift and don't step out of the window on the tenth floor. A breach of this law would be penalised with death. If we do not ride our dressage horse forward we are interfering with his natural destiny, and lack of progress will be our penalty. We cannot cheat nature.

On the same lines, have you ever worried about your balance? I am sure that you have not, except after a big party or some celebration when you were loaded with too much whisky. By ourselves we never think about being balanced. We have not contributed anything towards it. It is the design of our body, nature's wisdom. But when we have to carry something we soon realise that our feeling of being comfortable and safe on our feet has vanished and we are more or less staggering along. Why? Is it the weight? Yes, but more so, it is the fact that we have not been designed to carry something. Any additional weight will upset our natural balance. But with our power of reason we can do something about it. We can adjust our posture, get used to it, and find comfort under the changed conditions. If the weight on your back keeps still you will have no difficulty in adjusting yourself, but if the weight moves from one side to the other you will never find your balance—not until you have fixed the weight in a firm position.

If you have never carried anything on your back, then try it straight away; experience is the best teacher for what I am trying to say. If the Lord has designed us to move through life without a burden on our back, we can safely say the same for the horse. There is no reason why the horse should not have been developed to move through life with the same effortless ease as we do. Otherwise the horse would have broken down, could not have made use of his speed, and would not have survived the millions of years of evolution.

If the horse is well balanced by himself, there is no reason why he should not feel as uncomfortable as we do with an additional weight to carry. As I have said before, we can use logic and adjust the weight into the right position, or adjust our posture, or both. The horse does not have the mental power of man, therefore the rider has to do the thinking for the horse. He has to put his own weight in the right place and adjust the horse's posture.

There we have it again. Dressage means the realisation of nature's wisdom by re-establishing the horse's natural balance with the additional weight of the rider on his back. That is the essence, the fundamental requirement of dressage. The horse must carry the rider with ease, move gracefully, and go forward. That is the basis, the idea. It means submission to nature. That is common sense, and that is why it has lasted for 2500 years and will last as long as there are horses or people prepared to train themselves in the art of dressage. That is the foundation. How to achieve it is a different subject, and is not the object of this chapter.

Dressage means the horse's submission and the rider's control, but before we can control anything we must be able to control ourselves, we must be the master of our body, we must be able to put ourselves in the right position and maintain that position, because if this additional weight is tossing about, it will be impossible for the horse to find his balance. To control the different parts of our body is not enough. We also have to control our temper. This is very important, and unfortunately many riders do not pay enough attention to it. Dressage means education, but no rider can educate a horse if he has not educated himself first. Whatever one wants to educate one has to be fond of, otherwise we won't have the patience that is essential for any teacher.

We must be absolutely consistent in what we ask the horse to do, why we ask it, and how we ask for it. The 'What' and 'Why' are a matter of thinking first. 'How' we ask for it will be a matter of body control which will enable us to be consistent with our aids. Above all, we should be very diplomatic. I could add a lot more, or go into more detail, but I have already shown you that there is nothing for nothing. Dressage means more than not falling off. It requires self-education. That is why a lot of people do not like it. It also means that the dressage rider cannot blame the horse; he must blame himself. Naturally it is a lot easier just to ride, and, if things don't work out, to say that the horse has no brains, than to say that one is riding dressage, and that the horse has got the better of the rider. It is a psychological characteristic to blame something else for one's failure. It makes life with oneself a lot easier. In his book *The White Spider* Heinrich Harrer says, 'the glorious thing about mountains is that they will endure no lies'. Horses will endure no lies either. They show off the rider's shortcomings. One has only to look, think a bit, add two and two together, and one gets a pretty fair idea of the rider's personality. You might think that it is just plain philosophy or psychology, but the less brain and intelligence the pupil has, the more brain and understanding the teacher must have—otherwise, as my Old Instructor, Mr Lindenbauer, once said, 'If two fools are together there is certainly one too many'.

Another fact that has helped to keep dressage up to date for so many years is the fact that a dressage horse must maintain his true natural walk, trot, and canter. There are no artificial movements such as cantering on three legs. All these different artificial movements are circus tricks, and as such are an art in themselves. But they have nothing to do with classical high school.

The various dressage tests all require the execution of different movements on one and two tracks. All these movements are gymnastic exercise for the horse and lead from a simple line on one track to the more difficult movements on two tracks in the advanced tests, and finally to the very difficult ones such as piaffe (trot on the spot), passage (Spanish trot—very elevated trot carried forward), pirouettes (small turns on the haunches), and the flying change of leg at every stride of the Olympic dressage test. With every exercise, from the simple to the more advanced, we improve the horse's suppleness and his balance, all within the rider's control. I was asked once, 'What's the sense in schooling a horse to such a high standard? We do not need piaffe or flying change every stride when we are working cattle, playing polo, or jumping'. I answered with a counter-question, 'Why do people pay $500 000 for a painting by Rembrandt? I would paint them one for much less money. Why does a springboard diver jump from the high tower and perform a double corkscrew and a somersault and land head-first in the water? Isn't that a very complicated way of getting into the water?'. There are countless examples of doing things the hard way. Why? Well I suppose it is the age-old instinct for achievement. The attempt to be better than the other fellow, the thrill of having the mind mastering the body. A dressage rider must be master of his own body and master of the horse's mind and body—twice the thrill of accomplishment. The better the rider's control over his horse, the better the horse's balance will be; the better his education, the better the rider's performance must be, whether it is hacking or jumping, playing polo or cross-country. That is plain common sense. If it should not prove to be the case then the dressage training must have been incorrect (but that would have been the rider's fault and not the fault of dressage).

Dressage means exercise and discipline. In other words, the object of dressage is to develop the horse's mental and physical capabilities to the full extent through systematic schooling, and by means of education to get him to submit himself freely to whatever you might ask him to do. I underline 'submit himself freely', and quote Xenophon in 400 B.C. A horse must make the most graceful and brilliant appearance of his own free will, with the help of aids. We teach him what we want him to do. We prepare him through gymnastic exercise and he won't have any difficulties in executing the different tasks we put him to. If we only want to get from A to B it won't make any difference how we get there. The horse can pull and play up and fight, but it will not matter so long as we get there—in other words, so long as we do not fall off. But if we have to negotiate an Olympic steeplechase and cross-country course with forty-eight solid obstacles, then we need a bit more than 'not to fall off'. We need the horse's co-operation. We must have his mental alertness and his free submission, otherwise the result will be a disaster of some sort. Certainly there will be no gold medals. The fact that dressage asks for free submission by the horse should contradict the statement by an Australian that Continental riders are all dictators. The basic idea is as democratic as can be.

Perfection is something that does not exist. We are one-sided. Some people write with the right hand, some with the left. We do not walk straight but that does not interfere with the requirements of our everyday life. Should we decide to do some special feat like balancing something on our head, then we would have to come closer to perfection of balance and posture, by means of exercise. We are not the only ones to be one-sided. Look at a dog trotting along. You will notice that his hindquarters are to one side; he is moving crookedly. The same applies to our horses, but it is not so obvious because we cannot look down on the horse as we do on a dog. Most horses carry their hindquarters to the right side. Experts argue about the reason for this. It would take too long to state the different opinions here, but we can accept the fact that horses are one-sided—as one-sided as people, or dogs, or whatever you want to put under close scrutiny. It is good enough for horses just as it is good enough for us, so long as we do not want to do some trick of balance. If we *do* wish to do something, it is easy enough, because we can think it over and find out what we have to do in order to achieve our goal. But horses cannot think for themselves and find out how they have to adjust themselves to the condition of carrying a rider. That is why the rider has to do the thinking for the horse.

If the horse is to be balanced under the rider, then the horse will have to distribute the weight evenly on all four legs. Left to himself he will be inclined to carry more of the extra weight on the forehand than on the hindquarters, which would put such a great strain on the front legs that the horse would break down. It is impossible for the horse to distribute the weight evenly on all four legs if he is not straight in himself.

There is an old saying: 'Ride your horse forward and make him straight'. Only when the horse is straight in himself will he be truly balanced and the rider will have control over the hindquarters. Why should we control the hindquarters? Because that is where the Lord put the engine. The hindquarters develop the thrust, the impulsion; if you have no control over the engine what will be the result? If you think in terms of a motor car you will realise how dangerous that is.

To make him straight and at the same time go forward is the first requirement for any horse that is to give you an easy ride. After that we can advance him a bit more by flexing him in his longitude—of utmost importance for any advanced training. In going still further, we can shorten his step or stride and elevate his move-ment; in other words, collect him a bit more. Collection means more engagement, more activity of the hindquarters, and the head not pulled in. So far all movements are one track and that should give us a pretty good control over the horse—already sufficient but essential for any hack or jumper. To get even more suppleness we can give him more gymnastics by working him on two tracks, such as shoulder-in, hindquarters in, half-pass, half and full pirouettes, and so on to the very top. Every exercise that is carried out properly will improve the horse's suppleness and balance, the rider's control, comfort, and enjoyment.

Everybody must have done gymnastic exercise at some time, and therefore will know that our muscles do not readily agree if we start to pull and stretch them. They hurt, and the natural desire is to give up the exercise. No action, no reaction. But we also know that there is nothing for nothing, and so if you want a supple body you have to pay for it with a bit of pain and strain. There is no difference in the working of the muscles in man or horse. The horse will feel as uncomfortable as you when you ask him to do gymnastic exercise, and will try to get away from it.

If people think that horses have no brains they are mistaken. Horses know well how to look after themselves. We must realise that the horse does not want anything from us, but we want a lot from the horse. To avoid resistance, the rider will have to be very tactful in how much he asks the horse to do. The work will have to be carefully planned and thought-out in order to build up the exercises systematically.

To get a horse fully trained to the highest standard takes a long time, about three years. But if the training is done properly the horse will maintain the high standard throughout his life, providing for at least ten to fifteen years an easy ride and consistent performance—whether in dressage, showjumping, or combined training.

As you can see we need much more than just to sit on a horse somehow. We have to sit in a certain way, supple and at ease within ourselves. We have to be the absolute master of our body and the better we master our body the better we will master our horse. We have to think a little in psychological terms; we have to control our mind before we can control our body. We must realise that every single movement, everything we do, is governed by our brain. There is a reason for everything we do and how we do it. I said earlier that it is easier to live with ourselves if we can blame something else for our failure. Excuses are a psychological means of self-protection, restoring our ego or soothing our conscience.

Horses endure no lies. If you are mentally tied in knots your actions or reactions will reflect your state of mind. We can't have a supple body if we do not have a supple mind. The same applies to the horse. His body is also governed by his brain, and that is why we have to put him mentally at ease before we can do anything else. Only then will he have a hope of understanding what we want from him, and only then will he be ready to co-operate. Horses are good pupils and learn very quickly and willingly. Horses also have an outstanding memory. They will remember what they have learnt and never forget it. Make sure that you teach them only the right things, because they remember the bad things even better. Respect the horse's personality as another one of God's creation. Treat him well in order to gain his confidence. He will never let you down, and that is more than we can say of our fellow human beings. Horses repay you 100 per cent for whatever work, love, and understanding you give them. If your training has been good you will have a horse you can rely on all his life. If the training has been bad the result will be bad. Do not blame your horse for something he is not responsible for.

I have tried to explain to you that dressage means 'to train'. I have tried to make you see the problem from my point of view. You may not agree and I do not mind because everybody is entitled to his own opinion. But perhaps you will give it a thought. It may mean that you have come one or two steps up the ladder. And to admit that one has been wrong has not hurt anybody yet and never will. Dressage means the appreciation of everything of value in life.

The Aims and Requirements of Schooling

The aim in schooling is to have the horse going forward happily and freely, always alert and attentive to the rider's wishes. Throughout the horse's schooling his movement and bearing will improve. Having confidence in the bit he gradually learns the engagement of his hindquarters, to lengthen and shorten his stride and neck without restriction. With smoothness and energy he goes through the transitions from one pace to another without loss of cadence. The whole picture is one of harmony between horse and rider, the horse giving the impression of enjoying his work.

To achieve this ideal the rider must be self-disciplined and capable of giving his full concentration to the horse. He must be able to follow the horse's movements with his weight evenly distributed through his seat. Through a still position the rider is able to keep his hands still so that the horse always has an even feel in his mouth. This enables him to develop a soft feel of the rider's hands. When the rider gives thoughtful preparation for transitions, corners, circles, or any change of movement the horse is never startled, and never unbalances himself. He performs his movements with calmness and deliberation. The suppleness which he acquires enables him to carry out his work with the least possible strain on muscles and limbs, thereby prolonging his usefulness.

The well-schooled horse will always be a joy to ride and a pleasing picture to watch. If he is to remain so, the rider must be a joy for him to carry.

The Portrait of a Well-schooled Horse

Lifting and putting down his feet in a regular pace, with lightness and steadiness, the horse moves well forward on the track, going freely and willingly without haste or disturbance. His neck arches well in front of the rider with a supple poll. The position of the head is such that the line of the face remains a little in front

Franz Mairinger on Gay Pam. The well-schooled horse, showing the balance of the rider and straightness and evenness of the horse. The horse is at working trot

of a vertical line drawn to the ground. The ears will be at their highest point, neither pricked forward nor laid back, but revealing by their natural position the horse's attention and obedience to the rider's will.

The eyes, full of confidence, are turned in the direction of the movement, the mouth is closed but wet, indicating that the horse is chewing the bit without grinding his teeth. The reins must maintain a steady and even contact; those of the curb reveal by a slight vibration that they are applied only lightly, maintained in a certain tension by the horse himself, stepping full of confidence up to the bit. When the rider gives the reins momentarily, the horse maintains the position of his head as well as the regular tempo of his pace, thus revealing that he does not lie on the rein but carries himself. If the rider lengthens the reins the horse must stretch his neck without boring into the ground or throwing his head up. He must keep the contact with the bit.

Closing the hand lightly will make the horse go at a slower pace or bring him to the halt where he will stand still in the correct position, carrying his weight equally on all four legs. A light pressure of the rider's legs will make him move forward immediately in the demanded pace. All movements are free from constraint and make the horse's back swing elastically.

The rider, by sitting quietly and comfortably, proves how much he feels at home on his horse and how pleasant his movements are, and yet the horse is full of impulsion. Every step and every bound is brought about by the hindlegs springing energetically under the body and bent well in their joints. According to the tempo and the degree of collection of the pace, they develop a strong pushing and carrying power. In extended paces he will fulfil that task which is to relieve the forehand of the weight, and in collected paces he will increase the bend of the joints to increase the carrying power without, however, limiting the impulsion. This will help the forelegs to be lifted lightly off the ground, allowing them either to gain ground freely to the front or, in extreme collection, to lift the forearms nearly horizontally, hardly touching the ground with elastic steps.

Seen from the side the rider gives the impression of sitting in the centre of the horse; the outline of the horse's back undulates smoothly from the ears to the tail, which is carried proudly and naturally. The withers will be higher than the highest point of the hindquarters. When looking at the horse from the front no hindleg must ever be seen to step to the side of the track of the forelegs. The horse holds his head straight so that both ears are the same height. The neck is directed forward in prolongation of the horse's body. When ridden in the correct position the inside part of the horse, the inside shoulder and the inside hip, must be in the same line. The rider's shoulders should be seen symmetrically on either side of the horse's neck. His head appears above the horse's ears. Horse and rider seem to be one being. They form a well-balanced entity, a living work of art, showing the beauty of life, with harmony of form, and graceful movements which at the same time are both energetic and precise.

SUMMARY

This chapter on dressage repeats much that has been said in Chapter Two. It covers all the basic principles and the reader will do well to study it all again.

1. The word 'dressage' is often misunderstood. It is a French word meaning 'to train', and to train means to educate, instruct, to form through exercise, and to discipline. That is what dressage aims to do for a horse. It is not to teach him fancy tricks, as is often believed.

2. Australians first started to learn about dressage when we had to prepare a team for our first Olympic appearance at Stockholm in 1956. Many Australians were scornful of the work and claimed that our way of riding was adequate. But the classical training of the horse has lasted 2500 years, so it must be good.

3. There are different types of riding for different jobs—stockwork, racing, polo, and so on—but dressage training is the best training for the horse whatever he may be asked to do eventually.

When the Australians first went abroad and did so well they did not prove that the Australian way is the best, because they had greatly changed their style. What they did prove was that they are good horsemen and can do well and adjust themselves to any style. [They also proved that, in Franz Mairinger, they had one of the best trainers in the world.]

4. Dressage is training the horse according to the laws of nature. He is designed to survive through his speed; therefore in training we must keep him going forward. All his energies and attention should be taking him forward.

The great aim of training is to teach the horse to adjust his posture so that he is balanced under the weight of the rider. He is not designed to do this and so we must teach him to engage his hindquarters better so that his hindlegs will do their share of carrying the extra weight. If we do not teach him this his forelegs will do far too much, and so he will be likely to break down early in his life.

We feel uncomfortable with a weight on our back, and so does he. We can think out a way to adapt ourselves and so become more comfortable. He cannot reason this out, so we must think for him and guide him to adjust himself. He does this by engaging his hindquarters more. *Thus another fundamental requirement of dressage is to train the horse to carry the rider with ease, and to go forward with grace.* These principles are simply common sense and are the reason why this art has lasted for 2500 years.

5. Dressage means the horse's submission to the rider's control. To be able to obtain the horse's submission the rider must be able to sit still through his own body control. He must also control his temper. He must be fond of and interested in his pupil. Patience is a 'must' for every teacher.

6. We must be absolutely consistent in what we ask of the horse and in how we ask it. This is a matter of thinking first. How we ask, is body control, so that we can be consistent with the aids. We must also be diplomatic and never ask too much. If things go wrong we must not blame the horse. If the rider thinks and sits correctly the horse will understand and co-operate.

7. Classical riding does not include unnatural movements like cantering on three legs. These are circus tricks and, though clever, have nothing to do with dressage. In dressage the horse must maintain his natural walk, trot, and canter.

All movements asked in dressage tests are gymnastic exercises designed to improve the horse's suppleness and balance within the rider's control. This applies to work on one or two tracks, right up to piaffe and one-time flying changes.

People ask, 'Why take the horse's education so far?'. It is a challenge to trainer and rider. The rider must be in full control of his own body and also of the horse's mind and body. This is a double satisfaction.

The object of dressage is to develop to the full extent the horse's mental and physical capabilities through gymnastic schooling, and by education to get him to submit himself freely to whatever the rider asks.

If we only want to go from A to B, no matter how we or the horse do it, we need make no effort. If we want to compete at the Olympic Games we must do much work and go much further.

8. We and the horse are one-sided. We get along quite comfortably until we wish to do something special, such as walk a tightrope. Then we have to straighten up and we do it instinctively to balance. So it is with the horse. He is mostly bent to the right. Now he has to balance himself and the rider. He cannot think how to do this and so we have to teach him. We have to make him straight so that the weight is equally distributed over the four legs. He must be straight so that we can control the hindquarters, for this is the engine. When he has learnt this first lesson he is useful for most things. Also, we have the foundation and can go on to the top if we wish.

9. Gymnastic exercises make all muscles work.

If the horse is working his muscles more, or in a different manner from what he is used to, the muscles will get tired and hurt. We must keep on working if they are to get supple and develop more strength. But we must not do too much at a time or the horse will get upset from his aching muscles. To take a horse from novice to Grand Prix takes at least three years. It takes much work, but then he will last and perform for ten or fifteen years.

10. To train the horse the rider must control his own mind, his body, and his temperament. No excuses are permitted. The horse must be mentally at ease before he is receptive, and so the rider must be calm and thoughtful to gain his confidence.

Teach him only the right things and his remarkable memory will never let you down. If there are bad results the rider is entirely to blame. If the rider can cultivate this self-discipline he will be rewarded in everything he does.

Franz Mairinger says, 'Dressage means the appreciation of everything of value in life', and he makes this very clear to us—his trust in the Creator, his respect for the laws of nature, his appreciation of the personality of the horse, and his thoughtfulness for the horse. If we can follow his teaching it must surely improve our relations with our fellow men.

11. The portrait of the well-schooled horse: the reader should study every word carefully to the end of the chapter.

CHAPTER ELEVEN

JUMPING

Jumping is closely related to dressage. A jump is just a gallop stride, a bigger gallop stride. The sequence of the footfalls is clear: if he takes off with the near hind starting the stride, the off hind follows immediately, the diagonal being broken by the period in the air. The horse lands on his near fore, and the off fore takes over to complete the sequence. Then he starts again—near hind, left diagonal, off fore. You need impulsion and physical strength from the horse; and the better controlled he is, the better the jump will be.

We have seen that we cannot teach the horse to walk, trot, canter, or jump. However, we *can* teach the horse to jump when we want him to. What is the most important thing with jumping? The jump itself or the way we come towards the jump? It is the approach.

Why is the approach so important? Because when you approach the fence you give the horse the length you require. You give the horse the impulsion and the speed, and you bring him to the right take-off point. The point of take-off is the most suitable point for the horse to take off. That is very, very important. If that is the fence *there* and I want the horse to take off *here*, on which of the following horses will it be easier to achieve? On a horse that has all the gear in the world on his head? Or a horse whose rider comes round the turn smoothly, and collects, and says right away, 'Three short strides' or 'Three long strides'—and over he goes with no excitement, no resistance, no fuss, and no fight? Which horse will be the more comfortable and happy? The latter.

In competition it is often a shock to see riders having to check, check, check sharply, because the horse is tearing around too fast. How such riders ever make them jump I cannot even guess. In many cases the rider cannot hold the horse in any way, other than by all the gear on the horse's head. The riders hold, hold, hold, hold, then let the horse go. That is one way of jumping, and sometimes it is very successful too. But for only one horse out of every ten equally good showjumpers will it work. Nine will chuck it in because they don't agree with that treatment. I think that is why a lot of top-notch jumpers are not really thoroughbreds. A thoroughbred would not stand for that treatment —you cannot knock them about. A placid horse with a bit of common blood in him does not really get stirred up, but with the blood . . . *whoosh*!

In Vienna there is a saying, if something goes wrong, 'Three times cut off and still too short'.

If you reverse it you can say, 'Three times check him and still too long'. The more comfortably a horse goes and the less his resistance is, the easier it will be for the rider to bring him to the right spot for a take-off. Once the horse starts to take off, it is the finish of the rider's work up to that point.

How can the rider help the horse to clear the obstacle? In a way the rider cannot do anything about it. The rider cannot help the horse to clear the fence, but he can do a lot to make it very hard for the horse to clear the fence. The only way the rider helps is by achieving the right speed with the right impulsion and by taking off at the right spot. From there on the rider cannot help the horse at all. All the rider can do is not interfere.

How would a horse look when jumping by himself? Have you ever seen a photo of a horse jumping with his ears back and his eyes staring, his back hollow and his mouth open—if he is just jumping by himself? No. A horse that jumps freely looks happy.

We must remember one very important point: the horse always stretches his neck, and always rounds himself. That should lead us to a very simple conclusion—that the horse must have freedom of head and neck.

I mentioned earlier that it has taken the horse fifty-five million years of evolution to get to his present stage, so why should we say, 'We will jump him with a hollow back and with his head up'? Perhaps we cannot prove that a given horse would have jumped for another six to eight years if he had been jumped correctly, but we must use common sense. If we let the horse use himself in his natural way, then the horse will surely last.

I have heard the best dressage opposers, sitting watching in the stand, say, 'Why doesn't he give the horse its head?', when a horse has got into trouble at a jump. Even they realise that if only you give the horse his head he can really use himself. If you give the horse his head when you get into trouble, then why don't you give him his head *before* he gets into trouble?

How can we sit so that we do not interfere with the horse? Two, three, or four strides in front of the fence the rider should let his weight down and push the horse together from the seat. Approach is most important. We have to push on, or we have to shorten, but we shorten him without pulling from the front. That is taking impulsion away from the horse. The more impulsion we take away, the more momentum we take away, and the more the horse has to rely on his physical strength. Maintain the same stride. The change of stride should come from the weight. As the horse starts to raise himself and stretch, the rider follows with his hands, and always in the direction of the horse's mouth. If that is not enough, the body follows. Don't stand up. The angle of the rider's thigh and leg position should not alter. There is no justification for thinking that the horse must have his back free, with you standing up telling him the latest news. As you sit in the way shown in the photograph below, and go forward, you have already taken the weight off the horse's back. The importance of the

Good jumping position

position is here—the leg and thigh. As you
have the knees close on the saddle when you
are on the flat, so you have them close over
fences. You can give in the way shown in
the photograph on page 132, but most riders
are too stiff. They unbalance the horse, particularly if it is a big spread. If you stand up or hurl
yourself forward whispering in his ears, you
will upset the horse's balance.

You hear that a horse has lost its confidence
at big jumps, but it is usually the rider who has
made it impossible for the horse to retain his
balance.

The horse comes up with the neck for the
simple reason that as he comes up in front he
comes under with the quarters. It makes it
easier for the horse to take off. The leading leg
at take-off is of the utmost importance because
that leg determines how high he can jump. The
front legs are there to catch the weight. There
is no joint in the body as with the hindlegs.
Power comes from the hindquarters. The front
legs are hanging free. It is his ability to give that
makes you think he can push off with his front
legs. A stallion at the School, when resisting
being bridled, crouched down and hurled five
men in all directions when he thrust up with his
hindquarters. Power comes from the hindquarters. The position of the rider must be
such that he gives the horse a chance.

The rider must be good with his hands, letting
the horse stretch. The rider should not move.
The horse is off the ground with all four legs.
There is proof that he is off the ground before
he starts to take off. The horse lifts the forelegs
off the ground and the hind then come under
him for the thrust to jump. The sequence of
legs jumping is, therefore, near hind, off hind
(breaking diagonal), horse stretches with near
fore, lands on it, off fore takes over and completes the stride.

When I push my 72·5-kilogram body off the
ground, I must support it somewhere. If something is delicately balanced in movement, and
suddenly there comes a thrust of 72·5 kilograms,
what is supporting it? The horse is still supporting it. I have said that in a normal stride the

Action of the horse over the jump.
Franz Mairinger riding Coronation

horse is still moving forward when he is in suspension. His thrust is right underneath him and he really can assist himself over.

The rider follows through the whole period of suspension and the horse will land with the off fore, if he took off with the near fore leading. The rider should have contact with the horse. Follow him through and, as the horse starts to land, the rider takes him up. The rider takes over and from there he decides whether it is a short stride or long stride to the next jump.

As he starts to land, the hindlegs are still coming forward over the fence. If the rider has thrown everything away, when does he take over again? When the horse lands he is on one leg. If the rider takes the power away he is not happy. All power comes from the hindquarters. When he is landing we must be very careful. You establish contact as the horse lands with his first leg on the ground. Then you have him and he does not run away forward. The importance of being able to make long strides or short strides without going yank, yank at his mouth is shown where there are jumps with good combination fences. Some horses check, check, then pop over, rush again, jump, check, check, and pop. Others can flow over, lengthen stride, jump, shorten stride, and jump in complete control.

If you cannot go with him, take him up and go, you cannot jump combinations successfully. So we prepare ourselves as soon as we can for the big spreads. Sometimes he will want to stretch as far as he can. There is usually one fence where the rider has to make the horse go. The horse can only do it if he is supple.

How high must a fence be so that a horse really has to thrust himself and not step over? Higher than his legs. I have to lift the bulk of my weight to jump over a certain height myself. You hear people say, 'He is a terrific jumper, he always clears everything by a foot'. The horse should only jump as high as his body must to clear the obstacle. The horse can get his legs out of the way but not his body. The horse will jump it in that way if he is calm and judges the height and puts in only as much

effort as is necessary. The horse will probably jump eight out of ten without bringing even one rail down and will jump this year and equally well next year and will last a long time. A horse that is stirred up and preoccupied with fighting the rider has to put in a lot more effort than he normally would—physical effort, not to mention nervous strain.

The horse catches the whole weight, which is increased by the speed and the height, as he is coming down on one leg. That leg has to take the impact of the lot. The other leg comes shortly after, but the first leg has to take the lot. The less high he jumps the more the horse looks after himself. If you jump down with stiff joints, and then you jump down with swing, which will feel more comfortable to you? The jump with swing. There is much more strain if everything is jammed. The tendons have to take the lot. If the horse is supple he will swing into his landing and stride quite comfortably.

Contact should not be a jerk on landing. The horse will pull the hindlegs over the rail and roll it off if the rider takes hold with a jerk. The rider will pull his hindlegs down. So you must not interfere with the horse's movement. You can have the horse so comfortable, supple, and obedient that you can indicate the turn of direction coming over the fence, and he will immediately obey you and you can lead him over that way as he lands *if he is supple*. Some horses are supple and so when they jump they are supple, but some horses are stiff on the flat and so they stay stiff over the jumps.

As I tried to explain earlier, the horse raises his forehand and brings the hindquarters underneath, and the less the rider disturbs the horse the more he will be able to bring his quarters under him and the more the horse will be able to propel himself away.

Xenophon, who lived 2400 years ago, said, 'Jumping: if he uses his whole body going up and down it will be much safer for the rider'. Am I telling you anything different today? Much as I admire Xenophon, I don't agree with the rest of his statement about getting a green horse to jump a ditch. The rider is supposed to jump over first and encourage the horse to follow him: and if he does not go, then you get someone with a whip to urge him on from behind and make him leap over. But I admire Xenophon because of his principles and his thoughts about education, balance, and so on.

Let me finalise the section on jumping. Always start with a little. Whatever the horse does he must do easily and comfortably. You have to prepare the horse's body, and you must also educate and school his brain.

How should you go about making him strong, supple, and relaxed at the same time? There should be a little pole on the ground and you just walk him across. As the horse goes towards the pole he will probably be looking at it, then stretching his leg to step over it. Now that look is of the utmost importance. The moment he looks his mind is on the job. The horse probably thinks, 'It is just a simple pole and I will step over it'. When he does this quietly and sensibly you can add another pole, and then another, so that he may step over three poles. Don't make it three poles if he tries to jump over, or if he stops first to look. You must not rush it. The horse should walk across still having a look. Widen it and narrow it to make him think. At the same time he must make long steps and be flexible. You can make him step over a big log or a cavaletti for variety. If you watch him go over, you will see how he has to lift his front legs, stretch out and step over, and that is gymnastic exercise. It makes the horse supple and relaxed and it makes him loose in the shoulder. At the same time you must make sure that the horse's mind is on his job, and when it is he will look and be relaxed in the back. This forces him to relax the back. He cannot do it in any other way. He may knock the pole a little at first, but he will learn.

If he steps over the pole calmly we can raise it a little bit higher and so progress in the same calm way. The horse should eventually come to a 1·8-metre brick wall and should think, 'Well, I have to put something into this', and jump over.

If you bring the horse up a little at a time from kindergarten to the puissance event, that is fine; but if you rush him, because you want to win a quick blue ribbon, then you are not using common sense. Don't expect the horse to be better than you are yourself. If he cannot do it, for God's sake don't say that he is a silly stubborn fellow, but be brave enough to say instead, 'What have I done wrong?'. That must rule your whole riding career. The less you blame the horse and the more you blame yourself, the more quickly you will progress. You will look for the fool everywhere except in yourself unless you use common sense. Riding is a lot easier if you try to find an excuse.

I sometimes had trouble with the Australian Team and then I would say, 'Horses have very little brain, man supposedly has a lot. That is why the horse has to take the blame'.

As you get the obstacles a little higher the horse will jump spread fences more easily than straight fences. As you increase the height, you can increase the spread. Remember: rhythm and submission. The horse must not fight. The moment he fights, his attention and concentration are not on the job ahead of him; he is preoccupied with trying to fight the rider. The horse should take it calmly. The rider should have rhythm, and in front of the jump should sit down, collect the horse, and push him to go, thereby giving him a chance. They say that one picture is worth a thousand words. Well, I took 5000 or 6000 photos in 1956 at the Games, and I did not get one absolutely perfect picture of rider and horse. It is really hard to get a perfect position and maintain it, but we should work towards it and watch for that goal in our progress.

Is there any merit in keeping a horse down to a trot when training him to jump? Yes. Don't canter till you can push the horse on, extend and shorten him, without jumping. That enables you to place the horse. If you cannot do that before you start to jump, he will still jump if he has lots of heart, but he will go without your telling him to, and go too soon. The horse will see the first fence and off he will go. So don't jump him over obstacles at the canter before you have him under control. If the horse stretches out, it is because he wants to stretch out, and the rider should not interfere. But don't let him stretch out before he has gathered himself underneath for the take-off; then let him stretch out. Some horses have a naturally long stride, and some have a naturally short stride. Which horse will you be able to place better at the fence? A short-striding horse. Coronation was a very long horse. A long horse is hard to push together. I did not train him over jumps until I could push him on and shorten him and he was obedient.

Can you work the horse too much on cavaletti? Xenophon says 'Too much of anything is not good for man or horse'. Cavaletti is hard exercise. If you do too much he will get sour. I have never had more than four cavaletti in a row as I think it is a very hard exercise. If he should slip or make a higher step or stiffen and get himself unbalanced in a cavaletti of, say, ten, he would make a mess of it and get scared. The horse would then probably rush through. If you have only four, he can safely pop out and no harm is done. As with everything else, think it out with feeling.

Try it yourself. Do ten push-ups with a heavy bar all at once; then do four push-ups, have a rest, and do four more. You will see that it is too much and too tiring if you do it all at once when you are not fit for it.

What about the height of the cavaletti? Make it 0·3 metre high, or even 0·45 metre when the horse is ready. A distance of 1·2 metres is a safe distance for trotting over and you can alter it. You cannot have a horse that does not use his shoulder. He goes well when he relaxes, and sometimes if you ride sitting trot over the cavaletti he will go over it like a Spanish Riding School horse with a beautiful long, comfortable swing.

The jumps should be as firm and as natural as possible, and also inviting, so that the horse will want to jump. Don't put any trick jumps in. Be fair to the horse.

When putting up a course, the first thing to think about is what kind of competition it is going to be. Try to put up a course to suit the horses that are going to compete. It is easy if there is plenty of material. Don't make the course so that the horse has to be pulled around too much. The first thing to do is to make a clear line, then you can put the obstacles in.

Realise the nature of your material and the class of horse to compete. Make the fence as appealing as possible. The first fence is to get the horse going, and numbers two and three are to keep him going and to introduce him to the type of fence he is going to meet. So prepare him for the bigger fences and the combinations. Introduce a straight and a spread and then a test. The riders who have control will do well, but the others will fall down.

SUMMARY

1. The jump is a large gallop stride. The sequence of foot falls when the off fore is leading is: near hind, immediately off hind (then he crosses the jump), near fore, and off fore takes over to complete the stride. So he crosses the jump in the middle of the diagonal which is beat 2 in the canter stride.

2. The horse needs impulsion, strength, and control. He can jump, but we have to teach him to jump when we want him to, and so the approach is all-important. In the approach the rider must control impulsion and speed and he must bring him in to take off at the right spot. The right spot is the place from which it is easiest for the horse to clear the jump. The horse must be calm, with no resistance. The more comfortably he goes the easier it is for the rider to bring him to the right spot for take-off.

Many horses jump even though the rider is always check, check, checking—trying to bring him right—but this must be wasting energy and causing mental strain.

The rider cannot help the horse actually jump: he can only help by bringing him in with the right impulsion and speed to the right spot. Then all he must do is just not interfere.

3. Jumping free the horse always stretches his neck and rounds himself. Therefore he needs freedom of head and neck over the jump. If he does not have this he is forced to jump with his head high and his back hollowed. By restricting his neck the rider has made things difficult for him. He must not interfere with the reins. If in trouble, then the horse needs freedom even more—so that he can lift his hindlegs over the jump.

4. How should the rider sit so as not to interfere? In the approach he may have to push on or shorten stride, but he should shorten by letting the weight down, not by pulling at the front. This would take away impulsion and so increase the physical effort needed. Do not stand up.

The angle of the lower leg and thigh should not alter. The upper part of the body only goes forward with the horse and the hands stretch towards his mouth. The knees stay close to the saddle. When a horse loses his confidence it is usually because the rider has made the big jump impossible for him to manage.

The rider follows him through and as he begins to land he gently takes him up, ready to control the stride for the next jump. This must be done with great care because if it is rough or jerky it will cause the horse to pull his hindlegs down on to the jump.

5. When the horse lands with the first foreleg the hindlegs are still coming over the jump. They are the power, so at this point the rider must be very careful not to unbalance the horse, but he must get control of the stride, especially when riding a combination. Here the ability to lengthen or shorten the stride is essential.

6. The horse who is calm will only jump as high as is necessary. He will not be wasting physical effort nor be undergoing mental strain. The front leg on which he lands takes the lot. He must be supple for the tendons to take up the shock. Anything that is tense will be jarred far more. The less the rider interferes, the better the horse can bring his hindlegs under him and propel himself away.

7. Of course, start slowly. We have to prepare the horse physically and mentally. Walk him over poles and let him look. If he looks, his back will be relaxed. Increase to two or three. If he is quite calm, raise them slightly but do only a very little at a time. Go for a ride and give him a change. When out, you may find a small log to cross. Make the jumps very small at first and only trot him. Increase the spread with the height, but all very gradually. If you rush him you are certain to have trouble. Do not canter over jumps until you can push him on at the trot on the flat and extend and shorten the stride. If you can do this you can place him

at the jump. If you can't, he will take over and learn to rush.

8. *Cavaletti* This is hard work for the horse so do not use more than four, or at the most six, in a row. The height should be 0·3 to 0·45 metre. A distance of 1·2 metres apart suits most horses.

Never have two horses on a row of cavaletti at once.

9. The jumps must be firm, well filled in, and inviting.

When building a course, first make a clear line where the horse must go, then build the obstacles. Do not make a course where the horse has to be pulled around.

The first fence should be planned to get him going, the second and third to keep him going. Then come the bigger fences and spreads.

CHAPTER TWELVE

COMBINED TRAINING

'Combined training', as the words suggest, combines the training of a horse on the flat (dressage), over jumps (Olympic jumping), and in cross-country. Needless to say, such a horse and rider need very careful selection and a lot of well-planned schooling should they wish to excel in international competition. In such competition the combined training takes the form of a three-day event—so called because the event goes on for three days and consists of the dressage test on the first day, a speed and endurance test on the second day, and show-jumping on the third day.

On the Continent this type of competition is known as 'military', because originally it was a competition for mounted officers only. The idea was to test the officer and his horse to see whether the rider had his mount under control and was able to carry out all movements involved when on parade—represented today by the dressage test of the first day. The next day the same horse and rider were ordered to deliver an urgent message to the commanding officer of another troop. This message was vital and it had to reach its destination—whether it got there depended on the quality of the horse, its training, and the courage and judgment of the rider to use the horse's capabilities to the

best advantage. Today this is the speed and endurance test of the second day.

In the past things would probably have happened in the following way. An officer would receive his orders and the message, and set off at a brisk trot towards his destination—at a trot for the simple reason that he had to travel about 35 kilometres and might be forced to call upon the horse's speed during his trip. So in order to save the horse's strength he started at a rather comfortable trot on his all-important task. This is represented in the three-day event as Phase A: Roads and Tracks. Trotting along, the officer was spotted by an enemy patrol, so then he had to ride for his life. And ride he did, jumping every obstacle in his way until he succeeded in shaking off his pursuer. He slowed down and continued to trot along the road. The fast gallop is today Phase B: Steeplechase, followed by Phase C: Roads and Tracks. For the officer the day was not yet over. Another enemy patrol tried to intercept him and he had to cut across country to get away from them. Again he had to call upon the horse's speed and his own judgment. He had to find the shortest way. Time was precious and could not be wasted by skirting around obstacles. He had to jump them. Finally he succeeded in slipping through their lines and, approaching his destination, eased up and let the horse canter along. He delivered his message and after the hectic ride could now relax. The ride across country is Phase D: Cross Country, followed by Phase E: Run In, which is the completion of the second day's test of speed and endurance. (Phase E was dropped after Rome 1960.) Naturally, the same horse and rider had to be able to continue their services the next day. To prove their ability to do just that we have the showjumping on the third day as the final phase of the three-day event.

As I have explained, in days gone by there was a very good reason for this type of competition but why do we still have a competition whose fundamental idea is to test a cavalry officer and his horse? Well, on the Continent this type of competition is known as 'The Crowning of Horsemanship'. There is no other horse sport where horse and rider must combine such a lot of qualities to be able to compete — let alone win. So long as there are riders daring enough to gallop fast over solid obstacles and enjoy it, and who at the same time are prepared to work hard enough to get the horse and themselves fit, the three-day event will survive. Mounted troops or no mounted troops, the spirit of a true horseman will never change.

The special challenge in this event is the fact that the rider must be a good all-rounder. To be a specialist in one of the three sections is insufficient. The three-day event calls for a real horse and a real rider.

For a clearer understanding of what horse and rider have to do, I will explain in more detail.

First Day — Dressage

This is carried out in an arena 20 by 60 metres. It is a test of medium difficulty to show how well the horse is under the rider's control; how supple and balanced, how obedient and submissive the horse is; and to evaluate the efficiency and general appearance of the rider. As a rule it is judged by three judges who award marks for approximately twenty col-

In the dressage arena

lective movements. The good marks gained are subtracted from the possible total and converted into penalty marks. The lowest penalty score on the first day is the best.

Second Day — Speed and Endurance Test

Before the start of the competition the riders are allowed to inspect the course, but the horse must not be brought near any obstacle. This would be penalised with elimination. A timetable is set for all competitors, fixing all starting and finishing times at the different phases.

Phase A: Roads and Tracks This is a distance of about 6·5 kilometres at a speed of 262 metres per minute. No bonus points can be gained for going faster, but penalties are incurred for going slower. The same applies for Phases C and E.

Phase B: Steeplechase This follows straight after the completion of the first phase. It is about 3 kilometres, at a speed of 656 metres per minute with ten to twelve obstacles. Brush fences have a maximum height of 1·37 metres, solid obstacles 1·22 metres, and water jumps are up to 3·9 metres wide. For going faster than the speed required, bonus points can be gained, up to a maximum speed of 755 metres per minute. Taking longer than the time required will incur penalty points.

Phase C: Roads and Tracks   This goes straight on from the steeplechase, over a distance of about 16 kilometres, at a speed of 262 metres a minute.

Phase D: Cross Country   This is about 8 kilometres at a speed of 492 metres per minute. Bonus points can be gained for a faster pace, up to a maximum speed of 624 metres per minute. The maximum number of obstacles to be cleared is thirty-five, with a maximum height of 1·22 metres and a maximum spread of 2·29 metres. Open ditches or water jumps are up to 3·96 metres wide. All obstacles are to resemble natural objects, as far as possible.

Phase E: Run In   About 1·6 kilometres distance, with a speed of 360 metres per minute.

Besides penalties for going slower than the minimum speed required, penalties are incurred for refusals—twenty points for the first, forty for the second, eighty for the third. A fourth refusal would mean elimination. Fall of horse or rider is penalised with sixty points and after the third fall over the whole course the rider must retire.

Third Day—Jumping Contest

This is over about twelve obstacles. The maximum height is 1·22 metres and maximum spread 1·98 metres, with a speed of 440 metres per minute. No bonus points are gained for going faster but penalties for a slower pace can be incurred, plus a penalty of ten points for every refusal and every rail knocked down.

The final score is obtained by adding up all penalty points from all phases of the three days and subtracting the bonuses. If the score is minus, the lowest score is the winner. If there is a plus score (which does not happen often), the highest score is the winner.

If you try to visualise this competition, I think you will agree with me that it needs a real horse and a real horseman. Now the best horseman is no good without a good horse, and that leads us to consider the qualities of the horse.

The horse must be fast—the faster the better —to be able to gain bonus points in Phases B and D. He must be able to gallop long distances; he must have stamina. He should be a free mover, be able to jump, be bold, and have plenty of personality for the dressage. To sum it up—a horse with speed, stamina, jumping ability, and boldness, a free mover with personality. Very simple! We are looking for the ideal horse—a horse that won't run last in a 6·5-kilometre steeplechase, that can win the Champion Hack at Sydney Royal Easter Show, that is a medium-class dressage competitor, and a B-grade showjumper. All this, mind you, more or less in one day! And for him to be able to compete we must add another virtue: he must have an outstandingly good temperament. Now we really are up against some odds. We are looking for the perfect horse, the horse every horseman has looked for all his life. But we never find him because perfection does not exist.

Seeing that we won't get anywhere like this, let's regroup the necessary qualifications according to importance. Experience shows that proper and well-planned schooling can improve the whole performance of the horse and so overcome shortcomings in his conformation. What cannot be improved on are his breeding, his substance, and his stamina. A horse without these three points is a waste of time and money.

From these points I put his boldness first. He must have the heart to have a go at anything, no matter how big and wide it might be or how awkward it might look. However beautiful he might be, if he is chicken-hearted he won't get around the cross country on the second day. His breeding will secure us speed, without which there can be no bonus points. His substance will help us to keep him sound and will also have some bearing on his stamina. Stamina is so important because he must be able to keep going over a distance of up to 35 kilometres. These three points are a must.

From there on we have to judge the horse and look for the good points first. What is the most important good point? Free movement. The more freely a horse can move the easier he will be to school. Look at his good points and then look for his bad points, and then ask yourself the question, 'Can he still do the job or are the weak points such that he can't?'. In seventy-five out of a hundred cases you will tell yourself that he can still do the job. It would lead us too far off the track to list all the good and weak points and find out which good points cancel out which weak points. This alone would fill a book. My advice is to see the horse in action and see whether he has rhythm and suppleness, whether he is loose.

Temperament should have been mentioned before, but I have not done so. Some might argue about it and say, 'What's the good of the best horse if he does not settle down? He is good for nothing'. And I fully agree. I fully realise the importance of a good temperament in the horse, but I also fully realise that most bad-tempered horses are made and not born.

I mentioned personality earlier on, but I think we can dismiss that, because I have not yet seen a bold horse without personality. Intelligence is another point to be mentioned, but, as with temperament, stupid horses are made and not born. Exception proves the rule of course.

What breeding should the horse have? After what I have said there should be no need to say it at all but to make sure: for cross-country competition it should be a thoroughbred, preferably from a bloodline of stayers. If for some reason there is no thoroughbred to be found anywhere and you must settle for mixed blood, then Anglo-Arab will do—but nothing else. Most definitely no cold-blooded horses. The speed of the horse decreases as the amount of cold blood increases.

When I say, 'a thoroughbred and nothing else for cross country', I most definitely do not mean to say that another breed cannot do the job. For instance, the gold-medal winner in the 1956 Olympics—the Swedish horse Illuster—and the winner of the silver medal—the German horse Trux von Kamax—were both part-bred horses. What I want to point out is that for cross-country work a well-schooled part-bred horse won't be able to win against an equally well-schooled thoroughbred, simply because of the fact that the thoroughbred has a greater top speed. By comparison, it would be like me taking my little Austin A50 and trying to get to Melbourne as quickly as somebody driving an Aston Martin. He would cruise at 120 kilometres an hour while I would be flat out trying to get 120 kilometres downhill. Well, I think I would get there, but if I wanted to drive home again I would have to install another motor because I would have completely ruined the first one by driving at top speed all the time. The Aston Martin on the other hand would turn around and cruise home, again at 120 kilometres an hour. And why not? Its top speed is over 220 kilometres an hour. The Aston Martin is the thoroughbred, and my little A50 is everything else. Any horse can get around somehow, but 'somehow' is not good enough. We want to win, we need the speed, and therefore we must have a thoroughbred. He should be a horse between 16 and 16·2 hands. Smaller horses may feel the weight over the distance—they have to carry around 75 kilograms. Bigger horses are inclined to lose their agility and are hard to keep on their feet. I have nothing against mares but prefer a gelding and would like a stallion. Mares have to be handled with a bit more diplomacy. One can rough up a boy if necessary, but a girl!

Where do we find this type of horse? It's simple enough—on the thoroughbred stud. This is the ideal solution, but will involve big expense. As a rule one buys the blood of the yearling's ancestors and that costs a lot of money. The next place to look is the racetrack. Many horses that are taken into training are found to be too slow to win at a metropolitan meeting and are then sold at a reasonable price. This is just the horse to look for. He is still faster than any other part-bred horse, and that is exactly what you need. You want to win and not be listed under, 'Amongst the other starters were . . .'.

142

Unfortunately, horses are raced as two-year-olds. Now, nobody can tell me that a two-year-old is fully grown and developed. The stress of hard work and the excitement of the racetrack take their toll on an underdeveloped body and mind. The horses get nervous and excitable, hard to manage, break down, and are turned out as 'no goods'. It is a pity that the horses are not kept until they are fully three years old, and then raced. Fewer horses would break down and get rattled, more horses would come good, less money would be wasted, more money would be won. Last, but not least, we would have a lot more horses to choose from for the Olympic Three-Day Event. Well, maybe one of these days!

I have been told that on some of the big stations in Queensland hundreds of thoroughbreds are running wild, but I have not seen them yet. Perhaps a Queenslander may get the idea and truck a load of them to the Royal Easter Show. If the horses are as good as I have been told, they will sell like hot cakes.

Wherever you get the horse from, make sure that he is sound. A horse that has broken down once will break down again. Bear in mind that a major part of the success lies in the fitness of the horse and that requires a lot of work. If the horse is not truly sound you will never get him to the post, and a lot of work has been done for nothing. No matter how good the horse may be in himself as a type, his future will rest upon his training.

The schooling the horse receives for a particular job will determine his success, and also how long he will last in his career. As we have seen, a thoroughbred is essential for three-day eventing, but we must be clear about the fact that a thoroughbred needs more care, more knowledge, and better handling from the rider. They have more personality than any other breed, with the exception of the Arabs. They are more sensitive and more intelligent, and therefore have to be treated accordingly.

The foundation of all success is a proper grounding in the work on the flat. This means that the horse must be well balanced under the rider, well educated, supple, and obedient. In other words, the rider must have complete control over the horse's energy. This will place the horse's tremendous power at the rider's disposal. This in itself is the essence of schooling, our goal. Major Cornel von Feurchtersleben wrote an article published in the German *Sankt Georg Almanach 1959* in which he discussed the Olympic prospects of the Australians in Rome. Among a lot of other things he said that the E.F.A. had decided to concentrate its preparation on the three-day event only, and that to school the team the E.F.A. had employed an Austrian from the Spanish Riding School. The impression given was that one can get the highest degree of knowledge about three-day eventing from the Spanish Riding School in Vienna.

The results from Rome seem to show that the Spanish Riding School does know more about three-day eventing than any other school. To be honest, I must say that the Spanish Riding School does concentrate on classical high school only and does not teach anything about the details of a cross-country ride. But they do teach how to get a horse supple, balanced, and obedient; how to educate the horse, to make him willingly submit himself to carry out whatever the rider might see fit to ask him to do. It is nothing else but systematic development of the horse's physical and mental powers.

Whether the rider wants to concentrate on high school as the Spanish Riding School does or on three-day eventing, the foundation should be the same. And with that foundation success will come. It is nothing but common sense, and a horse prepared in such a way will be a reliable instrument in the hands of a skilled rider. No matter in what sort of competition the rider should choose to participate, a rider who can use the horse's power at his pleasure will be able to concentrate all his attention entirely on his job. He will be able to take advantage of every little short cut, he can choose his approach and take-off precisely. He can do so because he does not have to do battle with the horse. What is right for the rider is equally right for the horse. The horse, too, can concentrate on what he is doing if he is not employed in a tug-of-war with the rider. Such a combination will also be a safe one. They can rely on their skill, developed through proper schooling, and therefore will have the luck.

Hand-in-hand with the horse's schooling on the flat goes the preparation for his cross-country work. To start with, his flat work is carried into the open. Riding across the country will help to balance the horse and his suppleness will be improved by going up and down hills, through gullies and water, down little slides, and so on. This will improve him all round and also sharpen his senses; he will learn to look after himself. This is very necessary, because later on in the heat of the battle the rider has no time to look out for every little stick or hole in the ground. The horse's natural instinct will make him avoid such things if his mind is not preoccupied with fighting the rider. As the horse learns to handle himself on all kinds of terrain he can slowly be introduced to hopping over little natural obstacles—logs, little ditches, and the like. By slowly increasing the demands, the horse will learn to take everything in his stride. There is really nothing to it.

The horse must never rush at his fences. If he should do so, and the rider cannot stop him, it simply means that the horse lacks education. In that case forget the jumping for a while and do more schooling on the flat until the horse does not dictate the speed but submits himself to the rider's orders. That in itself is a very important fact. The horse must not go faster or slower than the rider wants him to go. Of course to be able to achieve this, the rider himself must know how fast he wants to go, otherwise he won't even notice that the horse is choosing his own speed.

If you let a child do as it pleases for a while and then try to stop it, the child will resent it, because it cannot understand why suddenly it isn't allowed to do what it has done just a minute ago. Your horse won't understand you either if you suddenly want to make him go

slower because you know that there is a big drop on the other side of the obstacle, and that if you keep up that speed there will be trouble brewing on the other side. The rider tries to pull the horse up, and the horse thinks, 'What's got into you? Let go of my head!', and goes a bit faster in an attempt to get away from the pull. With every stride the distance decreases, the rider's desperation increases, and he pulls a bit harder. Suddenly the horse wakes up and thinks that he should not jump at all because the rider is pulling so hard, and obligingly he stops. The rider becomes airborne and when he hits the ground on the other side he realises how big the drop really was, and then he scrambles back into the saddle and abuses the horse. He may even use the whip to punish the horse. For what?

Now this little episode is not as far-fetched as you might think. It, or something similar to it, happens over and over again. Why? Only because the rider did not educate the horse to submit himself freely to the rider's will. As mentioned earlier, a properly schooled combination will also be a safe one.

A disagreement between horse and rider does not necessarily always result in a fall that may bring bodily harm to both; but even if it only causes a rail to be knocked down, or something like that, it means losing points, and a loss of points can mean the difference between winning and losing.

To determine the horse's speed is only one little part of schooling, but it is of the utmost importance.

Before we go any further, let me warn you *never* to overface your horse. Do not get impatient. The slow process is the fast one in this case. If you ask too much too soon you will encounter resistance, and you may have to retard your whole programme of schooling.

As you go along with your programme and the horse comes along nicely you must think of competition. No horse can be fully schooled on the home ground. Competition forms an important part of his training. Whether preparing for the show, or just working, do not

Diagram 19: A horse refusing to jump

forget that the horse is not a machine. Like you, he gets tired. The safest way of keeping a horse on his feet is to finish working him while he is still fresh and eager to go. This is not only the best safeguard against breaking down; it also keeps the horse in good spirit. The horse should enjoy the work as much as the rider, and he will if the rider does not forget the simple fact that the horse is the one who does the running. Whatever you do, start with just a little and increase your demands only by degrees. With competition as with everything else, we proceed slowly.

No rider in his right mind would choose a three-day event as the first start for his horse. He would look for the easiest competition he could find and he would not try to win at the first time out. The first competition should be used to sound out the horse under strange con-

ditions, to discover the shortcomings in your work. The dressage results will yield a mine of information, and the same applies to the cross-country ride and the showjumping. You will see what kind of fences he dislikes and, above all, when it is over you will know how he has stood up to the little competition. Was he fit enough or wasn't he? For the competition as for ordinary work, he must finish fresh. If he is tired you know that next time you must give him more work beforehand. Not only will you find out a lot about his schooling and condition, you will also see how he loads and travels. Did he get excited? Did he eat and drink? Will he need bandages or bellboots, studs, and so on? All these little details have to be thought out. They are the facts. It is a simple matter to arrive at the logical conclusion and act accordingly.

If, for example, the horse did not take the ditch too well, then find a ditch and school him over it to get him used to ditches and give him confidence. There is one thing that the rider must never do. He must never blame the horse for whatever may have gone wrong. The horse does not know what he must be able to perform, but the rider does. Instead of abusing the horse, think matters over and go to work on it. Your performance is bound to improve from one competition to the next until you have a horse that is well schooled, experienced, and full of confidence.

The horse comes first, the blue ribbon next. Do not ride the horse all out to win if he is not ready for it, because in the long run you will lose much more than you can win that day. But when you know and are sure within yourself that the horse has had the necessary preparation, and not before, that is the day you have been waiting and working for. 'Come on, fellow, let's show them what we can do!' How the horse performs, looks, and behaves is the rider's mirror. The horse will be as good as his rider and not a jot better.

The training of the rider is of course of major importance. The more he knows himself the better use he can make of his horse's capabilities. Without that training, even with the best intentions he will have to travel the hard road of trial and error. It can be a very frustrating and disheartening affair. Yet it is just plain common sense. I could not teach anybody how to fly an aeroplane because I cannot fly myself. If a rider does not know the principles involved in training a horse, there is not much hope. Like everything else in life, it is the approach, the mental approach, to the subject at hand that will determine how matters will be dealt with. In dealing with the horse this mental approach will grow in importance because we are dealing with something alive, something possessing a certain amount of intelligence of its own. And last, but most certainly not least, it possesses tremendous strength to fight us.

No matter what kind of sport one wants to be good at, one has to train the body, adopt certain positions or carry out certain movements which are necessary for what one wants to do. For example, if one wants to be a good golf player one cannot just go out and hit the ball anyhow. Well, one can, but such a player will never amount to anything.

Unfortunately, with riding, people very seldom understand and accept these facts, probably because we can blame the horse for our failure—whereas we cannot blame the golf ball for not going in the right direction.

In summing up we come to the conclusion that the development of a firm and independent seat will be the all-important part of the rider's training. Without a properly developed control of mind and body the rider will have no hope of controlling the horse's mental and physical powers in an easy and comfortable way. The best way to develop this independent seat is to ride without stirrups. With the stirrups off the rider is forced to let his weight down and really to sit in the saddle. Naturally it will be uncomfortable and it may be painful at the start, but it is like taking an ill-tasting medicine in order to get rid of an ailment.

On the whole the rider's schooling should be advanced slowly, just like the horse's schooling, because the rider can be overfaced just as a horse can. A schooled horse will make the schooling of the rider very much simpler. The schooled and well-educated horse will give the rider the feeling he needs. With the aid of the instructor the rider will learn to feel whether the horse is right or wrong. Having to school the rider and the horse at the same time requires an instructor who has been blessed with endless patience. Proper, planned schooling on the flat, over jumps, and in the open—including the judgment of speed—will soon have the rider prepared to take part in small competitions.

As with the horse so with the rider; it is not enough to be good on the home ground. Both must be good when the pressure is on. Experience will get rid of nervousness. Excitement will build up confidence, and in the long run enable the rider to ride with cool-headed

First Australian Olympic Team, 1956: Gwen Stead (groom), Bert Jacobs, David Wood, Ern Barker

deliberation and determination. The way to international competition is paved with hard work, but such is life. There is nothing for nothing.

The participation of an Australian equestrian team at the Olympic Games in Stockholm in 1956 was certainly the turning point for the equestrian sport in Australia. When I think back and recall my impressions at the first show I saw in Australia, and then confront this impression with the fact that eight years later Australia was able to capture two gold and one silver medal at the Games in Rome, I can hardly believe it myself.

When I arrived with the first team in England I met some Continental riders I knew. They all agreed on one thing—that I was mad to take on a job which was bound to end in failure. Their argument was that it would be impossible to pick up the experience of the Continental riders, accumulated by generations of riders. Quite a point! But the Australian riders proved them wrong. The success of the team, which finished fourth as a team out of eighteen competing nations, certainly got the ball rolling after their return. Most important of all was the introduction of three-day events in Australia.

The team that competed in Stockholm started work completely from scratch, without any previous experience at all. Mind you, they were all good horsemen; they could and would ride anything, and stay on somehow. But 'somehow' was not good enough for the Olympics, and so the poor fellows sometimes had to go through hard times. But they went through it cheerfully and the result in Stockholm was certainly a well-earned reward.

Short of competitive experience as we were, we had other problems. The outbreak of a respiratory epidemic which swept through the Continent and England, made it impossible for us to compete at the Harewood Three Day Horse Trials. This left only the Badminton Three Day Event in 1956 to gain experience for the great task ahead in Stockholm. Badminton was taken gently in order to save the horses for Stockholm, and we all got through it without any mishap.

The horses were bought in England and, with the exception of Radar, were not thoroughbreds. To buy a top-class thoroughbred like Countryman, Wild Venture, or Kilbarry (the three horses in the English team) would have been utterly impossible—certainly 5 minutes before the Games. As the situation was, with only three horses allowed to take part in each team, we had some hope of being in the money as a team if we got through clear the second day. We nearly succeeded too. One unlucky fall robbed us of a medal. We finished forty-seven points behind Canada, the winner of the bronze medal. Our team was faced with the biggest course they had ever seen, and an unlucky draw (we had number one), and little competitive experience. I am sure that their will to get around was governed by their determination not to let Australia down. Their effort and achievement has never received the credit it deserved, but they certainly paved the way for the outstanding success of the team in Rome and I salute David Wood (Captain), Ernie Barker, W. Thompson, and Brian Crago, the riders in Stockholm.

In Rome, with altered rules, four riders could take part in every team and the best of three were counted. Rome had to be looked at from a different point of view altogether. I was anticipating that, because every team had one spare rider, everybody would ride a lot faster than they did in Stockholm. This surely called for thoroughbreds. Three-day events were in the meantime a standard fixture in Australia,

giving horse and rider the chance to gain experience in that particular field of horsemanship. It also made the selection of horse and rider much easier than it had been before Stockholm, because now horse and rider more or less selected themselves with the results they had on the board.

When eight horses and five riders left for England to undergo the final preparations I felt much more confident than when going to Stockholm. The first attempt had been a gamble, but now we were starting with a fairly good foundation.

As with the first team, we were again stationed at Aldershot and started our preparation for the major competition before Rome with the Badminton Three Day Event. The result must have come as a shock to many Continental riders. Bill Roycroft, riding Our Solo, was first, Laurie Morgan with Salad Days second, Neale Lavis on Mirrabooka fourth, John Kelly on Adlai eighth, and Brian Crago on Toscanella ninth. This result was just what we needed. It boosted confidence and gave a bright outlook for the future. It also showed clearly where we had to try and improve our performance, and try we did. After a spell in the paddock the horses were brought back into work and slowly worked up into their peak condition for Rome. As much as I would have liked to spend more time in the dressage ring to polish up on the finer points, condition had absolute priority and the work in the ring was reduced to a minimum. Naturally we had our little ups and downs as we went along, but finally arrived safely in Rome. Faced with the fact that the three-day event horses were 50 kilometres away from the Olympic Village where the riders stayed, we were forced to travel 200 kilometres every day in order to work the horses twice daily. The riders had to go back for their breakfast and lunch—200 kilometres through the traffic of Rome every day! That alone could wreck a fellow's nerves; it was like a madhouse.

The cross-country course was not as big as the one at Stockholm, but formidable just the same. Most of the fences were well built and must have been a joy to ride over. Why the rest of it was left flimsy and uninspiring I could not understand. Nor could I understand why the most difficult combination of fences was left as thirty-two, thirty-three, and thirty-four. A tired horse was faced with a practically impossible task. A lot of horses fell there, and this could have been avoided if the fences had been earlier in the course. The standard of the dressage phase was not as good as it had been in Stockholm, nor was the performance in the cross-country. Quite a number of horses were unfit for such a test and consequently came to grief during the cross-country. But not only were some horses unfit; some of the riders were not in condition to last through the second day. It was a most disappointing sight to see the poor horses labouring along with exhausted riders on their backs.

Contrary to my anticipation, riders did not go as fast as one could have expected under the changed rules. Some did go faster. Perhaps the rest did not do so because their horses were not thoroughbreds.

The jumping on the third day was not too difficult. The course was very good but unfortunately had two compulsory turning points which I think were unnecessary. There was no reason to trap a rider after he had successfully negotiated the cross-country course on the second day. It does not conform with the original idea either — to test whether the horse is still fit enough to carry on, rather than to trap purposely. That only serves to spoil the happiness of a great finish.

Our starting order was:

Bill Roycroft   — No. 1
Neale Lavis   — No. 2
Brian Crago   — No. 3
Laurie Morgan (Captain) — last

The performance in the dressage was satisfactory but not outstanding. Compared with some of the other performances I feel we could have been marked a bit better but, as I mentioned earlier, some of the points were knowingly sacrificed during the training period in exchange for the fitness of the horses. The scores were as follows:

	Penalties
Laurie Morgan and Salad Days	—106
Bill Roycroft and Our Solo	—114
Neale Lavis and Mirrabooka	—124
Brian Crago and Sabre	—137

In the cross-country on the next day Bill and Our Solo went magnificently, and very fast, until fence thirty-one, where disaster struck. Bill, in an attempt to avoid an official who ran across the track, had to swerve and so came too close to the fence. Our Solo hit the rail hard and broke it (one of the flimsy ones), landed in a hole on the other side, and came down heavily. Our Solo cleared out towards home, trotting leisurely just about 5 metres in front of me, until at the gate somebody stopped him (in the excitement I did not realise who it was) and took him back to Bill who remounted and finished his round. Bill was taken to hospital with a broken collarbone and concussion. The start did not look too good. Neale, next to go, returned a fast clear round and prospects looked a bit better. Brian and Sabre went very fast and clear, with maximum bonus points, but Sabre pulled the ligaments in his fetlock and was very lame when he returned to the stables. The situation looked very grim.

Laurie Morgan and Salad Days were last to go, and did they go! They gained the maximum bonus points and the fastest round of the day. With the exception of Sabre, who could not be started the next day, the horses were sound, but Bill was in hospital and that left us with only two horses — which would have meant the elimination of the team. Bill, knowing the situation, said that he would ride and I do not think that any doctor could have held him in the hospital. Sabre's injury was a cruel blow for Brian but he took it like a real sportsman.

The final day's jumping took place on Rome's beautiful international jumping ground, the Piazza di Siena, and was watched by a closely packed audience. Our Solo was the first of our horses to go. He had a clear round, excellently ridden by Bill in spite of his broken collarbone and heavy fall the day before. Neale and

Australian Olympic Team, Rome, 1960: Laurie Morgan, John Kelly, Neale Lavis, Bill Roycroft, Brian Crago

Mirrabooka did the same—a clear round, very calmly and exactly ridden. Now it was up to Laurie Morgan and Salad Days to secure two gold medals (his own medal as the individual winner and, as the third member of the team, the medal for the team). Laurie's nerves must have been taut, but he came home and brought everything with him. Despite having a rail down and some time faults the final result for Laurie was excellent.

Final Individual Score
  Laurie Morgan
      1st—gold medal +7 min. 15 sec.
  Neale Lavis
      2nd—silver medal −16 min. 50 sec.
  A. Buhler
      3rd—bronze medal −51 min. 21 sec.

Final Team Score
  Australia
      1st—gold medal −128 min. 18 sec.
  Switzerland
      2nd—silver medal −386 min. 2 sec.
  France
      3rd—bronze medal −515 min. 71 sec.

When the Australian flags were hoisted it was one of the greatest moments of my life, probably the greatest day for the riders, and certainly a great day for all Australians.

The tragedy of the great day, which was felt so deeply by everyone there, was that Mr Sam Horden could not be with us to share the triumph of the team. He, as the President of the E.F.A., had been the driving force behind us all, but fate deprived him of seeing the fruit of his work—he died in a car accident shortly before the Games.

The first team that had competed so honourably in Stockholm paved the way for the success and triumph of the second team in Rome. The second team—led by Laurie Morgan, whose determination inspired every-body—set a standard for the future that every coming team will have to live up to.

When I say, 'I salute the second team (Laurie Morgan, Bill Roycroft, Brian Crago, Neale Lavis, and John Kelly) for their mighty effort', I hope I can say the same to the teams that follow.

Good luck to you all.

SUMMARY

1. The three-day event was originally planned to assist the training of cavalry officers and their mounts. The phases could be typical of a hazardous ride through enemy country with an urgent message.

2. There is no other horse sport where horse and rider must combine so many qualities before they can hope to compete. The event calls for a real horse and a real rider.

A full description of the phases of the event follows.

3. To become a successful three-day eventer the horse needs speed, stamina, jumping ability, boldness, free movement, and personality. He also needs a good temperament. All this sounds like the perfect horse, and where can we find such a horse?

Proper and well-planned schooling can improve many things about the not-so-ideal horse, but to be worth working on he must have boldness (so that he is game to tackle anything), breeding (for speed), and substance (to keep him sound). These three qualities are essential.

4. In judging the horse, look for the good things, then the bad things. Then you must decide which will dominate over which.

What about the breeding? To gain full bonus points in the steeplechase and cross country he must be a thoroughbred. The well-trained cross-bred horse can do very well and may beat many thoroughbreds, but the thoroughbred who is equally well trained will always win. You can get this horse from a stud or from the race-track. Unfortunately the latter may suffer ill-effects from having been raced as a two-year-old. Wherever he comes from, your horse must be sound. He has to do a lot of hard work to become fit. All your time will be wasted if this is going to break him down.

5. If you choose a thoroughbred you must remember that he will take more care, more skilful handling, than another horse. He is more sensitive and intelligent, and must be treated accordingly. The rider must have complete control over the horse, and he must educate the horse to make him submit himself willingly to whatever the rider asks him to do. If the rider can use the horse's power at his pleasure

151

he must be successful in his part of the job because he does not have to fight with the horse. The horse, too, is confident, and so the pair can rely on their skill and do their best.

6. The training of the rider, both mentally and physically, is equally important. The more knowledge and skill he has, the better he will train his horse. The horse's tremendous strength to fight must be overcome by skilfully executed education.

The rider must also train his body for it must be as fit as the horse's. Properly planned activity for horse and rider on the flat, over jumps, and in the open will soon have them ready for small competitions. To be good at home is not enough. Competition experience is essential for both.

7. The horse should never rush his jumps. If he does, he needs further education on the flat. At no time should he go more quickly or more slowly than the rider wishes.

Take the training slowly and you will strike no resistance. Never overface him and he will come along nicely. If you do not tire him he will enjoy the work. Always remember that the horse is the one that does the running.

Soon you will take him for an easy competition and here you will discover how your work is progressing. The dressage remarks will help you. How did he shape up in the cross country? Was he fit? What types of jumps worried him? And so on. Take note of every detail to help your further schooling. The horse comes first, the blue ribbon second. It will be some time before you ride him flat out to win. When you feel that he is ready—and not before—give it a go.

8. The rest of this chapter tells the story of the first Australian teams to compete in Olympic Three Day Events.

CHAPTER THIRTEEN

THE YOUNG HORSE

Everything I have said earlier goes for a young horse also, but naturally you have to be much more generous with a young horse.

In the Spanish Riding School they always watch a young horse to see what his natural capabilities are, and then they develop them. It is better to break your horse in at three years, rather than at two years. The Lippizaners are broken in at four years.

I will tell you what *I* do with a young horse. Other people have different methods. I lunge the young horse with a saddle and bridle on, and a cavesson with three rings (one ring in the centre of the nose, and one on either side). The reins should be loose for the first few days.

Some people mouth their horses, but I don't, because if you put the horse in a yard with a bit in his mouth he will discover how to get behind the bit, and will run around that way, and that is useless.

I put the bit on for lunging. Later I put on side reins, then gradually shorten them, two holes at a time, until finally the neck is rounded and the horse is on the bit.

You may have to use an assistant to lead the horse out when you first start lunging. During the first week I don't ask anything. I let the horse walk, trot, or canter as he wishes. During the second week the horse can trot around, and you can push him on with the whip from behind, but don't let him get frightened of the whip.

Continue lunging the horse for six to twelve weeks, depending on the horse. After that you can ride him and only the exception will buck. By then the horse will trust you and not try to get rid of you. If you have his confidence the other schooling will go much better, and the horse won't get scared and silly. If the horse is quiet and full of confidence you will have a good foundation to work on.

The first time I ride, I ride the horse for 5 minutes. Gradually I extend this until I am riding him for 10, then 15 minutes. For the first four weeks I ride the horse for only a short time. Remember that the horse has to get used to your weight, otherwise he will get stiff. Take him on carefully and don't let him get tired.

The first thing the young horse must do is to go forward. Remember that he doesn't have a clue as to what he should do, so be careful. And be as gentle as possible with your hands. Try to go forward on a straight line. It is a great advantage to have a large paddock where the horse can go forward without continually being pulled up or having to turn corners. If he will

Andrew Hoy and Davey receiving the Franz Mairinger Memorial Trophy from Mrs Franz Mairinger, Melbourne Three Day Event, 1981

154

go straight forward that is all you want. Sit still and be comfortable; if you bounce about he will try to get rid of you.

Don't ride a young horse at the sitting trot for at least three months, as he will only get sore and his back will stiffen up. If the back gets stiff, the horse will only use his legs and the movement will not go through the back. You will spoil his natural impulsion and beauty. It is the worst thing you can do. The time spent training a young horse the right way will repay you later on.

Your horse should not be scared of the whip. I bundle up the lash and pat the horse all over with it. Swing your whip so that it just touches him, and if he is not active enough just drop the whip on his hindquarters. At the moment he drops the bit you must push him forward. Get him on the bit, not behind the bit.

Work out a programme for a young horse. Don't ride him too long because he will get tired and start to resist. Even when he is stronger, never work him for more than an hour. It is a good idea to work for half an hour in the morning and half an hour in the evening. Better still, work him 20 minutes at a time, three times a day.

Never ask too much at first. It is always better to work the horse the next day when you have left a good impression the day before. Make the horse go forward and stop, and go on the line you want him to.

When you teach him to turn, make a large turn at first. Your turns will be rough but you can polish them up afterwards. Have a lot of patience and be generous. If you have patience you cannot go wrong. You cannot force muscles to develop—you have to work them and develop them gradually. Then, when they are ready, you can go ahead.

There is an old saying, 'No walk, no canter', because there is no free stride. If I buy a horse that has already been broken in, I first look at the movement and then I look at his neck. The better the horse's natural movement is, the better he will be later on. If there is nothing there you cannot improve it.

Don't jump the horse too early, and never ask more than the horse is ready for. If the horse can jump 0·914 metre, attempt a jump of only 0·9 metre; and when the horse can jump that properly and quietly you can allow him to go up. However, do a year's work before starting to jump. Popping over 0·61 metre is all right.

SUMMARY

1. It is better to break in a horse at three years than at two. Even at three years the work should begin very gradually.

Lunge him with saddle and bridle and cavesson, starting, of course, with very short periods. For the first week he just learns to run around at the gait and pace he chooses. He is slowly pushed up to contact on the rein. Side reins are slowly introduced and this is how he gets a mouth.

Lunge him for six to twelve weeks, according to his progress.

2. Now he will have confidence in you and understand your voice orders. You can ride him now and he will seldom object—5 minutes the first day and increase very slowly. Do not get him tired or upset. He learns to go forward on a straight line. Sit still and be comfortable and he will be calm. No sitting trot, as it is far too much for his back; it will stiffen it and he will not use it to swing along as he should.

3. He must not be afraid of the whip; he must just respect it. Train him slowly. Then you can drop it on his hindquarters to keep him going and up to the bit. If he drops the bit he must be sent on immediately. Never work, even later on, for more than 1 hour—and even that would be better in two or three parts. He must go forward, stop, and follow your line.

4. Teach him to turn on wide turns. Do everything slowly and with patience. This will slowly but surely develop his muscles and his mental understanding.

Do not jump more than 0·5 metre for the first year.

CHAPTER FOURTEEN

DRESSAGE JUDGING

The main job of the judge is to try to help the rider along by carefully observing the test. It is very difficult to write a lot of remarks at the time because the movements follow each other very quickly. If possible you should have a short summary at the end of the test and try to point out to the rider the main weaknesses in what the horse has done—or in many cases what the rider has not done—or why the horse does not perform as well as he should. Often you can see that if the rider had tried to push the horse a little more, or had been a little more sensitive with the hands, the horse would have performed better. The rider should read his papers carefully and work accordingly.

As judges you should try and point out to the competitor what has been good and what has not been good. If the rider, after the test, reads the papers and sees that in one place the judge says the horse is 'on two tracks', or says it twice or three times, or if the judge says that the horse is against the bit or is not flexed to the left—or whatever else he may care to criticise— then the rider can draw his own conclusions. Then he may say, 'Next time you are not going to catch me with a crooked horse; I'll make sure that my horse is straight. I'll make sure that my horse will flex to the right and to the left and that he will accept the bit', and so on. And after the next test when he reads the remarks of the judge carefully he may find only one reference where the horse was 'on two tracks'. The rider continues to work on his problems and eventually with the help of the judge, through the tests, he irons out every criticism and goes on from one level to the next. If he keeps on working and working (many riders do not work enough) he really should reach the top—with a lot of work. Naturally, though, not all horses reach the top.

It does not matter if a judge has not had a lot of experience. He can still see something and point it out. I remember when I rode for the first time in a performance in Australia. Everyone I knew came to see me, and somebody who had never been on a horse in his life said something to me that was very much to the point and which nobody had said to me before, and it was a great help to me.

Theoretically, the more practical experience the judge may have, the better judge he will be. Not necessarily, but it will certainly help. This is particularly so in cases where the judge tries to suggest to the rider ways of overcoming the difficulties which have cropped up during the test. The more practical experience the judge has had the easier it will be, because he has dealt with the same problem so many times before. If the judge has not had the necessary practical experience he should at least have a thorough knowledge, a thorough theoretical knowledge, of the requirements.

One thing I like to do is to judge dressage. If you are judging, or are going to judge, the more interest you put into it, the more you ride, the more you look (even if you are not judging), and the more you observe, the better equipped you will be. Judging, like everything else, is a matter of experience.

One of the best judges they had in Germany was a judge who had done very little riding. But he was one of the best. He was not so much a horseman in the sense of a rider on a horse, but he was a tremendous horseman in another way. He could say to somebody (and I have seen it) 'That horse is never going to learn piaffe'. Nobody could see why that horse shouldn't be able to do piaffe, but he never did. That judge had something beyond most other people, some sensitivity, and because of that he was special. But on a horse he was something else again—he was merely going for a ride and not much else. That judge had really studied the whole thing and he did understand it.

The more theoretical knowledge you have the better it is when it comes to assessing. If you make some mistakes when you first begin don't be disheartened. Everybody needs to practise. To practise seeing. In the beginning you look at the horse's gait, look at whether he is flexing, look at whether he is maintaining his rhythm, and by the time you have seen all this the horse has gone through the movement and you may not have seen much at all.

It is a matter of practice to be able to absorb the whole picture in one go, and then to continue concentrating subconsciously on whether the horse keeps going, whether he is on the track and flexing and so on. You must absorb the picture in one go. You look at it as you look at a painting—it's the whole impression. An expert looks at a painting and he knows what technique the painter was using. If *I* wanted to find out, I would probably go up and take a close look and then say, 'He did this'. But did he do that? The expert looks and can see the technique, the expression, and everything. It is a matter of experience, of practice, so that in the beginning you do your assessment step by step. You will find out as you go along what are the more important things, and what are not so important; where you can be tolerant and where you cannot be tolerant.

You sit there the first time, and you may have the shakes: 'Now what do I give him?', 'What do I do now?'. As you go along it becomes much easier. You can grasp the picture and put it into the shaker and come up with a cocktail of 'One' or 'Two' or 'Ten'. It really is like looking at a painting. If you are an expert you may look at the painting, study the technique of the artist, then go back and view the painting as a whole, the general impression of it. The same applies to the test. You watch the individual strokes of the artist as he goes through the turn, and down the straight line, and you view the test, the general impression of the test —horse and rider together—what they have done well, where there is room for improvement, and so on.

A very important thing, and probably the hardest thing for the judge, is to be able to detach yourself completely. You should be able to sit down in a chair and if your daughter comes in, then as far as the test is concerned, you don't know it is your daughter, you don't know the horse, you haven't seen them before. It is a matter of concentration. One should never say, as someone once said to me, 'If my children ride they always win'. It is understandable, because no child could be as good as your own child. That is where the difficulty is—it may be partly your character, partly failure to take it seriously enough.

I have seen judges giving two or three for a movement where I would have given at least an eight (probably a nine) and I have the film to back up my judgment. If it happens once: all right. The judge might have been blowing his nose and didn't quite see what happened. But if it happens a few times! Whether you love the person who is coming towards you or hate him, it shouldn't make any difference to your judgment; as soon as it does make any difference you are no longer a good judge. You are not judging what has been put in front of you, even though that is why you are sitting there. Instead, you are judging what you feel inside. You should judge what you actually see and not what you want to see. There is a big difference.

If someone whom you are fond of comes in, naturally you will be looking for the good points, and you will certainly see them. If somebody whom you don't like comes in, you are going to look for the bad points and you are sure enough going to find them.

A typical example, one of the things I remember so clearly, was Bill Roycroft in Tokyo riding Eldorado. He came down the centre line full of impulsion, on the bit, like a clock and dead straight, absolutely dead straight, and he came to 'X' and the halt was a little bit abrupt. That is what the judges wanted to see. That is why I say, 'Don't look for the bad things; don't look for the good things; see the test as a whole', and be brave enough to say, 'That was good', and be brave enough to say, 'That was no good'.

It is more important than anything else that you should be absolutely honest, and correct, and try as hard as you can—forgetting what you know about the rider, forgetting what you know about the horse, and really seeing and assessing only what is put in front of you. Don't say, or think, 'I have seen that horse go a lot better'. *NO:* you have never seen that jolly horse in your life. Don't think that he could do a lot better, but try to concentrate and assess and give your judgment exactly on what is put in front of you. If the horse has done, or could do, better that is none of your business. As soon as you make it your business you are no longer judging what is really put in front of you.

I went into a Prix St Georges once—the first Prix St Georges in Australia. It was in about 1962/63. Someone said, 'No wonder Franz is

winning; Mr X is judging'. Somebody else replied, 'You are making a mistake. Mr X gave him twenty points less than the other judges'. Finally Mr X said, 'Yes, but I know that horse can go a lot better'. He was right—the horse could go a lot better than in that test, but that was quite irrelevant. You should not know that a horse was going beautifully yesterday, or last year, or last month, and that today it is not going so well. By contrast, if you see a horse going with the hindquarters in one day, don't have it in your mind and say, 'Aha, this is the one that went crooked last time'.

That was one of the reasons why I found it almost impossible at the schools I held to get people to bring their horses. Everybody was scared stiff that if I said, 'Now look, that walk is uneven, and that trot is crooked, and he is doing this or that', the judges sitting there would remember and say, 'That is the horse Franz Mairinger said was crooked'. It is very hard, a matter of concentration, to be able to detach yourself and see only what you see and nothing else. You don't know what he did yesterday, and you don't give him points for what he might do in the future but isn't doing now.

When judging dressage tests you have to be able to follow the test and then view it as a whole. If you don't try to look at the whole performance you get carried away with too many little technicalities. You have to see the whole horse in the movement and at the same time you have to see what the legs are doing. Don't concentrate only on the hindlegs or the front legs; try to see the whole horse, or the whole picture. View the particular movement and then try to put the whole thing together and see and get the feeling of the whole performance.

The more experience the judge has had in riding dressage, the higher the tests he has been competing in, the better it will be, because then he is in a better position to see and judge what is minor and what is major. Sometimes you will see a horse and you will have the feeling that all the rider needs to do is stretch out a bit and take him with the legs, and his nose will be in the right position, and away we go.

The main object of your judging is not to find out who is first, second, and third. That is only the side product of your judging. The main reason for your judging is to tell the rider where he is going right and where he is going wrong. From your remarks the rider should draw his own conclusions. Your remarks are his guideline. From your remarks he will know what he has to concentrate on, what he has to work on to try and improve. If the rider *does* work according to what has been written on the judging sheet, next time he takes up the paper he may find that the horse was crooked only five times instead of seven. And as he keeps on working, the remark that the horse was crooked will disappear, and with that you have helped him on his way.

The real reason for your judging is to *point out* the weak spots. But even the more serious dressage rider is a human being, and as such needs a little pat on the shoulder every now and then. So if you can find something good, please say so—'A good straight line, but unfortunately not standing still'. It may be that you give with one hand and take away with the other, but try to give something. I know what you might want to say—that sometimes it is very hard to find anything good at all—but, even so, try to come up with some kind of encouraging remark.

There is never enough time to write down everything. Try to keep your remarks to the essential things, to the important parts. Don't contradict your mark with your remark, and don't double up on it either. Don't give an eight and write 'Good' in the margin—because you have already said 'Good' with your eight. On the other hand don't give a three and say 'Very good' or an eight and say 'Very bad'. It could happen that some part of the movement is so outstandingly good or so outstandingly bad that you feel you should reward or punish it and you go up or down with the mark. But you have to point out why it was bad or why it was good so that the rider can see why you gave either a high mark or a low mark.

Most riders know what they have done so we shouldn't kid them. On the other hand we shouldn't murder them either. As I said earlier, keep your remarks to the essentials; you don't have much time anyhow, so keep them on the job. Don't do what I saw on some dressage sheets in Melbourne some time ago. There were scores—1, 2, 2, 0, 0, 1, 2, etc.—down the page but nothing on the side at all. The whole sheet had been turned over and written across the page was, 'Horse and rider need a feed'. Another said, 'This rider cannot ride at all'. And yet another, 'This test has nothing to do with riding, let alone dressage'. Ernie Barker was the subject of that last one.

That of course was ridiculous. It is not your job to judge whether the horse and rider need a feed, but to assess how much work the rider has done with the horse.

It should not happen, as unfortunately it has happened, that somebody says, 'Make sure the right people are in the right places'. It is not your job to get the right people into the right places. You assess the performance and by assessing the performance you are helping the competitor on his way to Grand Prix.

Don't be too dogmatic. I saw this not too long ago. The horse came into the halt at 'C', and the halt could not have been any better. It was a really beautiful halt—coming underneath with the hindquarters, coming into the bit and staying there. The problem was that the halt was not at 'C', it was about 1·5 metres after 'C'. But the halt was still so outstanding that I would have given him an eight and if he had been on the spot he might have got a ten (which happens once in a blue moon). I found out that the judge had given him a five and had based his judgment on the fact that the horse was not on the marker. Base your judgment on the important things—in this case the transition and the halt. If the transition, which was beautiful, had been carried out on the spot, his mark would have gone up. But the transition that was carried out so beautifully, but not quite on the spot, deserved a good mark also.

A transition that is carried out badly but on the spot is useless as far as the future development of the horse is concerned. Don't be too dogmatic about the markers. That does not mean that you should overlook them altogether, but don't cut somebody's throat because he was not on the spot despite the fact that he was doing whatever he was supposed to do.

When you finish a test make sure to check whether you have given all movements a mark. A competitor came up to me after a show and said, 'Look, you did not give me a mark for my extended trot'. I thought he was being funny, but he was right—there was no mark for the extended trot. The paper had gone through the adding-up process and been checked, because it was at the Royal Show. I had missed it, we had all missed it. Fortunately, the competitor had won anyway despite my missing mark. However, if the rider had not won, I would have been in hot water because the judging would have left grounds for a protest. So make sure, and check.

Keep your remarks short, and as clear as possible. As a judge, don't make the mistake of saying, 'What did I give the first one?'. Have a theoretical picture in the mind, and make your judgment on that picture because it will never change. It will always be the same because you put it there yourself. Because of that theoretical picture your judging will be reliable and even throughout. If, however, you try to remember what you gave this one or the other one you are certainly going to get all muddled up and your judging will go up and down like a yo-yo.

You may be a little hard in your judgment and so your marks are a little on the low side. That is all right. If you have a variation of a point per movement do not worry about it. What shouldn't happen is that you are down all the time, then *zoom* you are up, and then you are down, then you are up. If the other judges are zooming up when you are, though, that is all right.

Another thing: it is always strange that the marks are better after lunch than before. There should definitely be no stimulation in the form of alcohol and so on in between.

Finally, if I say the good Lord created the horse, I do not want to preach to you. You can replace the good Lord by Nature or whatever you prefer. But we are faced with facts, facts that we cannot alter and we shouldn't try to alter, because they are a matter of creation and if we try to alter that fact we pay for it. Whether riding or judging, remember what Roy Stewart, the old vet, said to me: '*People always think that horses are made for man, but that's not true. Horses are made to be horses*'.

SUMMARY

1. As a dressage judge you must try to point out to the competitor what has been good and what is not good. With experience you will be able to make remarks as the test goes along, but it is often difficult to think of the right words quickly enough. A short summary at the end can cover much.

You must watch the performance closely so that you an assess the good and the poorer parts. Then you must try to analyse why things went well or not. Then you try to give advice for improvement. This improvement will almost always necessitate improvement in the rider's position and co-ordination.

The competitor should read the sheets carefully and so plan to work towards improvement.

Even if you are not experienced you can see much that goes on. Remember to remark on the good equally with the bad.

2. The more experienced you are as a judge and a rider, the easier it will be for you to find the right advice to help the competitor. If you have not been a rider up to the standard you are judging you must read and study very carefully to acquire the necessary theoretical knowledge.

3. You need practice in 'seeing'. You have to observe the whole thing. Is the horse going forward? Look at his gait. Is he on two tracks? Is he flexing? Is he even? Is he straight? And so on. At first you need to look step by step, then the whole picture comes to you. You will learn what is important, where to be tolerant. You get the picture of horse and rider together, and what they have done well, and where improvement is needed.

4. As a judge you must be completely detached. You must not take any notice of past reputations, or of what horse or rider is in the ring. You are just judging what you see, with no thought of other occasions. This is very difficult but it can be done with concentration. If your feelings for horse or rider have any effect on your mark then this is not fair judging. Don't look for the bad points only; look for the good first. Try to see the test as a whole.

5. **You must be absolutely honest and assess what you see before you with no thought for anything else. You must not think, 'This is the horse that usually goes crooked', and so look for crookedness, and so on.**

6. **Do not get carried away with small technicalities. You have to see the whole horse in the movement. Don't concentrate on the front legs, nor on the hindlegs. View the movement and try to put it all together. As in No. 2 above, the more riding and judging you have done, the** better you will be able to judge what is important. For example, the horse comes beautifully up the centre line to a good square halt, but the downward transition was a little abrupt. He could have an eight or nine.

7. The main object of judging is to help the rider to do better next time — to point out what was good and what needs improving. To find the place-getters is of far less importance or value.

From the judge's remarks the rider should learn on what aspects he must work. If in one test he gets five references to 'falling in on the corner', and in the next he gets only three, then he must have improved. Remember that you must find some good points to remark on, or you may discourage him from ever trying again.

8. There is no time to write down everything, so you must learn to pick out the most important parts. You must explain why marks are lost, especially if the mark is four or less. The mark and remark must follow the tables of values. They should not repeat nor contradict each other. 'Very good . . . five' and 'Poor extension . . . six' are both wrong. By the tables the marks should be nine and four.

If half the movement is good and half poor the mark can be in the middle. 'Good active walk and straight, but halt crooked and not square' could be five or six.

If you give eight (or any other mark) there is no need to make the remark 'Good'. The eight has said that. Use your time and space to say something more: 'Good circle' or 'Good rhythm'. Or if the mark is three do not only say, 'Fairly bad'. Say why it was fairly bad.

9. You must be reasonable in the marks and remarks and stick to the performance before you. Never be facetious or sarcastic. Do not over-emphasise accuracy of position on the markers. Other things are of greater value.

10. On completing a test, always check to see that every movement has a mark. If one is missing and you cannot remember what it should be, give an average mark but do not send the sheet away with a blank space.

11. Make the remarks short and clear. Before beginning you must form a picture in your mind of what you expect from a performance at this particular stage—novice, medium, etc. Then mark your horses against that picture. Never try to compare one performance with another. If you do, you will never keep an even standard.

It does not matter if you are a little harder than your co-judge and so your marks are lower, so long as this is constant and you do not shoot up and down.

Remember that a horse is a horse and do not judge him except on his natural paces. Artificial movements have no value.

Lastly, do not take any stimulants during judging time or it may affect your judgment and so upset your standard.

CHAPTER FIFTEEN

CONCLUSION: THE INSTRUCTOR

The greatest problem that presents itself to the riding instructor is the lack of variety in the subject being taught. If we teach geography we have the whole world to roam over in our lessons. In arithmetic there is an infinite range of problems. In riding, the pupil strives to improve his seat and, through this, his ability to train his horse. Of course there are different aspects to it, but broadly speaking we do the same thing all our riding lives.

The beginner makes quite rapid progress, and can feel himself improving with each lesson. He learns how to sit and to manage his horse, and he learns to ride at the walk, trot, and canter.

For the next two or three years he must slowly improve this basic work. He can begin jumping, but he is not yet ready for more advanced riding on the flat. The rider's progress cannot be more rapid than is the development of his mind and body. If this fact is not accepted, and the rider is taught beyond his capabilities, he will be forced into so many mistakes that it will be very difficult for him ever to become a good horseman. In all probability he will never make the necessary effort to overcome these bad habits.

This part of his riding career is one of hard work, of persistent and consistent endeavour. For a long time there is very little apparent reward. The rider must achieve a steady and deep seat in the saddle to enable him to control his horse's movements by co-ordinated rein and leg aids, and to have full control of his weight. He must develop his 'feel' so that eventually he knows exactly what his horse is doing under him . . . the list could go on for pages.

Many actions and reactions must become instinctive. How does the rider achieve these instinctive reactions? Once learnt, it is always done like that, and quickly becomes instinctive. It is always done because it is uncomfortable not to do it. Why does the rider do all this hard work and apply this concentration? Only because he believes that it will all be worth while, repaid by the joy and infinite satisfaction which will be his when he acquires the ability to ride a well-trained horse; when he appreciates its training and ultimately trains his own horse. The rider believes this through the inspiration of his instructor, through reading books, and through watching top riders.

But the rider must do the work. He must do the concentrating necessary to make these reactions instinctive, and he must do this without the inspiration of success, which is very slow in coming. After this we hope that he will begin to feel the benefit of all his efforts. The rider will strive for an effect and get it, and know that he has done so. By then he has battled through the hardest stage.

The light dawns; our rider is no longer working in the dark just believing what the other fellow says. He has experienced some success as the result of his labours and he realises now where he is going. The rider will still have his setbacks, but he will find where he is wrong and correct it, and before very long he will have felt the harmony and thrill of being one with a horse that is doing its best for him. He will come to the final stage and join the ranks of those who can never give up riding so long as they are physically able.

Those of you who instruct carry a great responsibility. It is especially great because you are the teachers of our young riders, the riders who will carry Australia's flag one day.

I have tried to tell you *what*, and *how*, and above all *why* to do all the things I ask of you, in order to show the necessity of doing them in a certain way because of the relationship between riding and nature. I have told you stories, and attempted with them to prove to you that if you believe you can do it—if you want to do it, and are prepared to produce the necessary effort (which is the price you have to pay)—then you can achieve success. You will then have succeeded in making young riders understand that a horse is more, or can be more, than a mere object of convenience, and you will have succeeded in making the young riders understand their horses. Most of the

young riders' difficulties will then be removed and you will be halfway to success. If you can lead your pupils to really understand their horses, you will have succeeded in producing a horseman and not a passenger, and this in itself produces a sense of responsibility and consideration in the young rider. It is therefore character-forming.

Furthermore, if you succeed in making the young rider understand, and thereby appreciate the fact that work comes before the prize, you will have developed more than an understanding horseman. You will have developed a very useful member of the community—someone who deeply comprehends the fact that privileges carry duty and responsibility. With that knowledge young riders will have the essential requirements for a happy life and surely won't become the so-called 'drop outs'. I am convinced that riding can be formative in a great many ways.

As you know, the Bible tells us that the Lord created the world and that He looked down and saw that it was good. Personally I don't know why He had to look. Then I think the Lord looked down on a Sunday morning and saw that something was missing—something that represented His patience, His understanding, His love, His everything, indeed all that was good—and He created the horse.

On my first day at the Spanish Riding School the Instructor said to me, '*The Instructor lives on in his pupils*'. If you carry my thoughts to your pupils it will mean that when I close my eyes one day I will close them in the happy knowledge that I will live for a long time in the thoughts of my pupils.

SUMMARY

This needs no summary. It should all be read and studied carefully. How true are the last words. Franz Mairinger and his wonderful teaching and philosophy will live on in the thoughts of his pupils for as long as their lives last. We trust that all the good he did will live even longer—as we, his pupils, endeavour to pass it on to our pupils in turn. He was a very wonderful man. May his memory and influence last as long as men ride horses.

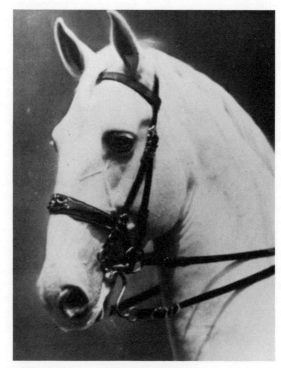

An old friend

INDEX